W9-AZJ-712

ASPECTS OF

CULTURE AND PERSONALITY

Also by Francis L. K. Hsu

UNDER THE ANCESTORS' SHADOW

AMERICAN AND CHINESE:
TWO WAYS OF LIFE (1953)

RELIGION, SCIENCE AND HUMAN CRISES

ASPECTS OF
CULTURE
AND
PERSONALITY

A SYMPOSIUM EDITED BY

Francis L. K. Hsu

ASSOCIATE PROFESSOR OF ANTHROPOLOGY,
NORTHWESTERN UNIVERSITY

ABELARD - SCHUMAN, NEW YORK

Library of Congress Catalog Card Number: 54-10232

The publication of this study was made possible by funds granted by the Wenner-Gren Foundation for Anthropological Research. The Foundation is not, however, the author or publisher of this publication, and is not to be understood as approving, by virtue of its grant, any of the statements made, or views expressed, therein.

PRINTED AND BOUND IN THE UNITED STATES OF AMERICA

DESIGNED BY ANDOR BRAUN

CONTENTS

EDITORIAL ADVISORY COMMITTEE

EDITOR'S PROLOGUE

Francis L. K. Hsu

THIS VOLUME contains the bulk of the results of a *Conference on Anthropology and Psychiatry,* held under the auspices of the Wenner-Gren Foundation for Anthropological Research, which took place on May 17, 18, and 19, 1951[1], at Northwestern University as a Centennial event. The proposal that this conference be held followed from a paper on "Anthropology or Psychiatry," delivered by the editor at one of the Foundation's supper-conferences in 1950. This paper was later published in the *Southwestern Journal of Anthropology* (Vol. 8. 1952, pp. 227-250).

The purpose of the conference was a simple one. It was to see if some of the accumulated knowledge on culture and personality could be integrated by a meeting of the psychiatrists and psychoanalysts on the one hand and the sociologists, psychologists and anthropologists on the other. It was also hoped that some of the arguments given in the editor's paper on "Anthropology or Psychiatry" might be advanced or refuted.

The editor cannot say that the projected objective of the conference was completely reached. For one thing, the clinicians and the social scientists have yet to develop a relatively more adequate means of communication. Often anthropologists use such psychiatric terms as super-ego, or compensation, without any precise definition, just as psychoanalysts frequently make too much of certain highly restricted data from anthropological literature which are either archaic, inaccurate or without the necessary context. It is apparent that for a scientific integration to be achieved students of psychiatric and social sciences need to have a better knowledge of each other's fields, whether as regards data, concept or method.

However, difficulties in the way of integration transcend mere matters of communication. Many general semanticists hold that once we are rid of the thinking habits built on Aristotelian logic mankind will have done away with most, if not all, of their current misunderstandings, tensions, prejudices. Yet this is not borne out by observable facts. The simplest test of its validity may be had in the marital relationship. Will husbands and wives adjust to each other more satisfactorily if they learn to clarify their intentions by employing proper linguistic usages? It is difficult to believe this. Actually, a couple about to separate will do so much more rapidly if they attempt to sharpen their means of communication. Most men know how easy it is to win an argument with their wives, but how difficult it is to come out victorious in a serious marital conflict!

In intellectual differences it is usual to find that disputes have non-rational as well as rational bases. Regardless of the subject matter, whether it concerns mathematical equations or the color of the moon, human beings, even the most detached, have a way of injecting their own emotions into seemingly objective problems so that demonstrable facts are never sufficient to settle an argument as to their interpretation. It is said when Galileo first attempted to convince those about him of the truth of the heliocentric theory of the universe by showing them the satellites around Jupiter, they refused even to look into his telescope. In the case of problems where emotions bulk larger than in science, the demonstrable facts are patently not enough. Here the difficulties will persist, perhaps even become stronger and more violent, when the intellectual error is pointed out.

This is an important reason why racial prejudice persists in the United States in spite of an excellent educational system and the overall importance of the ideological structure of freedom and equality. This is, to a considerable extent, why Christianity keeps dividing into new sects that continue to contend with each other in spite of their lack of basic theological differences. This is an important factor in most parent-child difficulties, marital quarrels, and management-labor disputes, no less than at the basis of many academic differences. Usually emotionality is not only characteristic of much of the attitudes present in disputes between psychiatrists and social scientists, it also characterizes disagreements among anthropologists who hold the positions of different schools of thought, in much the same way as psychiatrists who hold dissimilar views of the nature and functions of psychiatry.

Fortunately, the difficulties are sometimes outweighed by other factors, such as necessity. For example, it was the necessity for finding a key to go beyond surface description which led many present day anthropologists in the culture and personality field to borrow heavily from psychoanalysis, just as it was the necessity for a master concept to string the many miscellaneous facts together which prompted anthropologists of two or three generations ago to rely greatly on evolutionary biology. I believe that in time the necessity for a broader and more scientific view of man will similarly compel the clinicians to learn more from the social scientists.

Necessity is not the only way to overcome emotional problems, misunderstandings and resistance between members of the different disciplines. Closer and more frequent contacts through engaging in tasks of mutual interest can also help, within limits, to increase mutual confidence and friendship. The fact that there are so many conferences and symposia, where psychiatrists, psychoanalysts and social scientists in varying combinations are willing to discuss their common problems, is a happy omen of an increasing degree of cooperation which, though difficult, is not impossible to achievement.

The present conference was conceived and planned in this perspective. While the results may not have measured up to the highest expectations of the participants, some gains are evident. For example, in the body of the symposium, there is no lack of drastic disagreement which, in the main, consistently divides the clinicians from the social scientists. But as the symposium draws to its conclusion, this line of division is indubitably blurred.

This volume is presented to the public in the expectation that it will be of interest to students of culture and personality as well as to those concerned with the meeting of minds among men in different disciplines. To the former, it is hoped that many of the individual papers, as well as the discussions, will be helpful. To the latter, it is hoped that the symposium as a whole will contribute a little to their search for a common basis of understanding and cross-fertilization.

The editor is greatly indebted to members of the Editorial Advisory Committee, especially the tireless help of Drs. Robert F. Winch and William A. Hunt, for planning the conference and for helping to edit its results; to Dr. A. C. Van Dusen and his Centennial Office staff for facilitating the execution of the conference; to the Committee on Research of the Graduate School of the University for a grant-in-aid which made completion of the volume possible; to Mrs. Stephen Fentress, Mr. Arthur Tuden, Mrs. Alan Polasky, and Mr. and Mrs. Simon Ottenberg for bearing most of the burden of the secretarial work; to Dr. Paul Fejos for his many excellent suggestions; and to the Wenner-Gren Foundation for Anthropological Research for two grants which financed the conference and subsidized the publication of its results. The Wenner-Gren Foundation is not, however, the author or publisher of this book and is not to be understood as approving, by virtue of its grants, any of the statements made, or views expressed, therein. Last but not least, the editor wishes to thank all participants in the conference without whose stimulating contributions this volume would never have been possible.

ASPECTS OF
CULTURE AND **PERSONALITY**

I

METHODS OF APPROACH TO THE STUDY OF HUMAN BEHAVIOR

John Gillin

WE LIVE in a time of confusion. Every man and every society of the modern Western world is faced with bewildering choices between alternatives of action and attitude which are often mutually incompatible and inconsistent. Faced with such excruciating uncertainties, our people are showing an increasing tendency to individual breakdown, collective hysteria, internecine aggressiveness, and outbursts of childish emotionalism. Cross-cultural evidence seems to show that the resoluteness and integration of any people depend upon their confidence in a system of beliefs concerning the nature of the universe and the relations of human beings to it and to each other. The faith of the Western peoples in their traditional belief systems has been badly shaken, and their pyschosocial security framework consequently appears to be decidedly wobbly and unsteady.

I do not wish to exaggerate the confusion of the present time, but I do not believe that we can usefully discuss approaches to the study of human behavior without taking it into account. It is my belief that the sciences of human behavior are in a position either to aggravate this current state of affairs or, on the other hand, to aid the rebuilding of a culture capable of providing reasonable assurances to its participants of the realization of certain objectives of Western civilization: individual dignity and liberty, the full realization of human capabilities, and the elimination of fruitless conflicts and anxieties, whether of an individual or social nature.

To begin with, the sciences of man must consolidate their points of view regarding human behavior. No approach to an understanding of human behavior or of anything else, for that matter, can be made except in terms of some sort of theory, either implicit or explicit. If any contribution is to be made to the solution of the social and individual perplexities of this and future periods, it is high time that the theoretical preconceptions of the alleged experts in humanity be made explicit and put in order.

It is probable that much of the intellectual and emotional muddle in which our people find themselves has been stirred up by the irresponsibility of the human scientists themselves. All science has been subject to some internal theoretical confusion, but that in the human sciences has had the effect of inhibiting the application to the world of affairs[1] of much of the knowledge actually agreed upon among scientists. I am referring here, not to our failure to "popularize" our scientific knowledge of human behavior, but to our

[1] The most recent complaint from the point of view of "the intelligent layman" which has come to my notice is Joseph H. Spigelman, "Can Science Make Sense?" *Harper's Magazine,* May 1951, pp. 54-60.

reluctance to integrate among ourselves as scientists that which we know.

Our general culture is a competitive one in which certain techniques of aggression are taught to the society's members from their earliest years. It is a culture in which proprietary values are rated high. Having little other property, the average social scientist fiercely defends a proprietary interest in a theory or a collection of words, the "true meaning" of which he thinks he has discovered himself. Having been schooled from early childhood in the American creed that "you never get anything for nothing, bub," and "the Lord helps him who helps himself," he seeks prominence and such professional rewards as are available by the application to his colleagues of thinly disguised techniques of competition and aggression adapted from those current in the market place and in everyday life.

However, we can no longer afford the luxury of intrascientific warfare, but must focus our efforts on the integration of our scientific knowledge regarding human beings.

How may the goals of integration and systematic expansion of our knowledge of human behavior be achieved? I should like briefly to offer for your consideration the following suggestions.

First, the "academic and scientific culture" of the human sciences could stand some adjustment. The system itself is inconsistent with the goals we have mentioned. Mechanical steps have been taken to provide closer physical contact between various disciplines at a few universities. Experience has shown, however, that mere propinquity does not necessarily produce scientific integration nor even amiability, although the latter may be an occasional by-product. Such successes as some interdisciplinary organizations may boast have involved something more than providing mere cross-disciplinary contacts and opportunity for acquaintanceship between members of separate disciplines.

Among possible steps which might be taken to improve the academic culture from the point of view discussed here are the following. (*a*) Prizes and other rewards in the advancement or application of "the science of man," rather than one of its specialities such as anthropology, sociology, psychology, economics, etc. (*b*) A society and/or research council representing the common interests of all the human sciences could be established which would remain in close contact with organizations of more specialized sort such as now exist. (*c*) The administrations of academic and scientific institutions could be encouraged to aid interdisciplinary work in the human sciences among their staff members. At present, administrative authorities are wedded to a system of accounting monies and man-hours which is rigidly tied to departmental budgets. A man has, therefore, to make a personal sacrifice in terms of time, money, or nervous tension if he crosses disciplinary lines to collaborate with other students of human behavior. He is, in short, punished rather than rewarded for his pains.

The three steps just mentioned can be greatly speeded by enlightened grants from foundations, by action of the present research councils, and by the implementation and financing of special interdisciplinary commissions on the part of the present professional and scientific societies.

In addition, (*d*) I believe that those of us interested in the development of an integrated science of human behavior have an obligation to take steps on our home grounds. For example, I believe that every graduate student in the human sciences should have at least one course in theory which is of a positive, as well as of a critical, type. He should be taught how to take the best ideas and findings from the workers in his own and other fields and to use them as building blocks in his own work. Too often we have taught our students how to be critical, but not how to be constructive; we have hammered on the perfection of specialized techniques without providing a scientific rationale for them; we have emphasized one point of view within our own discipline without giving the student the methods or mental set for collaborating with workers of other points of view and other disciplines. This vicious circle must be broken. I should state right here that I am not advocating the abandonment of specialities if there is good scientific reason for their maintenance, a matter which will be discussed below. But I am arguing for the breakdown of scientific isolationism.

The setting up of favorable or permissive conditions for interdisciplinary collaboration will, however, achieve little beyond a cloudy type of "interfertilization" and perhaps some beautiful friendships if common understanding of terminologies and concepts cannot be obtained. The second major step required in the development of a useful science of human behavior, therefore, is a certain degree of integration on the theoretical level.

The first problem in this regard is one of sheer intercommunication. A number of procedures are available for securing agreement in the use of words and other symbols. Among them may be mentioned ostensive definition,[2] of which operational definition may be considered one type. Any operations, whether physical or mental, which are capable of being demonstrated socially may be symbolized by words or other indicators and receive consensual agreement as to their referents. Another way of agreeing about terms is not to attempt to define them formally at all ("primitive undefined terms"), but to derive common consent to their meaning from their usage in a system of logically ordered concepts. The fact that the social sciences deal with intangible objects which can often not be observed with relatively precise instruments is no excuse for fuzzy use of language and faulty intercommunication in the sciences of human behavior. No one has ever seen a gene, yet the geneticists seem to be in pretty fair agreement as to what they are talking about when they use the word.

Beyond mere intelligibility of terminology—and much more important—lies the necessity for an integrated body of theory. Any methods of approach to the study of human behavior, other than sheer random trial and error, must be guided by theory. A theory is a guide to possible discoveries in the empirical world and an aid in their interpretation once they are made. The following seem to me to constitute the simplest and most fundamental criteria of a useful theoretical formulation. (1) The postulates should be stated explicitly and unambiguously in terms agreed upon as discussed above. (2) The postulates and their corollaries should be related together in orderly fashion permitting log-

---

[2] "Any process by which a person is taught to understand a word otherwise than by the use of other words." Bertrand Russell, *Human Knowledge*. New York: Simon and Schuster, 1948, p. 63.

ical manipulation. (3) A clear statement should be made identifying the system of logic to be used. (4) The logical consequences of the postulates should be stated as theorems. (5) The theorems must be so formulated that they follow logically from the postulates and also in such a form that the possibilities they propose are subject to empirical verification or rejection. Unverifiable theorems are of no scientific value. (6) If, after empirical testing, a given theorem does not conform to empirical data, the theorem must be rigorously discarded or reformulated, as well as all the terms and postulates from which it was derived. (7) If, after rigorous empirical testing, a theorem conforms to the apposite data, it may be tentatively regarded as a reliable generalization, and the validity of the terms and postulates from which it is derived is correspondingly raised. (8) All terms, postulates, and theorems should be stated in such form that they may be meaningfully incorporated into other scientific systems concerned with relevant fields of knowledge. Thus, certain verified theorems of psychology are incorporated in the postulational system of modern psycho-cultural science. (9) Finally, the principles of simplicity and economy should be followed at all times. Two postulates should not be used when one will do, etc.

It will be seen that I advocate the use of empirically verifiable logico-deductive-empirical theoretical formulations, and the reason is that I believe that when properly employed they are the most rigorous, precise, and useful formulations available. They provide the theoretical framework for method which is at once inductive and deductive, and self-corrective in both directions at once.[3]

I am not, of course, saying that every statement made by a behavior scientist should be cast in the formal mode of a logico-deductive-empirical system. Informal discussion should be encouraged and exploratory reports should not be inhibited. But I do claim that a comprehensive system of theory should be formulated, and when serious investigations are started and seemingly important findings are made they should be referred to the system.

If this much is conceded, it follows that one of the major tasks before us is the integration of our approaches to the study of human behavior through the construction of a master system which would have the effect of rendering the various current and future approaches to behavior consistent within and among themselves.

What are the presently recognized specialities or disciplines whose integration would be desirable? Log-

[3] There has been a great deal of confused talking and writing among social scientists in which an alleged dichotomy is drawn between deductive and inductive theory. Even in some recently published books purporting to be contributions to theory I have noticed that the authors take defiant stances in defense of induction against that ol' devil deduction—as if they had heard nothing about scientific method since Francis Bacon. This empty crusade has got to be called off in the interest of scientific progress. No scientist has made contributions to our knowledge of the empirical world using only pure deduction or by using pure induction alone. Pure deduction by itself does not lead to empirical data; pure induction does not lead to meaning or interpretation. Those who claim to use only pure induction are actually guided by an informal system of deductive theory which is often not conscious to themselves and seldom explicit to others. The disorderliness of merely implicit postulates or of unconnected *ad hoc* hypotheses tends to confuse the investigator and frequently leads to waste of time and effort because the worker has no clear-cut guide to the relevance of his studies. The notion of many so-called pure empiricists that "the facts once discovered will reveal their own meanings" has been shown to be sheer nonsense as a general principle.

ically we should anticipate a working partnership among all the sciences concerned with human behavior, plus those specialities called the humanities.

Human behavior may be thought of as any autonomous (self-produced) activity of those organisms called *Homo sapiens.* I assume, however, that a restricted portion of the field of total human behavior is the focus of interest of those who might be concerned in the integrated science of which we have been speaking. We shall, therefore, narrow the total field to human social or interactional behavior—in other words, those activities which either directly or indirectly serve as stimuli to activities of individuals, or which are direct or indirect responses of the activities of other human beings, plus the material objects (artifacts) which are the products of such behavior or which serve under specified circumstances as the necessary adjuncts of such behavior. Such a restriction, however, definitely includes "mental" and other "internalized" behavior of interactional significance.

It is the present proposal that the theories, approaches, and findings of all the sciences and humanities which contribute to this broad field be integrated into a comprehensive framework of theory and findings. It is my contention that this will contribute to the advance of knowledge and to the solution of the crucial human problems of our time.

Since one of the advantages anticipated from such integration is organization of theory and knowledge, the foremost problem to consider is how best to *order* the contributions of our various disciplines. Here I would propose two types of order: (*1*) a logico-functional ordering ranging from the more tangible subject matter to the less tangible; (2) an order based upon levels of abstraction from concrete empirical data. It is quite probable that in a fully developed system both types of ordering will be integrated one to the other.

By way of illustration, we might think of our theory beginning at some agreed starting point with, let us say, a postulate of physical anthropology, such as "Man is an animal." The implications of this and cognate postulates would be fully and explicitly developed so far as they had significance for human social behavior. It should be recognized that such a postulate may in itself be a validated theorem taken from the system of zoology. Physical anthropology, genetics, physiology, and such other competent disciplines as would be agreed upon, would contribute all the pertinent extant knowledge concerning the organic bases of human social behavior: structure, function, capacities, etc., of the human organism for activity.

The next stage would be contributed by psychology, beginning perhaps with physiological psychology. Here we would expect a systematic formulation of present knowledge and hypotheses concerning the macroscopic conditions under which human behavior takes place, then a suitable formulation of the principles of learning, maintenance, and loss of acquired behavior. A certain amount of work would doubtless be necessary within psychology itself to achieve integration of various points of view such as those of topology, configurationism, learning theory, and the psychoanalytic approaches.

Next might perhaps appear the contributions of a certain phase of sociology, namely, that which has discovered something about the conditions of social interaction and the formation of groups. We should expect the sociologists to contribute something substantial concerning the conditions under which various types of interactional behavior take place, the formation and composition of human social groups, and so on. This would seem to be a logical preliminary to the formulation of the principles of patterned, cultural behavior.[4]

The next contribution could be expected from the cultural anthropologists, who would be expected to contribute their knowledge of the social conditions of the learning, maintenance, and functional operation of cultural patterns. Being an anthropologist myself, I shall at once admit the difficulties without attempting to specify them.

If the general principles of cultural behavior can be ordered into a consistent approach, the next procedure would seem to be to seek the contribution of the students of certain specific "institutionalized" behavior, if you do not object to the word. Here I think of sociological "institutionalists," political scientists, economists, religionists (if there exist any with pretensions to scientific outlook), experts on ethics (ethicians, if you prefer that label), jurisprudents, family experts (they need a Latin-derived name), planners (if there are any who know what theory and method mean as distinguished from technique), and so on.

Next would come the contributions of the students of symbolic behavior with their contributions from lin-

[4] Before any such contribution to integrated human behavior theory and research is made by sociologists, however, I believe it necessary that at least two groups within the profession will have to be brought to an understanding of what we are trying to do: (1) the vaporizing producers of free-floating theories which cannot (perhaps intentionally) be tested empirically; (2) the "empirical sociologists" who are busily counting instances and making correlations between "variables" which neither they nor anyone else can explain.

guistics, semantics, semiotics, etc. On this order we should expect to end up with a series of general theorems embodying all the unsolved questions of the preceding contributions.

If we look at the approaches to human behavior as ranged along a scale from concrete to abstract, we start with explanatory principles at the physiological and anatomical level and end with such concepts as "unconscious premises" and "structural objectives" of behavior expected in a cultural system. In this order of analysis we would expect to deal with the unobservable "dependent variables" of psychological theory, the "inferred structure of institutions," and the "principles of cultural integration."

Finally, we must find an integrated place in our approach for the products and adjuncts of human behavior. Archeology, for example, should find a legitimate role as the science which attempts to infer the social behavior of extinct societies from their material and (in some cases) documentary remains. Yet the process of inference should be based on the principles which have been tested on living, functioning societies. The humanities deal mainly with materialistic representations of intangible aspects of human social behavior—plastic and graphic works of art, music recorded on paper or otherwise, the writings of literary artists. I make no claim that humanists should be converted into behavior scientists, but I do feel that a comprehensive approach to human behavior should be so formulated that materials with which humanists for the most part are concerned should be amenable to investigation as data of human behavior, or the motives influencing it.

Thus, if the knowledge and possibilities of our field

were consistently organized, all students of human behavior could find a common meeting ground for judging the significance of their research plans or findings. The contribution of any one would be clear at once and the implications, varying from organic to abstract principles, would be explicit to investigators and readers of reports alike.

Some of the practical difficulties inherent in achieving an integration may be overcome by long sessions—perhaps three-month summer periods to be aided by foundations or other independent sources of funds—involving highly informed, congenial, and relaxed personalities from the numerous disciplines. These, however, are merely mechanical and financial hurdles to be vaulted. More important, perhaps, will be the objections voiced by the scientists themselves.

The proposal, in essence and simplicity, is that we organize our available knowledge and hypotheses concerning human social behavior in a consistent manner so that (1) we may understand each other, (2) new investigations may be provided with the widest possible rational basis for their significance, and (3) new findings may be interpreted in the broadest possible framework of possible explanation and prediction.

The first objection will probably be that "we scientists do not propose to be subjected to a dictatorship, even of the majority." My answer to this is that any individual scientist would and must be guaranteed the widest freedom to demand, on the basis of his empirical findings or logic, revision of the comprehensive theoretical structure any time that he presented adequate evidence of his views. It is an essential of this proposal that agreement on any organized approach be accompanied by consensus and that it must be changed at any time that acceptable scientific evidence so requires.

Another objection will be the allegation that a scientific "bureaucracy" will be required to achieve and to maintain such an integrated approach as here suggested. My own view is that an entrenched bureaucracy is by no means inevitable and should not in any case be formally countenanced in the plan. However, delegates from the various disciplines will be required to devote time and effort, at least in the first stages of formulating the integrated approach. Whether or not such delegated individuals—who also must be dedicated persons—will harden into a controlling scientific bureaucracy is entirely up to the organized social behavior of scientists of the country and the world. As of the present, the various specialists within this general field are democratically organized and quite capable of controlling the nominations and withdrawals of their delegates to a conference or board.

A third complaint may well be that I am proposing the abolition of specialities. But from the scientific point of view I do not see that specialisms will be eliminated at all. In fact, we shall need more of them, if anything. It is from the specialisms, as well as from other sources, that we may expect contributions to our knowledge. The man who out of sheer curiosity wants to know what happens when he tickles the fifth digit of the right hind foot on one hundred rats will be perfectly free to continue with his preoccupation. But if he thinks he has discovered something, he can refer it to the master system and see whether it adds to knowledge as so formulated, or whether his contribution requires a revision, however small, in the over-all statement.

Finally, it is necessary, once again, to consider the cultural and social system and the motivations of scientists who would be required to implement an integrated approach. Since they are men of modern North American culture we may expect them, with a few exceptions, to be motivated by the drives of money and prestige. How is a "brilliant" and "original" sociologist, psychologist, or anthropologist, for instance, to get either of these rewards if he is reduced to being a member of a "team" and has to submerge his flashing insights to the requirements of a dull logico-deductive-empirical approach? How is he to avoid the taint of fraternization with such "un-understanding" people as zoologists, physical anthropologists, or "rat" psychologists? The answer to this is apparent. If such geniuses have anything significant to say, their significance will be greatly magnified if stated in terms of a comprehensive approach which covers everything from human muscle to abstract logical constructs. If they have nothing important to say, they and others will soon find out why. Yet, their careers will not be ruined. They can become evangelists, writers of science fiction, or professional explorers who lecture before women's clubs. The present proposal is not intended to deprive any man of a livelihood. It is merely suggested as a reasonable means for increasing the effectiveness of the human sciences and for amplifying our knowledge of human behavior so that science may contribute effectively to the solution of the crucial human problems of our time.

Here at this symposium we have representatives of

several approaches to the study of human behavior. It is to be hoped that the "positive" aspects of our association will be emphasized and that at least some groundwork may be laid for a more integrated science of man.

DISCUSSION

Thomas M. French

Of course, I am very much in sympathy with Dr. Gillin's basic hope as presented in his paper—the idea of different sciences collaborating with one another in the study of behavior in society. Yet I am somewhat skeptical of his method. My fear is that premature organization and standardization will hinder rather than help the development of the social sciences. The growth of science is a biological phenomenon. We expect the best theories to survive; and the process of interdisciplinary co-operation could be compared to a process of cross-fertilization. Getting acquainted is more valuable than any organized effort to force people prematurely into a standard pattern of integration. Many fundamental scientific discoveries have been made by people who were looked upon as crazy, by people who were fortunately able to free themselves from the accepted beliefs of their day. Standardization tends to inhibit valuable scientific work. A group can not usually discover anything. Its members can stimulate one another mutually, but you can't map out and plan the discovery of anything really new.

Each science must develop its concepts in relation to the data which it is trying to explain. The concepts of sociology and those of psychology must necessarily differ at first because they are developed in relation to two different sets of data. The psychoanalyst must develop concepts that help him understand his patient, but the sociologist must try to understand people as they are related to one another through institutions. However, much that the psychoanalyst can learn from his patients has relevance also to the sociologist's problems; and much that the sociologist learns by studying institutions and group phenomena can help the psychoanalyst to a better perspective on his patients' problems. If now psychoanalyst and sociologist can learn each to translate the other's concepts into his own terms, a common language will gradually develop, to the mutual enrichment of both. For example, it is well known that Freud used the concepts that he developed in his clinical studies to throw light on a number of related fields. The same interchange of insights should also take place in the opposite direction.

Furthermore, in young sciences like psychology and the social sciences, the demand for strict formulation and systematization in advance of the precision of our data has its dangers. We are not yet ready to emulate the older physical sciences in this respect. If we formulate too far in advance of our data we are tempted to force our observations into the mold of preconceived theories, and thus blunt our capacity for really sensitive, careful observation, which is our most important task at this time. In the name of logic and scientific method we are in danger of losing our scientific imagination and of ceasing to look at our data.

As a second point, I should like to emphasize that we often overevaluate what science can hope to contribute toward the solution of social and international problems. Sometimes we imagine fondly that if the scientists of the world would only get together they could work out a "scientific" formula for achieving international harmony. Well, suppose they did, who would listen to them? And how would they persuade the rest of the world to follow their prescription? Pursuing this phantasy further, we might hope for a science of propaganda effective enough to make the rest of the world do what we scientists tell them. Personally, I hope that the science of propaganda will never be developed to this kind of perfection. If it were, how do we know that some other group of people might not get control of our propaganda machinery? And then we would have, not a solution for the world's ills, but an oppressive dictatorship.

Evidently we are in danger of thinking of the problems of social and international adjustment too intellectually. The process of finding formulae for social co-operation cannot be separated so sharply from the process of putting our formulae into effect. For example, we sometimes ask whether socialism would work or not. I am sure that a socialist experiment attempted by people who did not believe in it would never work. Today we are only beginning a series of national experiments to determine whether a people who really believe in socialism and are willing to make the necessary personal sacrifices can make it work.

In recent years there have been a continually increasing number of experiments in group dynamics, attempts to work out the principles that determine how people can best succeed in working together in groups. Such studies, I believe, point the way to the best contribution that the social sciences can make to the problems of a democratic society.

ADDITIONAL DISCUSSION

DR. MOWRER: I would like to express some observations very much in the vein that Dr. French has voiced. It seems to me that Dr. Gillin has quite admirably called our attention to one of the basic, if not *the* basic, problem in the whole field of social science. I think he stated the problem well, but don't believe he has given us the solution to it. He very precisely identified the problem as the lack of agreement between social sciences and the lack of a method which would bring about agreement. He makes a proposal in this connection. He says we need a validating operation for theory-making, and he suggests an "upward" validating system. He suggests we can refer our problem back to the more basic sciences and find alternative answers there. I think Dr. French was expressing the feeling that this is not really possible, because the problems and solutions in each field must essentially emerge from our research or work in that field. I do not believe that in the more basic sciences there will be ever found the solutions to various social problems. There are, in other words, in the field of social interaction and group dynamics, no *a priori* answers. This, I think, constitutes a serious, and in my mind insurmountable, obstacle to the validating operation proposed by Dr. Gillin.

The alternative that I see has a more promising future. It goes along lines that Dr. French also expressed. Here I would like to draw an analogy from the field of psychology, with special reference to the unique contribution of Freud. It seems to me that Freud advanced this field of psychology as remarkably as he did, not because he made an appeal to authority, not because he "looked upward" (to the basic social sciences), but because he looked downward with a new method. His problem centered his research. He did something, in fact, that nobody had done before: he took an individual with problems and attempted to learn from his observations of that individual struggling to solve those problems. Thus problem-centered, he developed a marvelous method of observation and manipulation. I don't think we can ever learn all there is to know in a field until we dirty our hands with the practical problems of that field.

This takes us into problems Dr. French pointed out. When social sciences begin to problem-center their research there are, to be sure, complications; and I would be the first to agree that practice alone, without conceptual interest and awareness, will not produce science in this or any other field. But, in the long run, we will learn no less from the complexities than from what is obvious and easy.

I think it is probably true that social scientists are in a weak position in assuming that we can learn more by watching than by doing, more by sitting back and observing than by participating. Social sciences are operating on the assumption that they learn more by observing, and letting lawyers and politicians carry on. If we can draw any kind of analogy of what has happened in individual psychology to the field of applied sociology, I would say that we are never going to get out of this quagmire as long as we sit back and watch. Referring back to the authority of the more basic sciences is not the way out, and I say this with all sympathy and admiration for the observational and deductive or inferential approach; but I don't believe more and more of that sort of thing will solve the problem. We must develop *social engineering* and get in and participate practically, which will greatly enlarge our observations and understanding. Difficulties exist, but the method has its rewards. Referring to the authority of the more "basic" sciences is not the way to solve the problem.

DR. GILLIN: I was not thinking in terms of reductionism. Take, for example, Freud. Everyone realizes now that he was guided in part by certain organic considerations current in the zoological sciences at the time. A curious thing was that this was taken for granted, i.e., not made explicit in the form of assumptions. If we are going to use current assumptions, my point is that we should see them for what they are—assumptions—and not necessarily invariable truths at a certain level of theory. However, it seems to me perfectly legitimate, and in fact almost inevitable, to incorporate as postulates in your own theoretical system validated theorems from other fields or levels of science, provided this is done explicitly and systematically.

DR. MOWRER: Will you give some examples of such assumptions taken for granted?

DR. GILLIN: The stage theory of development in personality growth is one. Freud's instinct theory is another example.

DR. MOWRER: I would see very little similarity to any zoological concepts. The notion of stages, yes, but that isn't all.

DR. GILLIN: How about the ideas of latency stage in personality development which were supposed to be inevitable, and have now been shown to be culture-bound on cross-cultural evidence?

DR. MOWRER: That again is empirical, not inevitable in my thinking.

DR. GILLIN: My proposition was that some of Freud's thinking was, as we should expect, drawn from biological sciences, yet neither you nor I regard this as reductionism.

DR. HUNT: I think you [*addressed to Dr. Mowrer*] are taking Dr. Gillin's remarks too narrowly. His principles on which an integrated science of behavior might be based would be broad ones. As a step toward integration, several disciplines might agree on certain behavioral areas for study. These could be identified and described in understandable and mutually acceptable terms. People trained in the use of these terms and studying the same phenomena should then arrive at common conclusions. This is what I think Dr. Gillin is calling for. It will not bring an overnight solution to the nature of man. The integrative principle involved is the common use of objective observation, logic, and the scientific method.

DR. HERSKOVITS: I have the feeling that Dr. Gillin's glasses are a little darker-tinted than mine when he looks at the matter of differences between social sciences. Through our integrated program here at Northwestern (a co-operative enterprise of the Departments of Anthropology, Psychology, and Sociology), I have observed that we have a much greater area of consensus than of differences—that the amount of overlapping between psychology, anthropology, and sociology is much more considerable than one might *a priori* have suspected, with more agreement between us than might be suspected.

It seems to me we have quite a number of integrating devices available to us. One such is the area program, which Dr. Gillin did not stress, but which is important as a focus to bring people together, since an area can be thought of as a region where a problem that touches on various disciplines is to be worked out. For example, the study of the movement of the Negro from Africa and the resultant changes in his culture in the New World necessitated the use of history as well as ethnology, a method we call ethno-history. It seems to me that if one follows the data of a given *problem* wherever they lead, one will finally arrive at a kind of integration which tends to get those who are interested in studying the same problem talking the same language, so to speak.

I may now perhaps turn to the point made by Dr. Mowrer concerning the place of preoccupation with practical problems in the research of the social scientist. We spoke, I believe, of the exact and natural sciences not having got anywhere until addressed to the solution of practical problems.

DR. MOWRER: I didn't say a word about exact or natural sciences.

DR. HERSKOVITS: Very well, let us take the matter of Freud. The contribution of Freud was based on the fact that he succeeded in developing a therapeutic technique. It seems to me that the contribution of Freud in the field of therapeutics was incidental to the basic workings of the psyche he revealed. In spite of the fact that his instinct theory, for example, doesn't hold true and that certain other assumptions he made have been found to be not valid, his basic discoveries about certain mechanisms in human psychology have been found to be useful and workable. I would like to suggest that in discussing problems we ought to differentiate between manipulation which Dr. Gillin spoke of, and the operation of what might be spoken of as the curiosity function of the scientist. It seems to me that the second is the basic one. Otherwise we tend to let practical considerations determine the problems we will study. As an anthropologist I have also observed too great an emphasis on problems of our culture. Problem-centered research—that is, research centered on practical problems—tends to allow the pressing situation to be more important than basic concepts and methods, which can be applied not only to the solution of immediate problems but to others of wider scope.

DR. HENRY: I didn't understand Dr. Gillin's proposal of setting up a master theory. Do you mean that in some way, possibly through the intervention of a foundation, individuals would be selected from various disciplines and this would be made . . . [*interrupted*]

DR. GILLIN: I made this as one possible suggestion. I am in favor of any plans that would produce a unified and mutually understandable structure for investigation. I certainly do not advocate a world bureau for how to think and behave. Any constructive plans that may be proposed have to specify conditions under which they are expected to operate, and it goes without saying that formulation of our knowledge is based on empirical knowledge of conditions as we know them at a given time.

DR. HENRY: All you suggest is that representatives of the different sciences get together and attempt to arrive at possibly better formulations of our present concepts, and then researchers in the various fields could refer to those formulations if they wished. It is not a program that you wish to impose.

DR. GILLIN: For my part, I would certainly avoid any scientific imposition or dictatorship at all costs.

DR. HENRY: Let us consider the period when Social Darwinism had pushed aside all other theories of social dynamics; you would have to assume the Social Darwinism occupied its pre-eminent position at that time because of the intrinsic merits of the theory.

DR. FRENCH: Thinking over the implications of your question, I would say that the contribution that causes a new set of concepts to be accepted for a time is often a one-sided contribution. For a time the merits of a one-sided theory are exploited, and there may be attempts to fit everything into the new framework; but the very one-sidedness of such formulation tends to highlight its defects, and then another orientation may become popular which is equally one-sided in the opposite direction.

DR. HENRY: Then you believe that a theory is accepted not because of its merits but rather because it is new.

DR. FRENCH: I say we tend to exploit one theory as long as it has merits, and then to give one-sided preference to another theory that is preoccupied with correcting the defects of the earlier theory. Then perhaps somebody else comes along with a theory that tries to synthesize the two conflicting notions.

DR. SCHNEIDER: May I understand this. In a very real sense you can't study men without getting to know and perhaps help them, a medical slang that you carry over to our field.

DR. FRENCH: My view is essentially this: that especially a young science should remain flexible, sensitive to ideas of many different kinds, and very tentative about its formulations. In young sciences like the social sciences and psychology, free scientific imagination is of the greatest importance; and premature formulation is likely to suppress the very ideas upon which the progress of the science depends.

DR. SCHNEIDER: Essentially the problem is one of adjusting people to one another.

DR. FRENCH: That is not science. I am talking not about people's getting along with one another, but about arriving at the truth by co-ordination of conflicting one-sided views.

DR. SASLOW: I believe it will take a much longer time than many expect to make clear the assumptions under which people professionally concerned with human behavior now operate. Ernst Mach pointed out, in his *History of the Development of Mechanics,* that the practical and effective use of levers, et cetera, antedated by centuries a clear theoretical understanding of the underlying principles. And P. Frank, in his *Modern Science and Its Philosophy,* describes clearly how the "common sense" of a particular period appears to have represented the crystallization of some earlier scientific theoretical system, now being subjected to the strain of data not covered by it.

Such observations suggest that attempts to standardize theoretical frameworks, as Professor Gillin appears to be advocating, are likely to be premature, and to be used against new discoveries acceptable only if the existing theoretical structures are altered.

DR. FRENCH: I am not critical of a theoretical approach, only it should be an individual's theoretical approach, which must then compete with other theories. A theoretical system agreed upon and imposed by any body of scientists would paralyze the individual scientific imagination upon which the progress of scientific investigation depends.

DR. GILLIN: I am entirely in favor of individual imagination. That is the only way we can feed in new material to new types of theory. Secondly, we don't have to accept the assumption that because in the past it took centuries to disprove or prove a certain proposition, it has to take that long in the future. We now know how to make short cuts. It is unrealistic to say that, because the groping scientists of the eighteenth century, for example, required decades or more to establish their assumptions, we have to do likewise. We have, I hope, learned something about scientific method in the last two hundred years that should add to our efficiency. Understand me: the assumptions we make still have to be subjected to scientific validation. But the techniques of this process have been greatly improved.

II

HOW FAR CAN THE SOCIETY AND CULTURE OF A PEOPLE BE GAUGED THROUGH THEIR PERSONALITY CHARACTERISTICS?

Otto Klineberg

THIS TOPIC suggests the old dichotomy between personality and culture. Many people have suggested that this is a false dualism; one hears a great deal about personality-in-culture, or culture-in-personality. Our discussion today indicates, however, that the dualism is a real one in terms of the focus of our attention. Some of us continue to be more interested in personality, and others in culture; we do not always agree as to what is important, nor as to how it should be approached.

In the past, the topic to which I am addressing myself was usually stated in reverse. It was presumably through an understanding of the culture that we would learn something important about personality. The problem was frequently stated in terms of what we could say about an individual if we knew nothing about him except the fact that he belonged to a particular culture; John Dollard, in his *Criteria for the Life History,* specifically raises the question in this form. More rarely, attempts have been made to proceed in the opposite direction, by looking at *individuals* to see what we can learn about the *culture.* Jules Henry has proceeded in this fashion (in "The Inner Experience of Culture" in *Psychiatry* for 1951), studying the flow of conversation between two individuals in the course of a psychiatric interview and indicating how much we can learn about a culture through such an analysis. The use of life histories by anthropologists may be regarded as another example of this tendency to learn about culture by studying individuals. Still another example is represented by the use of projective techniques, designed for the study of individual personalities, but, as applied by Hollowell, Hsu, and others, utilized in order to throw light on cultural processes, with special reference to culture change.

When individuals in various cultures are studied intensively, this is often undertaken in the hope of finding corroboration for what emerges from the study of a culture. It seems to me that this is essentially what is done by Kardiner, who develops his concept of what ought to be the "basic personality" structure from an analysis of cultural institutions, and then looks at the individual life histories or biographies to see the extent of agreement. The essential technique appears to be to determine whether impressions of personality gained from the study of culture are or are not borne out by the detailed life histories. In general, Kardiner finds such corroboration. On the other hand, L. M. Hanks, Jr., in an article on "The Locus of Individual Differences in Certain Primitive Cultures," published in the Viking Fund symposium on *Culture and Personality* in 1949, indicates that the life histories do not always corroborate the findings obtained by the ethnologist attempting to describe the culture in general. He was able to point out a considerable number of discrepancies. If the culture was correctly described, then apparently it does not reveal itself in the same manner in all individuals.

This appears to me to raise a problem of fundamental importance for the anthropologist concerned with the problem of personality. It seems to me not unfair to say that most ethnologists have shown relatively little interest in the phenomenon of individual variations in personality; they have looked for the common denominator more frequently than at the distribution curve. When I mentioned this to one anthropologist (Margaret Mead), I was told that the two points of view might be expressed in this fashion—the anthropologist was interested in the *grammar*, the psychologist (or at least this particular psychologist) in the dialects.

I am not sure to what extent this formulation would be accepted by other anthropologists. Within this frame of reference, however, I would make two points. First, if it is the *grammar* which we are after, we must make sure that the rules of the grammar are based on adequate evidence, so that there may be some hope of agreement on the part of various observers of the same culture. I shall return to this point in a moment. Secondly, I would suggest that dialects are also important, if we want to know how the members of a group actually behave and not only how they *should* behave. The variations among individuals in the same culture—not just the contrast between the "norm" and "deviations" from the norm, but the whole range of individual variations—represent an important area for research and study in the field of culture and personality.

Again I think it is not unfair to state that this range of individual variations has been ignored by many anthropologists, although there are, of course, a number of striking exceptions. Some of the material contained in anthropological monographs is based on so few informants that any hope of obtaining information concerning the range of individual variations is obviously ruled out. As an extreme case, Parson's study of Peguche was based on material obtained largely from a single informant. Even when a number of subjects have been used, as in the Abel-Hsu study of Chinese- and American-born males and females of Chinese origin, investigated by means of the Rorschach, there is a full and adequate discussion of the differences between the *groups*, but little indication of how the individuals within each group differed from one another. The individual tends, in fact, to be lost sight of in many of these culture and personality studies.

If any additional reasons are needed for the emphasis which I have placed on the study of the individual, I should like to point out further that one of the characteristics of a culture is its degree of homogeneity or heterogeneity. Cultures differ in this respect, but we cannot establish such differences unless we keep at least some of our attention fixed upon the individual, and upon the manner in which one individual differs from others. The anthropologist often makes an implicit assumption of homogeneity which, in my judgment, is not always borne out by the facts.

This raises the general question of methodology. A

good deal of anthropology is the result of a visit by one individual to a culture for a varying period of time, frequently working alone and bringing back in his notes and eventually presenting in monograph form the results of his observations. I think it is legitimate to ask certain questions of the anthropologist. Is his method reliable? In other words, if another anthropologist were to go to the same culture, would he necessarily get the same results? Is the method consistent?

It may not be easy to establish such reliability, since theoretically the observations by one anthropologist should be checked by others in order to determine whether the results can be accepted. My guess would be that the reliability would be very high for observations in the field of material culture, description of religious ceremonials, et cetera. When we are dealing with material in the field of personality, however, it seems to me it is asking a great deal of any one observer, no matter how honest or skillful he may be, to avoid completely the inevitable pitfalls of unconscious bias in his judgment of other individuals.

Surely we have a right to ask, in all fairness, that our anthropological colleagues who venture into judgments regarding personality characteristics should give us some indication of the reliability of their judgments. We demand this of psychologists. I am making no value judgment regarding the methodological superiority of one science over another, but I do believe that in this respect the care exercised by psychologists is greater, and the methodology more sound.

A second methodological criterion which concerns us is that the method should be valid, that it should really be capable of giving us the kind of information that we require; that the method be trustworthy. When a culture is studied for light on individual personality, there must be independent verification of the extent to which the individual really conforms to what is expected of him. This is, in somewhat different form, the point I have already made, that there must be studies of a number of individuals and that the variations among them should be noted.

I believe that my methodological demands upon anthropologists are justified if they are to deal with personality in a manner which will satisfy their tough-minded readers. Since I myself owe so much to the work of anthropologists, it may seem ungrateful of me to engage in this criticism. I should feel very pleased if this were regarded as criticism within the family, by one who feels closely identified with what the anthropologist has been doing. I know that in many cases anthropologists have satisfied the criteria which I am suggesting. Sometimes they have done so, however, without giving the rest of us adequate indication of just *how* they have done it. I think we need to know just how many informants they have had; the distribution of informants relative to the total population; the degree to which all the informants have been in agreement on the information they have supplied; whether they have agreed more regarding certain areas of the culture than others; the specific evidence on which judgments of personality have been made; an indication of data which corroborate or throw into question the personality judgments, et cetera. Anthropologists owe it to interested readers from all disciplines, as well as from their own, to bring back their protocols in such a fashion that we need not take their word for their conclusions, but that we ourselves may have the opportunity to make a critical judgment of the nature of the evidence for their conclusions.

There are special methodological problems which arise in any interdisciplinary activity. There are also methodological problems within the confines of a single discipline. I have tried to indicate some of the ways in which, in my judgment at least, the field of culture-and-personality studies may be furthered by a more adequate consideration of such methodological problems. In this whole area, it will be the anthropologists who have the opportunity to make the greatest contribution, since it is they who will have the contact with different cultures. It is because of the major importance of anthropology in answering the question: How far can the society and culture of a people be gauged through their personality characteristics? that I have ventured to make these few critical comments.

DISCUSSION

Oscar Lewis

THE QUESTION of the reliability of anthropological reporting is, of course, not a new one. Many years ago Dr. Paul Radin suggested the need for independent restudies in anthropology[1] (a suggestion which did not endear him to his colleagues) and more recently I have dealt with the same question in my restudy of Tepoztlan, the Mexican village earlier studied by Dr. Redfield. Dr. Klineberg's point concerning anthropological assumptions about homogeneity was borne out in our study. Using a larger variety and number of infor-

[1] Radin, Paul, *The Method and Theory of Ethnology.* New York: McGraw Hill Co., 1933, pp. 102-104.

mants, and guided by the assumption that all human societies are characterized by a wide range of custom and individual differences, we found, in fact, a much more complicated and differentiated society than Redfield's earlier study had led us to expect.[2]

I would also agree with Dr. Klineberg's statement that anthropologists have not concentrated upon individual differences in personality in the groups upon which they have reported. But it seems to me that this failure to study and report the range of variation raises a much bigger problem than has been indicated by Dr. Klineberg. It is not as if the anthropologists generally reported range in beliefs and custom within a community, but failed to be consistent when they reported on personality. Rather, the latter is perfectly consistent with the general failure to focus upon range in any aspect of culture, and to concentrate instead upon finding the culture patterns.[3] In a sense, then, Dr. Klineberg is challenging the adequacy, for some purposes, of a methodology which works almost exclusively on the high level of abstraction and generality implicit in the culture pattern concept.

That the neglect of range of variation is implicit in the search for culture patterns is made clear in an excellent statement by Ralph Linton on how anthropologists derive culture patterns. Dr. Linton explains that in order to describe and manipulate the variety of behavior found in a society, the anthropologist uses the "culture pattern construct" which Dr. Linton defines as ". . . the mode of the finite series of variations

---

[2] For a summary of the differences in our findings and the theoretical implications of these differences see the last chapter in my book *Life in a Mexican Village: Tepoztlan Restudied.* Urbana: University of Illinois Press, 1951.

[3] There have been exceptions, of course. See for example, the emphasis upon range and upon controlled observations in some of Clyde Kluckhohn's work on the Navaho, especially "Some Aspects of Infancy and Early Childhood" in Douglas G. Haring, *Personal Character and Cultural Milieu.*

which are included within each of the real culture patterns." Dr. Linton uses the following example:

> Thus, if the investigator finds that the members of a particular society are in the habit of going to bed sometime between eight and ten o'clock but that the mode for his series of cases falls at a quarter past nine, he will say that going to bed at quarter past nine is one of the culture patterns of their culture.[4]

Here Linton has shown us, perhaps inadvertently, one of the fundamental weaknesses of most anthropological field method and reporting. From Linton's use of the word *mode* the reader might infer that the anthropologist studied quantitatively the range of any particular behavior and then arrived at the mode which he reports as the culture pattern. However, it is well known that anthropologists rarely use statistical procedures, and by no means arrive at the mode in the traditional statistical manner. Furthermore, the "series of cases" in Linton's example are very often only a small number of all the cases. For example, when a monograph reports that children are nursed about two years, there is a high probability that this conclusion was arrived at after talking with a few mothers and making some casual and uncontrolled observations in the community. It would probably not even occur to most anthropologists, or *seem important,* to seek out and observe all the children being weaned at the time of the study and to determine their exact ages. Thus, by calling the culture pattern the mode, Linton is giving statistical dignity to what in most cases is probably no more than the anthropologist's guess. When Linton writes "... the total culture pattern construct is developed by combining all the culture construct patterns which have been developed ..." what happens is that we are adding up our guesses and arrive at a total guess, namely, the total culture pattern construct. That anthropol-

[4] Linton, Ralph, *The Cultural Background of Personality.* New York: 1945, pp. 45-46.

ogists sometimes guess brilliantly is to their everlasting credit and is a tribute to the element of art in the social sciences. But this is still a far cry from the more exact methods of the natural sciences—and perhaps it should be.

I suppose much depends upon the objectives of the study. When anthropology was expected to give us interesting descriptions of the esoteric customs of strange and rapidly disappearing cultures, such general impressions served a very useful purpose. For one thing, it drove home the point of the range in cultures. But now that anthropological data is increasingly being used by other social scientists who are attempting to check their own hypotheses with anthropological data, there is a much greater need for more careful and controlled investigation and reporting. This is especially true in the field of culture and personality, where detail and exactitude may be crucial. If, for example, it is reported that infants in a certain tribe are swaddled, and then we go on to suggest some relationship between swaddling and character formation, as some do, it would be good to know at least (1) how many children are not swaddled; (2) the range in swaddling practices and beliefs; (3) the range in duration of swaddling, i.e., how many children were swaddled two months, three months, et cetera; (4) and, finally, some comparison of two groups of children within the same society which were subject to different degrees and types of swaddling. Only in this way might one test the hypothesis as to the effect of swaddling. In other words, for some problems the range rather than the mode may be the crucial datum.

Our leading anthropologists have frankly recognized some of the limitations in the traditional derivation of culture patterns. Dr. Robert Redfield has recently emphasized the element of art in all the social sciences,[5] and Dr. Kroeber seems to accept these limitations as in the nature of things, hardly to be rem-

[5] Redfield, Robert, "The Art of Social Science." *American Journal of Sociology,* Vol. 54, November 1948, pp. 181-190.

edied by more informants or other improved field techniques. In discussing what he calls total patterns he writes:

> In proportion as the expression of such a large pattern tends to be abstract it becomes arid and lifeless; in proportion as it remains attached to concrete facts it lacks generalization. Perhaps the most vivid and impressive generalizations have been made by frank intuition deployed on a rich body of knowledge and put into skillful words.[6]

I might add that most of Dr. Klineberg's criticism of anthropology applies with at least double force to some of the very studies which he and other psychologists have been engaging in, namely, studies of national character structure. If, as I have suggested, it is extremely difficult to arrive at valid and reliable generalizations about the culture patterns of a small community of one or two thousand souls, how much more difficult must it be to arrive at such generalizations for an entire nation.

So long as anthropologists continue to be "a one-man expedition of all the social sciences," expected to report on "the whole culture," including ecology, economics, technology, social organization, religion, politics, the life cycle, personality, and so on, then there seems little hope of getting the more careful detailed and quantitative methods of study suggested by Dr. Klineberg. Perhaps the solution is to work on specific problems rather than the whole culture, and to spend many years with the same people, as Kluckhohn has done with the Navaho. But even more important is the need for more teamwork based upon a division of labor between anthropologists and psychologists in field studies.

ADDITIONAL DISCUSSION

DR. LINTON: In field work there are generally two avenues of information. The anthropologist may proceed by first

[6] Kroeber, Alfred A., *Anthropology*, 1948, p. 317.

establishing enough contact for rapport with some members of the society from whom he can get the information, and who will be his assurance that most other members of the society will not run away from him. Then he must take what people tell him as to what they do. From this he reconstructs what I have called elsewhere the ideal pattern. Secondly, he must observe what people do. When dealing with individuals and getting them to give him verbal statements and completely external observations of their overt behavior, he is up against the opposition of the personality of the anthropological investigator. I assume he should be psychoanalyzed, and his statements should be weighed against his personality. He will also find out that there are some people in the society in question with whom he can get along and some with whom he can't. His own personality limits the range of information he is going to be able to work with. The ethnographer who attempts more finds himself very much disappointed.

DR. HERSKOVITS: I find much of what Dr. Klineberg has said to be useful, and much with which I am in agreement. Anthropological tradition, without doubt, has been to give the consensuses of the modes of behavior that anthropologists have studied rather than variations around those modes. Yet it would be less than just not to recognize that this tradition reflects a very real and continuing need in cross-cultural analysis. I would like to suggest that one cannot study dialectic variants until the basic structure of a language manifesting these dialects has been established. We are, in somewhat different terms, being gently chided for not studying individual behavior as well as social consensuses. Yet until recently anthropologists have been few in numbers—cultures seemingly endless in their variety. We are only today beginning to be able to contemplate the basic scientific need of independent restudies of a given way of life, to test the validity of earlier findings.

This brings up a different methodological problem. Culture

is not a phenomenon subject to laboratory control; yet it is dynamic, constantly changing, and, to the point of Dr. Klineberg's paper, manifests variation from the patterned behavior of one individual to that of another. Culture is lived by human beings; it is studied by human beings. How, then, methodologically, are we to reconcile these variables—changes in time, differences in individual behavior, and the impact of the differing personalities of the student and those studied?

A concept I have found useful and have developed in a recent book, may be introduced here—the concept of *ethnographic truth*. We have, I feel, perhaps in academic psychology no less than in anthropology, been beset by the idea of "a" valid answer to a problem, "a" valid description. In the qualitative approach of psychiatry and psychoanalysis, of course, this question has not even been broached, which is one reason, perhaps, why the study of personality and culture manifests those methodological lacunae of which Dr. Klineberg complains. But the concept of ethnographic truth implies that the study of culture is essentially the study of the range of permitted variation in a given type of behavior or idea-system. Culture, in these terms, is to be defined not as a series of modes of thought and behavior, but rather as a series of limits within which differences in thought and behavior are recognized as permissible. This allows for the existence of different local and class patterns; for change over time; and for the play between tradition and differing personality types. It recognizes that different informants in the same society give different accounts of the common culture; that different students studying the same culture will lay differing emphases on its various manifestations.

These are some of the problems which anthropological thought, as concerns methodology, is considering. I feel it is through an approach of this sort that we will fully utilize the concept of variation in cultural behavior, something which, as

I have long realized and feel now, in full agreement with Dr. Klineberg, is one of our major needs.

DR. WINCH: I would like to ask Dr. Klineberg a question. I think I understand what you mean by reliability, but what about validity?

DR. KLINEBERG: I am very appreciative of the additional comments of my friends in that corner and have nothing to disagree with. The matter is somewhat simpler when you are making a test. As far as validity is concerned, in a test it means that it measures what is supposed to be measured. There is a statement made by anthropologists about the ideal type. It seems to me we want to know the negative of the ideal type. One way of discovering it is to find out what are the behaviors of the people in the group. To the extent the anthropologist says they do that, then it seems that a kind of validation of whether they are right or not is to see whether, in a range of individuals, a good many of them actually do that.

DR. BOYER: It occurs to me that we are looking for a utopia, and I think we might find it if we could send four teams of the disciplines to go into the field to work, accumulate data, and before publication have ample testing periods to validate all the material that has been returned.

III

FACTORS IN PERSONALITY: SOCIO-CULTURAL DETERMINANTS AS SEEN THROUGH THE AMISH

Manford H. Kuhn

THE FRAME of reference on which this paper is based is that of self-theory as developed by C. H. Cooley, G. H. Mead, H. S. Sullivan, T. Newcomb, *et al.* In shortest possible compass, self-theory can be stated thus. Human behavior is organized and directed; that which gives human behavior its organization and direction is the verbal internalization in the individual of the roles and statuses which he and those around him play; in fact, his view of himself as the common object among all of his acts, and thus in all his experience becomes an attitude which, in its most general form, constitutes, as Newcomb has put it, the most general of all attitudes, an attitude toward attitudes. In terms advanced by Sherif and Cantril, it is the norm or anchoring point with respect to which all judgments are made, all things perceived, and all actions taken.

The analysis of social organization in terms of roles and

statuses can be done, of course, without reference to what goes on within the individuals who make up the society under consideration. That is, it can be done in terms of recurrent intermeshing overt behaviors. In self-theory the problem is to discover what elements of roles and statuses have been internalized and, further, how these can be used to predict behavior—assuming that analysis of overt role-playing does not give us the precise and dependable predictions we seek, particuarly when there are choices open (open alternatives available).

It has been only recently that we have begun to see clearly the *class of phenomena* to which the self (that is, these internalized elements of roles and statuses) belongs. It is increasingly apparent that we may usefully treat the self as a general *attitude*, as I have already indicated. This means that we may apply to the study of the self many of the techniques which have already proved effective in the study of other attitudes: for example, we may use questionnaires, and may look forward ultimately to the scaling of self-attitudes.

It was with this frame of reference that I approached the study of personality among the Older Order Amish. This was my "way of seeing;" what I did *not* see—because I did not look—must now be apparent. I did not see what their toilet training and weaning procedures are, nor what possibilities and probabilities there are for infantile traumas. I did not examine how phases of their culture might serve as projective screens on which might be thrown their infantile repressions. I did not examine their myths to see what evidences they might bear of the Oedipus situation or some variant thereon. I did not attempt to discover whether they had some idiosyncratic forms of neuroses and psychoses peculiar to Amish society.

On the other hand, I did not attempt to break up their child training (socialization) procedures into the categories of drive, cue, response, and reinforcement categories. My frame of reference designates roles and statuses as learned matters, but the operations I was intent on making did not include the study of the long developmental process by which this learning takes place.

It is not my purpose to challenge the validity or usefulness of either the psychoanalytic or learning theory approaches, except to indicate that they do not demonstrably take me down the road I intend to travel. I was interested in getting some indications of role and status internalizations which I could compare with those of other groups, and with other forms of behavior. What I have been trying to indicate is thus neither a boast nor an apology; it is merely an attempt to delineate.

THE OLDER ORDER AMISH

The Older Order Amish are simply one of many branches of the general group of people usually referred to as Mennonites. There are seventeen generally recognized sects within this Mennonite group. The origin of the Mennonites is usually traced to the Swiss Brethren of about four centuries ago. The heterodoxy of the Swiss Brethren was chiefly their belief in adult baptism. This group underwent considerable persecution, and drifted down into the upper Rhineland, where it met and merged with a similar group coming up from the lower Rhineland. The Amish split from this general group because of differences of belief regarding the imposition of "shunning" or the "mite" (*Meidung*). The Amish, following Jacob Amman, believed in the strict application of this isolating practice to all church members who were in any way miscreant, while the other Mennonite groups were more lenient.

The largest emigration of Amish and Mennonites from Europe to this country came in the eighteenth century. A sizable group settled in the tolerant Quaker colony of Pennsylvania. It is from the original Pennsylvania settlements that most of the many other Amish settlements in this country have come. There is no hierarchical organization which holds these people together, but they maintain a fair amount of contact with one another. They also maintain essentially the same beliefs, manners, and dress of their earliest predecessors.

Their clothes are of the buttonless and ornamentless variety. The women tolerate no figure or print in the material from which their clothing is made; the men have no collars on their coats, and wear the traditional so-called broadfall trousers. Their clothing styles they share, however, with some of the other, less conservative Mennonite groups. The one distinctive practice, not visible to most casual observers, is that of holding religious meetings in homes (sometimes in barns) rather than in churches or other designated meeting houses. For this practice they are known as the "House Amish." They drive buggies and do not own cars, but this practice they have in common with a few of the most conservative splinters of the Mennonites.

Their houses are quite barren by our standards, though they are often large and well built. The Amish have no rugs on their floors, no pictures on their walls, no curtains at their windows—no furnaces, no electricity, no telephones, no modern conveniences. If they buy farms previously belonging to non-Amish, they first rip out the wiring, the telephone, the furnace, and the like before they move in. It is not that they have little money, for in monetary terms they are usually very well-to-do (this is evidenced by the fact that they sometimes pay as much as five hundred dollars an acre for farmland). Their plainness of living stems from their religious beliefs.

The religious belief most directly connected with plainness of living is the belief that man's worst sin is *pride*. To own an automobile, to have upholstered furniture, or even to have rubber tires on one's tractor (for they do have tractors) would be evidence of having an overweening pride.

Closely related is the doctrine of the "unequal yoke" which seizes on a convenient Biblical passage—"Be ye not unequally yoked together with unbelievers"—to buttress their separatism, their quaintness, and their nonco-operation.

Like the Friends and the Brethren, the Amish and Mennonites have been traditionally opposed to war and to participation in war. All of the Amish young men subject to the draft are conscientious objectors—this uniformity is achieved by ejecting from their group any who did not take the conscientious objector stand. All of them do register, however. (The Quakers contribute only one in ten of their draft-eligible numbers to the ranks of conscientious objectors, but on the other hand approximately half of all the nonregistrants are Quakers. The Mennonites are somewhere in between these extremes, but toward the Amish end.) The Amish are nonco-operative with government in other ways, also.

While they pay their taxes, they do not vote in state and national elections. They avoid the courts as far as possible. They even avoid the county agricultural agent, although their farming practices are for the most part excellent (they practiced rotation of crops, the liming of their fields, the use of legumes and manures, long before these were practiced by others). But they do not participate in farm organizations (invoking the principle of the unequal yoke), nor do they have anything to do with state agricultural colleges.

They are a close-knit, socially self-isolated group of people. Their social organization in terms of roles and statuses bears looking into.

AMISH ROLES

In scrutinizing a specified society, it is frequently useful to arrange the roles which the individuals play in a continuous age-graded series which then delineates the natural history of the individual's functions in that particular society. Among the Older Order Amish this continuous age-graded series of roles stands in marked contrast to that of ours in our urban, secular society. The Amish infant and child are immersed in their families, and their widest horizons are Amishdom. Even at the ages of fourteen and fifteen some of my Amish subjects in the Kalona area had never visited Iowa City, only sixteen or seventeen miles away. This is, apparently, a very deliberate practice, for adult Amish people shop regularly in Iowa City. The horizon of the Amish child is thus bounded largely by his family, and as a consequence his earliest roles are much less age-graded than are those of our children. He associates mainly with his fellow siblings, who are thus not as precisely his age-peers as are the associates of our children.

When he goes to school, he goes to one-room schools, where again his playmates may be drawn from any of several different age-groups. It was frequently apparent that older brothers and sisters were taking responsibility for the conduct and welfare of the younger members of their families who were in the same room with them—in striking contrast to the studied disdain for the younger ones evidenced by siblings on our playgrounds.

The Amish children go to school for the first eight grades, and then they universally leave school. The Amish believe in the value of the skills of reading, writing, and arithmetic, but they think of the content of the high school as being of "the world" (*die Welt*) and thus definitely bad for their children. Furthermore, high schools are of the consolidated type, and were they to send their children to these schools their children would be forced to associate in large measure with non-Amish, and thus tend to get weaned away from the faith. As a result of this belief, the Amish are everywhere apprehensive about the stiffening of the compulsory school-attendance laws of the states in which they live. Many Amish families have left Ohio and Indiana for Iowa in the last few years in order to avoid the school-attendance laws of the former states which would result in their children being forced to attend high school.

When the Amish child leaves school he becomes a youth. That is, now begin the roles of courtship and full-time apprenticeship for adulthood. The boys usually become hired men, often to relatives. They are expected to save a fair amount of money for the establishment of a farm and home. The girls are now expected to become full-time full-fledged household help. But the most interesting thing about this youth age-grade is that it is a period of semi-permissive orgiastic behavior, at least for the boys. For example, it is regarded as very wrong to have one's photograph taken, but since these young people have not yet joined the church they all manage to get their pictures taken during this period (and I understand that Amish families have rather complete picture albums collected in this fashion, but I have no firsthand proof of this). The boys frequently get into scrapes, or secretly buy and use automobiles, or use intoxicants, or go on (for us fairly mild) binges in larger cities. Their courtship practices are said to involve at least the possibilities of bundling. There are even some reports of sex orgies of a fairly wild order, but it is difficult to corroborate these reports or to elicit any valid information from so close-mouthed a people. Even in this period of half-permitted wild-oats-sowing the Amish have rarely any brushes with the law.

At about the time for marriage the Amish youths join the church. With baptism and marriage the young Amish couple are confronted with a new series of roles. They are now the mainstays of the church, and must lead exemplary lives as they begin to establish their families. Since there is no paid religious leadership, each man must be prepared to serve his turn as religious leader if it should be his lot, and this in addition to the hard life of the relatively machineryless farmer. The wife must expect to bear many children (the mean number of children per family in my sample was 6.9).

During this period of raising a family the couple must also save against the rapidly approaching day on which they must purchase a farm for each of the boys in order to get him "set up."

After the family has been reared and married off, there follows another period of either partial relaxation of the rigid rules, or else their quiet evasion, one cannot be sure which. The elder Amish are said to spend their winters in Florida frequently, and if my informants are correct, they enjoy electric lights and all the other modern conveniences—away from the scrutiny of the children and other members of Amishdom. In any event, the older pattern of building the "*Grossvater* house" for the grandparents somewhere near the main house, while still the rule, is—I am told—waning. Instead the older couples are increasingly going in to the nearby villages to retire.

As to the continuity of roles into the afterlife, I am sure that the Amish do not put very much stress on the afterlife, at least as compared with that put on such conceptions by most rural fundamentalistic and evangelical sects (the Amish are, of course, neither fundamentalist—in the usual sense—nor evangelical). While the Amish scorn *die Welt,* it is more from the frame of reference of their own group as the kingdom than from the position that all this life should be other-worldly centered.

It is useful to contrast this sequence of age-graded roles with that in our own society. It is at once apparent that our sequence is characterized by at least two and possibly three sharp disjunctions or cultural discontinuities in role-playing that have no counterpart, at least in comparable degree, among the Amish. Least sharp, but doubtless very real, is the disjunction between childhood and adolescence.

The cultural discontinuity between adolescence and full-fledged adulthood, and between adulthood and old age, are clearly major in their sharpness and contrast. For the Amish, however, work roles are so well established that they may be said to be nearly fully operative. These continue as appropriate roles until death, with only a minor shading off in old age. The age-grades of youth and old age for the Amish represent merely minor embroideries on the general and uniform pattern, while for us these age-grades represent different patterns altogether.

Fully as contrasting is the detailed and multifarious age-grading, almost down to a year-by-year scale—or even half-year-by-half-year in some instances—which characterizes the childhood roles of our society and dictates the character of childhood associations and play-life. The Amish, on the other hand, have no such meticulous age-grading of childhood roles, and may in some senses even be correctly said not to have a childhood at all.

About sex role differentiation I can give no such detailed account. It is clear, however, that the Amish are patriarchal and that the other aspects of their sex role differentiation are the rather usual ones to the agricultural end of our society. That is, the men do the "farm and barn" work while the women do the "house and garden and chickens" work. Men have the major roles in religious activity.

The young boys and girls of six and seven are about equal in their aggressiveness or, by our standards, lack of it. From eight years on, the boys are more and more to be contrasted with the girls in their spontaneity, outgoingness, and directness of both speech and other conduct. By the age of fourteen the girls are inhibited and shy; their faces are increasingly stern and unsmiling, their glances averted, their voices low and quiet, their motions checked and careful. Actually both sexes follow this pattern by our standards, but the girls simply are much more extreme in it than are the boys. I watched a ball game between a Riverside ("tough," "Gentile") team and a Skunk Hollow (Amish) team. The spectator activity was more intriguing than was that of the players. The Riverside rooters engaged in the usual loud, raucous cheering and booing, while the Skunk Hollow partisans encouraged their team merely by smiling broadly and politely applauding with a minimum of body movements. There were girls on both teams, in fact more on the Amish team than on the Riverside team; the Amish girls were, on the whole, better ballplayers than were the Riverside girls, despite the former's long skirts and this curious personality inhibition or restraint.

As for occupational role-playing, there is no such differentiating factor among the Amish, for the Amish are, with very unusual exceptions, all farmers (the one exception that I noted was a blacksmith who also farmed).

Nor does the question of class differentiation of roles detain us, for Amish society is virtually classless. Their religious leaders are chosen by lot, and rotate. Their potential economic differences are held at a minimum by their patterns of co-operative activity, and particularly by their injunction against pride as it might manifest itself in differential possession of items of conspicuous consumption. The Quakers have a reputation for extreme democracy, but I venture to propose that there are infinitely fewer "big wheels" in Amishdom than in Quaker circles.

This, then, is the picture of Amish social organization in terms of overtly observable role and status assignments.

It was my aim to attempt to investigate what elements of these roles and statuses had been internalized in Amish children.

AMISH SELF-ATTITUDES

I had been initially interested in studying Amish personality by observing the behavior of three Amish children who had been forced, by the closing of a one-room school, to attend the consolidated school at Riverside. Despite the peculiarities of their dress and other behavior, they were neither ridiculed nor picked on by the other students. Furthermore, although they did not possess any of the paraphernalia of childhood which we deem appropriate—such as bicycles, ball-playing equipment, multitudinous dolls, mechanical toys, guns, and other gadgets, they seemed utterly serene and happy about their situation. While our children had hours and hours of free time both before and after school and over the week ends, the Amish children spent this time in chores and farm work and gave little if any evidence of minding, resenting, or rebelling against this situation as seemed probable that our children would do. I was interested in discovering what kinds of controls were operative here that managed to sustain this kind of personality organization. In short, what kind of conception of self was built into the Amish child which made possible this stable organization and direction of behavior?

No claim is advanced that the operations taken constitute an inclusive investigation of this internalization. The research consisted of the administering of a questionnaire to three groups—fairly equal in number—Amish, Mennonite, and "Gentile" children, in fourth through eighth grades in fifteen one-room schools. The questionnaire consisted of thirteen open-ended questions having to do with preferred and rejected roles, anticipated roles, objects having to do with role-playing, models for role-playing, situations of happiness and embarrassment. The completed questionnaires, of which there were 201, were analyzed by thematic content analysis, with particular reference to age differentiation in role-playing.

The proportions of thematic responses to most of the questions were remarkably different among the three groups. They indicated that the roles preferred by the Amish children (*Table 1*) were to an astonishing degree

	Child World Roles	Adult World Roles	Other
AMISH	45.6	39.9	14.5
MENNONITE	49.5	32.9	17.6
'GENTILE'	62.0	17.2	20.8
		PERCENTAGES	

TABLE 1

Thematic Classification of Responses to the Question "What are the Three Things You Like Most to Do?"

roles which we deem to belong to adult world activity. But they also indicated that the roles avoided or rejected by the Amish (*Table 2*) were also of the adult world, suggesting that the entire range from which choices among the Amish are made are to a much greater extent made up of adult world roles.

	Adult World Roles	Child World Roles	Religio-Anxiety-Aggression Themes	Cleanliness, Eating and Sleeping Roles
AMISH	48.0	19.3	30.4	2.3
MENNONITE	45.8	28.8	22.2	3.2
'GENTILE'	40.9	36.9	14.8	7.4

PERCENTAGES

TABLE 2

Thematic Classification of Responses to the Question "What Are the Three Things You Like Least to Do?"

The Amish to a much greater extent than the "Gentiles" looked forward with preference to farmer and housewifely roles as adults (*Table 3*). Since most of the adult world

	Farm Roles	Non-farm Roles	Other
AMISH	45.6	23.1	31.3
MENNONITE	30.5	44.1	25.4
'GENTILE'	21.1	53.3	25.6

PERCENTAGES

TABLE 3

Thematic Classification of Responses to the Question "What Are the Three Things You Would Like to Do When You Grow Up?"

roles they now engage in are farming and housekeeper roles, it is easy to see that their lives are going to be far less internally complicated by cultural discontinuities than are those of the other two groups.

The Amish children named adult objects such as dishes, breeding animals, farmland, et cetera, when asked to name things they now owned which they liked most (*Table 4*),

	Adult Objects	Children's Objects	Books	Other
AMISH	42.0	32.6	13.1	12.4
MENNONITE	35.3	44.9	10.1	9.7
'GENTILE'	25.9	63.7	6.1	4.3

PERCENTAGES

TABLE 4

Thematic Classification of Responses to the Question "What Are the Three Things You Now Own Which You Like the Most?"

while the Gentile children—as we would expect—named toys and playthings.

It was expected that Amish children, when asked to name models, would name their parents, people in their primary group, or religious figures. Actually the Gentile children named parents and members of their primary groups more often than did the Amish, while the Amish tended to identify their models in terms of abstract, moral, religious attributes (*Table 5*). There are at least two al-

	Abstract Attributes	Primary Group Model	Secondary Model	Other
AMISH	57.9	26.3		15.8
MENNONITE	47.9	24.7	9.6	17.8
'GENTILE'	20.3	41.9	18.9	18.9
		PERCENTAGES		

TABLE 5

Thematic Classification of Responses to the Question "What Person Would You Most Like to Be Like?"

ternative hypotheses to explain this: one is that Amish upbringing is accompanied by more perceptive teaching regarding principles of conduct than is that of the Gentile child; the other is that the general consistency of the moral and ethical code is so much greater among the Amish that they are able to form a "generalized other" (in G. H. Mead's term), a consistent abstraction of ethical expectations and norms which is not possible among the Gentiles, living as they do in our secular world of ethical clash, contradiction, and moral uncertainty. It is interesting that the Amish also defined the persons they would least like to be like in the same fashion—that is, in terms of abstract attributes.

In connection with describing their choices for models, they were asked to explain "Why?" The Amish, in striking contrast to the Gentiles, gave reasons having as a common theme that, were they like their described models, then other people would be kind and friendly to them. This seems to indicate an expectation of aggression or unfriendliness from others. Whether the "others" in this case referred to other Amish or to outsiders was not perfectly clear, but the context suggested that it referred to other Amish. This raises interesting questions regarding the basic anxieties and channels for hostilities in a society which so completely forbids the overt expression of the latter, and which so sternly stresses nonviolence and nonresistance.

CONCLUSIONS

A reasonable inference from these data would seem to be that the Amish children are not wooed away from their —to us—stark manner of existence because, first of all, they are kept in partial isolation from our world until they have assumed roles in Amish society which give them considerable satisfaction and security through the related statuses. Furthermore, these roles are highly continuous throughout life and thus lend a high degree of potency to the expectations which even early playing of such roles engenders.

To a youngster who is already playing an adult role, the trinkets of our children must appear as highly superficial placebos. To our children, on the other hand, the playing of adult roles at so young an age must appear as a highly enviable thing—thus the respect and lack of ridicule which our children accord the Amish children despite their queer garb.

In short, the Amish conceive of themselves as young adults with many of the manipulative privileges that go with this status on the farm and with the developing skills to effectuate these manipulations. The Gentiles conceive themselves as children in a world in which it is highly desirable to be adult, a status which is dangled in front of them but which they are not allowed to come at all close to occupying. Their future expectations, unlike those of the Amish, are varied and nebulous. Thus the Amish self-structure gives a sustaining organization and direction to their behavior, while the Gentile self-structure, fragile as it is, permits our children to be peculiarly amenable to the pressures of our mass culture.[1]

Social and cultural factors become determinants of personality factors only as the individual comes to internalize the roles he plays and the statuses he occupies. He asks "Who am I?" and can answer this question of identity only in terms of his social position—that is, in terms of social space and social time. The answer to this question, and those to related ones such as "What do I do?" and "How do I feel about the person I am and the things I do?" constitute self-attitudes—or the "self." This paper reports an attempt to demonstrate the proposition that it is feasible to attempt objective identification and comparison of such attitudes. That such an approach to personality is uniquely compatible and consistent with social science theory seems to me self-evident.

DISCUSSION

Charlotte G. Babcock

I SHOULD like to speculate a little further on factors within the individual which are reflected in group behavior that

[1] It should be noted that while this research was not directly concerned with the problem of acculturation, a hypothesis regarding this problem is suggested by the findings, viz: a society's proneness to acculturative change varies inversely with the degree of cultural continuity of its roles, *ceteris paribus*.

may also contribute to the Amish personality organization. The notable factor in the descriptions of factors welding this group together is the absence (repression) of overt and conscious competitiveness and aggression. There is no hierarchy such as occurs in other societies as a device by means of which the individual may feel competitive, envious, striving, or superior, and through which various internal stresses and social role solutions may be worked out. A pertinent comment in Dr. Kuhn's remarks is that in this society no one dares not to be equal; to be unequal, or to be "unequally yoked," is a sin. Thus, the competition must occur in a negative fashion from that common to other societal experience, namely, one must compete not to be different. Competition may be involved in the value attitude of plainness which is based on an authoritative religious abstraction that Man's worst sin is (overt) pride. The pride comes out in maintaining the plainness. This is translated in the group into avoiding any open competition, any standing out; for example, each must take his turn as leader; one should not vote.

How are the feelings of hostility and aggressiveness expressed? One channel of outlet is in the phenomenon of *Meidung*, or shunning. Shunning constitutes a positive outlet for aggression against members of one's own group; even though the process is less frequently invoked now than in the days of the Old Amish, the fear of expulsion with resulting total isolation and abandonment, a virtual suicide, must serve as a powerful deterrent to the individual in expressing his hostile feelings. Equally, once invoked, shunning is a powerful source of gratification to the wish for hostile expression. By identification with the one being expelled, one can also expel from oneself the bad or unacceptable, a phenomenon common to witchhunting in any of its forms. Thus we can see that there exists in the society a way in which hostile feelings can in varying degree be expressed toward other individuals within the group.

A second method, perhaps more disguised and subtle, exists in the idea that one must hate the ways of the world. We do not have in this paper details of the phantasies of either adults or children, but much energy must be used in the concept of "expectation of aggression and unfriendliness from 'others,'" and much hostile feeling must exist when it is necessary to so "sternly stress nonviolence and nonresistance." The external world must appear as very hostile, but best handled by denial. In this connection one wonders about the limitation of curiosity. While this lends itself to closeness with the group, and to the partial isolation which allows time for the internalization of socially sanctioned roles so these become determinants of the personality, it also sacrifices the individual potential for imagination and growth to the demands of the group, and perhaps accounts for the violent measures of expulsion which occur when one trespasses or is suspected of trespassing.

It would seem that as an individual the child must be able to assume these roles largely through the strong identification patterns with the parents. This is accomplished partially by the clear definition of acceptable male and female functions and patterns of behaving, and again suppresses the capacity for development of overlapping activity and function. To the child, the parents, whose roles are so sharply defined and who deviate so little in relation to the multiplicity of stimuli with which a child is beset, must seem powerful. It is probable that there is forcing of the sanctioned behavior with a degree of relentlessness which makes the parent seem very strong. The wish to be equally controlling must play a part in the ease with which the adult role is so readily assumed. This is further elaborated as adulthood is marked by another and paralleling process of separation, that of self from external society, in which again the sanctioned behavior is very specifically defined and clearly demarcated. Recognition of the strength of the drives in adolescence is universal, however, for it is in this period that the Amish can sanction some need for deviation from the intense pattern.

The child is thus early pressed into adult behavior, but one wonders in terms of integration of his capacity to its optimum if he reaches true maturity. Rather, out of feelings of shame and unworthiness he may act as an adult; and out of the group conscience he may maintain his narcissistic economy by adult behavior rather than by internalized and rational use of guilt as may occur in other societal situations. Here the highly continuous role without age-grading and with definition of function not only leads to permanency in the maintenance of the role but gives security and self-definition by self-restriction. Through related statuses, a level of security is thus attained. It would be interesting to study the adult Amish and to assess whether or not there is internal rigidity in the character structure. Furthermore, the knowledge of the points at which overt or covert anxiety are experienced would be enlightening.

Some questions may be raised concerning the author's method in this paper. Does it measure aspiration? For example, do Amish children really not want toys, or are they too afraid or too proud to make known their needs? Is there genuine gratification only in relation to pleasing the parent? Since the children are described as not close to the parents, are the abstract models for the children's personality development representations of the parent's? Further, one could ask: Is what is good for the Amish society (limitation of individual potential) good for individuals, even though they are described as happy? Is it relevant to discuss status, with its usual connotations, in regard to Amish society if the roles are theoretically undifferentiated?

ADDITIONAL DISCUSSION

[Dr. Kuhn was asked to elaborate as to why he did not resort to Hullian Learning Theory in his interpretation of Amish material.]

DR. KUHN: I would like to indicate some of the reasons for which I do not find Learning Theory useful in structuring research in human behavior. In the first place, Learning Theory is built around a drive scheme, the validity of which is seriously to be doubted and which has in this respect many of the limitations of the earlier instinctual explanations of human behavior. In the second place, Learning Theory, based as it is on minute elements of the behavioral process, can offer no empirically grounded generalizations which are predictive for the complex phenomena of human social life. Hull's law of afferent neural interaction when translated into plain English goes like this: "When two or more stimuli are directed at the organism at the same time, God only knows what kind of a response will be made!" Since there are always many more than two stimuli existing at a given time for the human being, any learning theory generalizations must necessarily be *post hoc* in character, and thus are characteristically explanations by naming. In the third place, the attempts to use Learning Theory in dealing with human behavior have made the allegation that "culture is a maze." As Dorrian Appel[2] has pointed out, this verbal bridge is an untenable analogy. Culture partakes of the nature both of the maze and of the reward at the end of it, and indeed many other disparate things. In the fourth place, Learning Theory fails to structure the functions of language and of thought in the learning and behavioral processes.

A learning theory which could be of use to the social sciences would have to address itself primarily to *role learning*. In this regard I have several hunches. One of them is that the *label* of the role is of critical importance in learning the various elements of a role. Another is that there is a close functional relation between language, thought, and ideology on the one hand, and "reinforcement" and "extinction" on the other.

---

[2] "Learning Theory and Socialization." *American Sociological Review,* Vol. 16, February 1951, pp. 23-27.

Finally, an acceptable and useful learning theory must structure the distinction between those role blockages which lead to thought, critical reconstruction of behavior, and adaptation, and those blockages which lead to repression and substitutive, complusive, and obsessive behavior.

DR. MOWRER: I think it is very satisfactory and good to have a person of Dr. Kuhn's interest and background to point out the flaws and shortcomings of the Learning Theory. The discussion seems to me to have already pointed to the phenomenon or concept of identification as being a critical issue here. We have two lines of thought regarding identification; a present Freudian thought which uses such unsatisfactory terms as oral intrajection, et cetera. On the other hand, it is entirely possible to take basic Learning Theory and by extending it get a theory of identification which is entirely adequate and to your purposes significant, and superior to any theories like oral intrajection. Bill Hunt and I took part in a conference on Learning Theory and psychotherapy out in California, and Bill began to talk about the forthcoming marriage of Learning Theory and psychotherapy. Somebody said it would be a good thing for both parts, since it would make a man out of Learning Theory and an honest woman out of psychotherapy. I wouldn't want you to give up Learning Theory too easily.

IV

THE CHINESE IN HAWAII: A RORSCHACH REPORT

T. W. Richards

THIS IS in the nature of a progress report. During the winter of 1949, Dr. Francis Hsu obtained Rorschach and other records from a group of persons whom he designated as Chinese in Hawaii. After giving the project some preliminary thought, he and I decided that I should make a "blind" evaluation of each Rorschach record, knowing only the age and sex of each subject. This is part of a wider project. Within the limits of certain assumptions about the Rorschach test (which the reader may not be willing to make) this report will primarily be factual.

In all, thirty-five Rorschach records form the basis for this report. These were the first, alphabetically, of a much larger group tested (some one hundred and fifteen). Twenty-seven subjects are male, eight female; they range in age from sixteen to sixty. The mean age of the women is twenty-five years; that for the men, forty-one. They are of top-drawer educational and occupational status; most are high school graduates, many with several years of college and professional school, such as dentistry and medicine. A few have had graduate training in a specialty. Successful lawyers, physicians, bankers, politicians, and

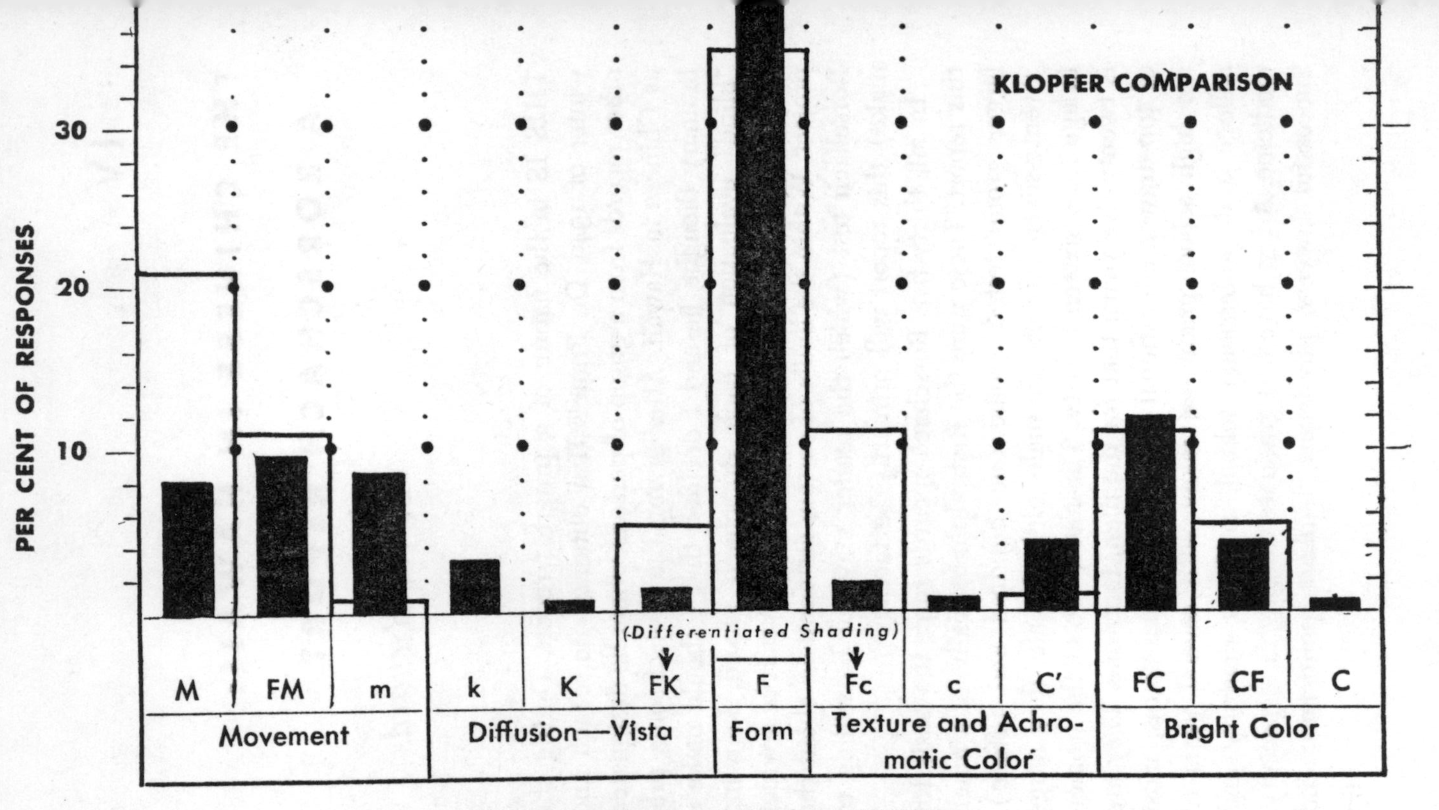
PER CENT OF RESPONSES
30
20
10
KLOPFER COMPARISON
(Differentiated Shading)
M
FM
m
k
K
FK
F
Fc
c
C′
FC
CF
C
Movement
Diffusion—Vista
Form
Texture and Achromatic Color
Bright Color
RELATIONSHIPS AMONG FACTORS

Figure 1

businessmen characterize the group. Few of the women were engaged predominantly in activities such as homemaking and child rearing.

The author knew nothing about these things while looking at the records.

RESULTS

(1) It would be close to impossible to pick up a Rorschach record and identify the subject as belonging to a group designated by Dr. Hsu as Hawaiian Chinese. The probability of error in this regard might be narrowed slightly by the fact that many of the records mention things specifically regarding the Pacific area; not only Hawaii, but Australia, the Philippines, Japan, Alaska, are mentioned. Of extreme interest is the fact that in these records China or Chinese (or something more specific, such as Peking or Canton or Nanking or Sun Yet-sen) is mentioned by half the women and by a third of the men. Furthermore, subjects who mention things Chinese tend to do so repeatedly, as if this formed a special sort of bulwark in the face of the inkblots. It seemed that being Chinese, in an historical sense, was important in the ego structure of many of these subjects.

(2) It might be well at this point to present some objective comparison of the group with norms.

Figure 1 shows how these subjects (black columns) compare with the profile (open columns) with which Bruno Klopfer* characterizes the personality of the healthy American adult. This figure compares *determinants*, or

* Data for the representation of Klopfer's hypothetical case were adopted from the chart provided by Bell [8]. (All footnote indications in this section refer to number References on p. 83.)

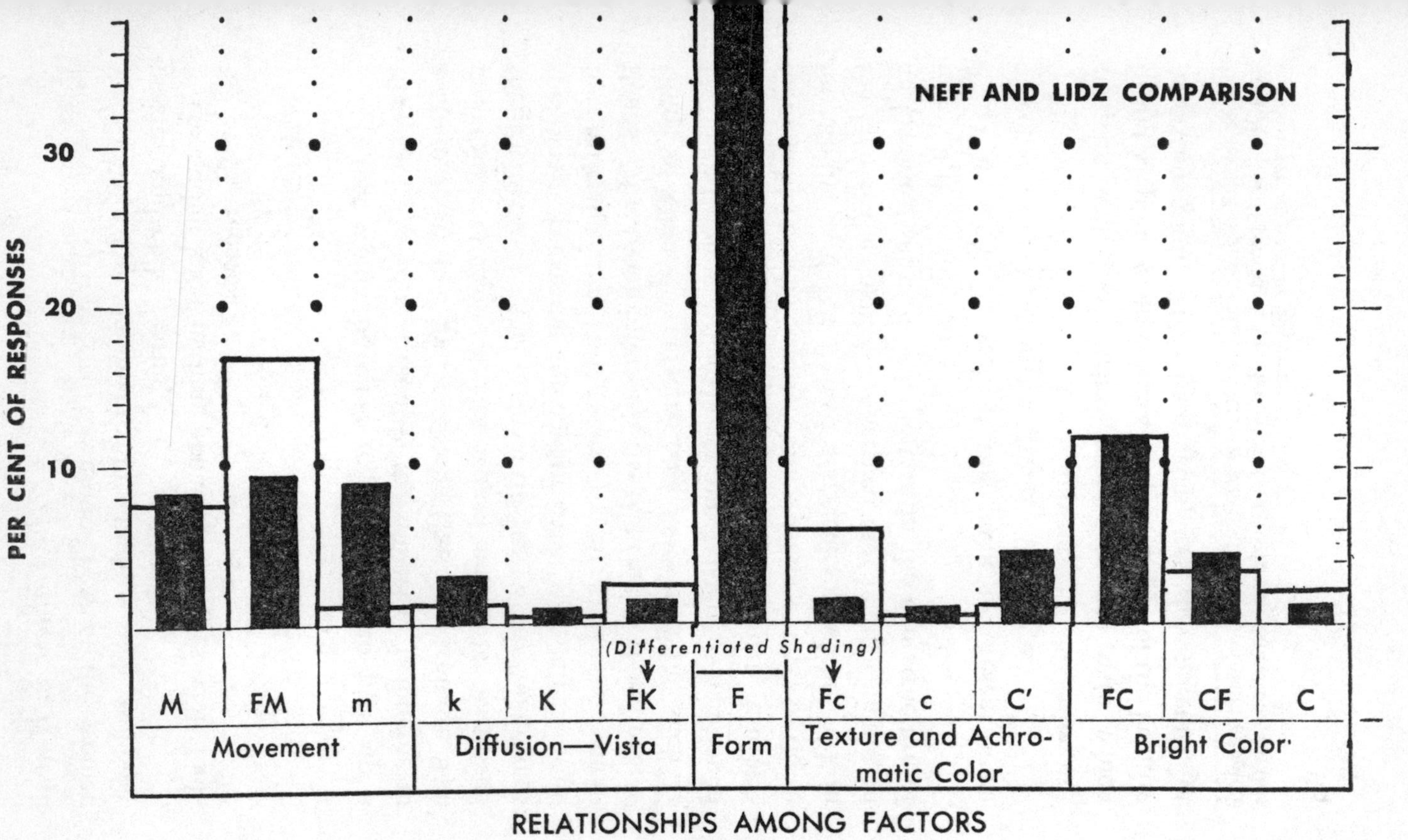

RELATIONSHIPS AMONG FACTORS

Figure 2

those scores of the Rorschach record which refer to what it is that determines the percept.

It is seen that these subjects use pure form (F) in greater degree than Klopfer's ideal; they use human movement (M) less. They show a definite tendency to give shading responses, particularly C′ (achromatic color) and k (third-dimension, such as X-Ray, topographical maps). The most marked deviation is in the abundance of m (inanimate movement) which these subjects give.

Figure 2 compares this older group with a group of soldiers (in the Pacific, as it happens) examined by Neff and Lidz ([5]). They are of above average capacity intellectually, and have a median age of twenty-seven. In this comparison our subjects are seen to be very similar to the soldiers on most determinants, even M (human movement). They differ from the service men most in the abundance of m, and lowered values for FM (animal movement) and Fc (form-texture).

With his colleagues, Beck ([2]) developed norms for 157 employees at various levels of the Spiegal Company Organization (a retail store). Their mean age was 30.5; a few scores (namely, M, FC, CF, and C) may be compared with our group (*Figure* 3). The Hawaiian subjects give slightly less human movement (M) and pure color (C); they give greater form-color (FC).

The foregoing comparisons are made in terms of the *proportion of total responses* scored for each determinant. As regards total productivity, the Hawaiians gave from 11 to 76 responses, for a mean of 29. The army men had a mean of 26, and Beck's Spiegal employees 33.

A general conclusion from these comparisons is that so far as these relatively objective indices are concerned, our subjects differ slightly from two quite different samples of the population. Their greatest divergence seems in the direction of increased C′, k, and m.

Rorschach students would conclude from this that we are dealing with a group of subjects who, so far as social and emotional sensitivity are concerned, are capable of a high degree of integration, but that this has been acquired painfully and in many instances traumatically. This suggestion comes from the increased C′. So far as inner living is concerned, these subjects intellectualize and impersonalize basic impulses.

So much for normative comparisons.

Rorschach workers feel that the most spontaneous projection of the personality into the record is the movement response, and that the clearest identification of the subject and his production is represented by human movement; in these terms, it becomes valid to examine its nature. Our 35 subjects gave a total of 82 human movement responses, ranging from none, for five subjects, (a retail dealer, a college teacher, a saleswoman, a tax consultant, and the business manager of a school) to nine

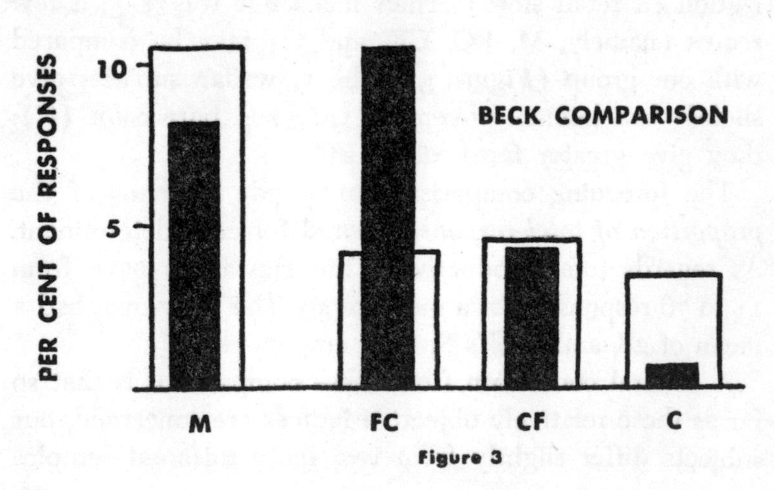

Figure 3

(a female school principal). The median number of human movement responses was two.

Movement tends to be *genteel.* Men, women, and children are seen dancing, playing, balancing, posturing, bowing, greeting, shaking hands, and the like. A little more pointedly, they often are *playing a game.* In one response two men "resemble ancient wild untamed men trying to assume some combat attitude," and another response by this same subject (a dentist) has "two waiters trying to be polite." This special sort of human movement, implying some quality of concern about the *intention* of social behavior, is revealed somewhat strikingly in another record: here are "two persons in a tug-of-war of some sort—conversation rather than tug-of-war" (from a welder). Another subject (an attorney) gives "witches, or two dragons playing together, rather than fighting." Another subject gives "two Chinese persons greeting each other or having a game." They are "Chinese because I have seen in painting old Chinese robes like this. I don't know what the lower red represents, form of blood or something. Maybe instead of a friendly meeting they are having a duel." (This from a businessman.)

One subject, (an insurance agent) sees "two persons having a scrap," then decides that they are "not persons but bears, but their heads do not look like those of bears." A minister sees "struggle—three parties or persons in physical battle. Poor guy in the center throwing up arms, two guys on the side are pulling. . . . We might define this as two men struggle over a girl." While this was seen on Figure I,* in Figure II this subject saw "two old ladies chatting and gossiping with each other" (followed by a

* Figure numbers here refer not to this text but to the Rorschach Test.

bomb bursting and flames coming up), and on Figure III he said, "These patterns suggest dualism of life-struggle between two parties—male and female, good and bad, day and night, et cetera. Two figures suggested by the image, facing each other on opposite sides. Also two colors, red and black." In the total group of records, these last responses are outstanding for the violence of activity, yet even here the subject reveals a need to make some sort of *justification*—he gives to the movement a meaning which is symbolic or abstract.

Subject J (a business executive, art collector, and furniture designer) saw Figure II as "two fellows arguing—they are having a drink, greeting each other, having a grand time; elbow resting on counter, holding up glass—'Health to you.'" On Figure III he saw "ladies from Africa having two children—two mothers separating two children fighting; each woman holding her own child."

Without doubt these are human movement responses, but they are not simple activities of humans—they have to do with *motives, effort,* and perhaps *ethics*. They reveal rather intensive *intellectualization.*

In this same direction, it is valid to examine in some detail the m responses. This inanimate movement is something which the subject experiences, but for some reason dehumanizes. Of these inanimate movement responses, eight subjects gave none, one subject (an insurance underwriter) gave nine, and one subject (a minister) gave ten. The median was 1.5.

Typical responses have volcanoes erupting, shells bursting, fires burning. One subject (a bank director) saw in VI "two creatures (notice he did not say "people") fighting over something. The two side blots symbolize revenge and hatred on the part of the two creatures." Later he said of this response, "Now I see a conflict in their hearts. They have hatred at their back, and yet friendliness in front of them, as shown by the center red. They may be really friendly." In this same blot was "a gangster—two eyes masked, two hands raised, two side red dots indicating his past—murder. Or the man is a good man; center red indicates he has a good and warm heart. The two side red dots symbolize his success built on bloodshed."

There was much *suspension* in these records: monkeys hanging by their tails, rats swinging in this fashion, persons suspended in midair, a bat hanging, birds being shot and hung up. Forces like fire shoot up, while also there is falling: a waterfall, and leaves falling from a tree.

Regarding movement, then, we can see in these records a tendency for the subject to remove himself—to dehumanize by symbolization or abstraction. Sensitive to dynamic forces within their personalities, these subjects give expression to them, but (for reasons of guilt or fear, perhaps) they must avoid responsibility for it. This comes out in the tentative, cautious, rationalized human movement, and in the abundance of inanimate movement in situations in which the human, and often the animal figure, is helpless and passive.

Hsu, in an earlier study of Chinese in America, done with Theodora Abel ([1]), found much of this sort of thing. In addition, it was shown in this study that *food* and things oral were frequently mentioned. The present subjects do this also. They mention flowers, often of a specific nature, with a high degree of frequency.

Because of interest in the relationship between anthropology, psychiatry, and psychoanalysis and, if you will, psychodynamics, the author explored in greater detail an area which has received increasing attention by Rorschach investigators within the past few years—namely, family relationships, and, more specifically, the image of father and mother. Some Rorschach investigators have felt that Figure IV has strong provocation for material relating to the father, while Figure VII is supposedly thus specific for the mother. Without entering into discussion as to the validity of these notions, it might be interesting to examine the responses of these subjects to these particular figures.

A first step here is to separate the men from the women; there are eight women, twenty-seven men. The women are younger, most of the women are single, and all are outside the home, as students or working. Most of the men, on the other hand, are married, and many are, perhaps, parents themselves.

In response to Figure IV (the father figure) the female subjects (75% of them) presented a shock reaction; none rejected the figure, but their reactions were depressed or hysterical: "a sad lady carrying a baby," "snail coming out of a broken shell," "giant's feet, sad, depressing; petrified stump, gloom, repulsive to me," "a monster, Frankenstein, I would be scared if I saw him." One subject intellectualized when she saw "coelenterate, anemone, protoplasm" (but she ended up with "Chinese food").

The men did not react as traumatically as the women to Figure IV, the father figure. While a third of them were depressed by it, almost half gave no indication of anxiety for this blot. Thus, assuming this reaction to be a valid index of the subject's easiness in the area of relationship to the father, we would conclude that the women showed greater anxiety in regard to the father figure than the men.

By Figure VII (presumed to be related to the mother) both sexes were much less shocked than by Figure IV, the father figure, and there was little difference in this regard between men and women. By these criteria, the mother figure was much less threatening than the father.

One subject (mother of two and a university instructor) said of VII: "Ha! This I like very much. Boys, children, or dogs, dancing happily. This is quite nice, I like it. I like this best; like in Heaven, more things. Castle and waterfall on top of it, like in Heaven. I like it. A house in the mountains, quiet. The whole blot suggests freedom of movement, lively." This same subject said for IV (the father figure): "No impression whatsoever. Two feet of a giant, that's all. . . . Like a monster—peculiar shape. I don't like too much black—depressing. Back of a monster, not the face. Once I saw a giant looking for Mickey Mouse. I can't forget that. He lifted up the house and walked over all the houses. Very childish on my part, maybe, but I have a picture in my mind."

Subject D (director of a school) saw VII (the mother figure) as "ballerinas—they are quite light. I see their skirts flying up in the air—a cloud above them. Light as a cloud, but something coming down. They dance like clouds, but they are earthy. The thing hanging down, like the man's penis, or something sexy. They are ethereal, but also sexy. That bone is sexy. It pierces through a vagina. It symbolizes they are having sexual intercourse, human." It was this subject, here aware of sexual yet ethereal possibilities for the mother figure, who gave for the father figure (IV) a Frankenstein monster. Her response to IV, in full, is: "Oh, God! Monster, Frankenstein or something. I would be scared to death if I saw him. Arms are limp, but feet and body are very strong. Strong spine. Head looks like a vagina, but that is not really strength. The bottom of his spine has two little things, looks like women's nipples. Can I say that? Therefore, he is feminine, but feminine nature is not as crude and cruel as this. This looks cruel and crude. Only in certain cases is the feminine nature that cruel." Later she said of this response, "A big dark mass. Broad chest, gnarled hands. Looks evil. But why does he have feminine things? He must be soft in heart. A very small per cent of women have as much evil as this. A small per cent is really destructive, though."

This obviously is a record in which sexuality is expressed openly. Yet the sexuality associated with the masculine is ominous and evil, while the feminine is pleasurable and even ethereal. In their overt sexuality the responses of this subject to these two figures are consistent with the total record.

The foregoing examples comparing responses to VII versus IV (the mother versus the father) characterize the women's records. Here is what one *man* does—an attorney. For VII: "Two highly tailored dogs, balancing on their heads. They may be Dalmatians. This way (v) it looks like two dancing girls with tall headdresses, swirling skirts, that come down to their knees." Later he added, "The center white space is like a picture of George Washington; outline of him. Also, it might be the helmet of Bismarck, with a point on the top of the helmet. This part here looks like part of a landscape in a Chinese painting—torn off the scroll. This way, the white space in the center is a table lamp, with a flat shade." Compare this shift from spontaneity to reasonable reserve with his response to IV, the father figure: "Can I look at it at any angle? (Several twists.) An impression that I am in a dense forest, with vines hanging down from the trees. The lighter portions show the sun coming through—we look up into space. . . . Also, the skin of a cow laid out on the floor." Additionally, he gave also a "man's boots. A picture of a man making a jackknife dive. . . . This seems to be an artificially built breakwater. A hand holding a torch. The other side will have to be the hand of another person. The tail end of a chicken—the South Pole of it."

When he first saw VII (the mother figure), Subject N (a news editor) rejected it: "I can't see anything." Later he said, "I was trying to be exact. Two goldfish, with big eyes. Not exact—any color." Certainly this was an inhibited, cautious, but unemotional response. Compare it with his response to IV (the father figure): "The picture of a large, vicious-looking bug," later elaborated by his saying "because of the vicious-looking outline of the upper part of the figure. My childhood vision of a bat. Something horrible-looking. My best vision—a young lady . . . no, could be a king and queen lifting up their garments; the king has a gown, the queen a skirt. Young girl in a play, a royal person, cousin of the king, about to dance . . . lifting up her long garment. . . . A ballet dancer tries to do some exercise, regular routine, legs stretched way out in back . . . a part of a woman . . . a show girl, burlesque . . . a show girl showing her legs, lifting up her skirt. . . . She is doing a burlesque in a dim light. She could be naked. That's why the dimmed light. Police regulations. Can't show too much. . . . The head of a dragon here."

As a final illustration of this discrepancy between the mother figure, on the one hand, and the father on the other, the responses of R13 (a bank vice-president) are interesting. He rejected IV entirely (the father figure); in VII, however, he saw two animals facing each other, and two girls dancing.

Regarding sexuality, it might be informative to look briefly at the responses to Figure VI (often referred to as the *sex* card). Some responses to VI have been mentioned in the foregoing material. Of the eight women, one (a married saleswoman) rejected the figure. One gave a response openly sexual and with considerable elaboration. Another gave the popular animal skin. Another response, given by a college student ("pigs tied together, burning") was considered traumatic. One woman was hysterical: "Intestine, exposed ulceration, amoebiasis—could be a dorsal view. We saw it the other day." The remainder intellectualized, seeing "Christ on the cross," "an Indian totem pole," "ladies peering at things," "a tailless plane."

While the women, with the exception of the college student, revealed anxiety in the face of sexual provocation, none was basically depressed. The men, on the other hand, were considerably traumatized by the figure.

R3 (an accountant) saw a "skin, a photograph of mountainous regions, an X-ray of infected lungs; oil, grease, crude oil. Wherever you have machinery, smudge." R1 (another accountant) saw an "X-ray view of a dead animal," and "a dry snake they sell in Chinese drugstores." R13 (a banker referred to previously) saw "a person squeezed between two forces." R11 (a politician, lawyer, and businessman) saw "an emblem," an "Hawaiian shrimp," "part of a war club," "an X-ray of an insect," "an amoeba," and "a crab." R12 (a lawyer) gives a few small details, then "insects trying to fly away from the neck of an animal. Deep blots here are grotesque, separate entities." Compared with his response to all other figures, his response to VI was one of confusion and disintegration.

A (an insurance underwriter) said VI could "pass for a couple of geese that have been killed and hung up side by side." H (a bachelor—teacher and editor) saw, among other things, "a dried snake." I (treasurer of a board of missions) said of VI, "a mass of ink, to me." P (a pastor) rejected VI entirely, but later, after urging, saw "a fish with whiskers—doesn't make sense to me."

V (another insurance man) saw VI as "an animal that is already skinned," but added, "a dagger which is penetrated through some piece of beautiful outer skin of an animal."

ERLEBNISTYP

One index calculated by Rorschach workers has to do with the introversive or extratensive tendency demonstrated by the subject. Rorschach himself suggested that the ratio of M responses (human movement) to color responses (considering CF 1, FC ½ and C 1½) would, when 1:1, indicate ambiequality. This index, for our men, is 1:1.6. For our women, it is 1:0.75. Thus, at the level of civilized—if you will, *conscious*—projection, our men are, therefore, extratensive, while our women are introversive.

At a more primitive level, a ratio as proposed by Klopfer ([4]) expresses the proportion of animal plus inanimate movement to surface qualities of the blots—texture and achromatic color. According to this index (1:0.4 for men and 1:0.34 for women), both sexes are introversive. We might conclude from this that, at a primitive level, both men and women are introversive; their behavior is governed largely by impulses within, which they are at pains to handle well. However, the women reveal this introversion in their social living; they exhibit at a conscious level a high degree of control and creativity. This is not true of the men. Socially and on the surface, the men surrender their power of creativity to the demands of the situation; they are, on the surface, extroverts.

CONCLUSIONS

1. It is impossible to decide that any one thing is characteristic of this group of subjects.
2. It is of crucial importance for this study that a group of non-Chinese Hawaiians be studied in a manner as similar as possible to that utilized in the examination of these subjects.
3. These subjects show wide variability and, hence, differences within their group—differences probably as wide as those demonstrated by other groups.
4. Measures of central tendency indicate that they do not as a group differ markedly from American groups with which they are compared.
5. There is a suggestion that they demonstrate more shading (black or white as color) responses, more third-dimensional response, and more inanimate movement, than we might expect of a healthy group in this country. Yet there is no evidence that the anxieties of these people differ essentially from the anxieties of many Americans today.
6. There is a strong suggestion that the women (for the most part a career group) react with anxiety and depression to what is supposed to be the "father figure." They seem to be highly introversive. It might be inferred that they are particularly addicted to a "masculine protest" sort of psychology. This may or may not be unfortunate. Perhaps our anthropological colleagues will know how much strain is imposed by "emancipation" on the woman of Chinese cultivation.
7. The men in this study are uneasy in the sexual situation—indeed, in situations of simple social, interpersonal relationship. They are preoccupied with *role-playing,* with

prestige, with the subjugation of basic feeling to demonstrations of *politesse,* of *manners,* and of *strategy.* Spontaneity is fearsome. There is security in making the right impression.

8. A final conclusion is that we have no evidence that these are not just good Americans, worried about things that, in our culture, are troublesome to all of us. Most people in test situations feel a need to maintain *face,* and this may be important—in Pittsburgh and Cicero and Chicago and Fargo—just as it is for these Americans in the land of Sweet Leilani.

REFERENCES

1. ABEL, THEODORA, and HSU, FRANCIS L. K., "Some Aspects of Personality of Chinese as Revealed by the Rorschach Test." *Rorschach Research Exchange and Journal of Protective Techniques,* Vol. XIII, No. 3, 1949, pp. 285-305.
2. BECK, S. V., RABIN, A. F., THIESEN, W. G., MOLISH, H., THETFORD, W. M., "The Normal Personality as Projected on the Rorschach Test." *Journal of Psychology,* 1951, Vol. 30, pp. 241-298.
3. BELL, JOHN ELERKIN, *Projective Techniques: A Dynamic Approach to the Study of Personality.* New York: Longmans, Green and Co., 1948.
4. KLOPFER, B. and KELLEY, D. M., *The Rorschach Technique: A Manual for a Projective Method of Personality Diagnosis.* Yonkers-on-Hudson: World Book Co., 1942.
5. NEFF, W. S., and LIDZ, T., "Rorschach Pattern of Normal Subjects of Graded Intelligence." *Journal of Projective Technique,* Vol. 15, 1951, pp. 45-57.

DISCUSSION

Richard P. Wang

TO GIVE a bit of my personal setting: From 1949 to 1950 I was in Hawaii in connection with a 1,100-bed psychiatric hospital. In addition to my clinical work I also had some opportunity for rather intimate association with the Chinese in Hawaii through the many relatives of my wife who live on various islands of the Territory. Therefore, although I was not engaged in field work there, I do have some knowledge of these people from among whom the Rorschach material under question was obtained.

I think this is an excellent Rorschach report, all the more because I can quite appreciate the difficulties Dr. Richards has necessarily encountered. One of the difficulties is that of not even knowing the exact perspective for the study nor the criteria of selection for these subjects, except that these thirty-five are "the first alphabetically of a much larger group tested." Another difficulty is that of getting adequate controls. The author mentions the need for a group of non-Chinese in Hawaii to be studied in a similar manner. Perhaps we would like to study a group of Chinese in China, if that were possible. Needless to say, there is also a need for establishing the so-called norms for Americans.

The results of Dr. Richards' analysis, after allowing some of the practical as well as theoretical limitations, such as validity of the test (interpretation basing upon the various determinants)[1], correspond amazingly to what I know about the Chinese in the U. S. A. and in Hawaii.

For example, his remark that half the women in these records mentioned such matters relevant to China or Chinese, while only about one-third of the men did the same, seems to correspond also with the impression that I got from the Chinese-Americans in New York, particularly the second-generation or American-born ones. The boys frankly expressed the opinion that they are not interested in China or what is going on over on the other side. While one of the girls' informal associations or clubs regularly contributes a substan-

[1] Holtzman, Wayne H., "Validation Studies of the Rorschach Test: Shyness and Gregariousness in the Normal Superior Adult." *Journal of Clinical Psychology*, Vol. VI, 1950, pp. 343, 348.

tial amount of money to China each year, none of the boys' groups did anything of the sort.[2] This may reflect the more reserved, conservative attitude of women in general. This may also mean that the women, being responsible for the methods of child training, being the carriers of culture, so to speak, do bring out more of the Chinese aspects of their original background. It may also mean, as mentioned in the paper, that this feeling of being Chinese supports the ego structure of these individuals.

Dr. Richards' analysis of the responses to Card IV on the father figure and to Card VII, the mother figure, also agrees well with my observation. The fathers among these Chinese in Hawaii I know of are, in many cases, rather frightening sorts of persons. The mothers, on the other hand are warmer, more affectionate, and more giving persons. It is no wonder then that these people reacted with less anxiety to the mother figure. That the men reacted less traumatically to the father figure may possibly be due to the process of identification, or substitution, to the thought: "Someday I will be a father too."

In general I am skeptical about statistics. Particularly in the case of Rorschach, I would much rather see the detailed analysis of the entire Rorschach protocols of a few selected individuals like that done by Oberholzer for Cora Dubois in *The People of Alor*. In that way, you are seeing the Rorschach findings as a whole, with each determinant in its proper perspective as related to the other parts in the whole composite picture. After all, from a Gestalt point of view, the whole is not equal to the sum of its parts. Yet it is remarkable that, according to the Rorschach findings as they are, they demonstrate a significant difference in having more black and white responses, more third-dimensional responses, and more inanimate movement responses, than we might expect

[2] Wang, Richard P., "A Study on Chinatown Associations," a paper presented to the Annual Meeting of the American Anthropological Association at Toronto, Canada, December 30, 1948.

of a highly hypothetical norm in this country. Here is one place where I am inclined to disagree with Dr. Richards when he concluded that "We have no evidence that the anxieties of these people differ essentially from the anxieties of any American today." His Rorschach findings lead me to think otherwise. However, this difference in interpretation will not be settled till Dr. Hsu publishes his final results.

Instead of making more specific comments, I would like to devote the rest of the space to two proposals:

1. As I understand that a total of more than one hundred subjects were tested, I wonder if it is possible, after all the material is lined up, that we group them together into: (*a*) First-generation Chinese-Americans in Hawaii, (*b*) second-generation Chinese-Americans in Hawaii, and (*c*) third-generation Chinese-Americans in Hawaii.

Besides knowing some of Dr. Hsu's work in the past as well as perhaps predicting some of the work to come, I think it would be exceedingly helpful to establish something like this. We were told that the Chinese-Americans in New York approach nearest in their personality structure to the Chinese in China, and that the Chinese-Americans in Hawaii approach closest to the Americans in their personality structure, and that the Chinese-Americans in San Francisco are somewhere in between. It would be extremely interesting to have a series of Rorschach studies done among these three groups of people and then to find out whether the above-mentioned prevalent impression is true; if so, we can then come back to the subject matter in this paper and find out what factors in the personality structure of these "Chinese in Hawaii" are closer to that of American personality structure, and what factors are closer to the Chinese personality structure. That would be a very interesting comparison. Perhaps we can then know how many of these personality features are the result of the people's cultural heritage from China, possibly as a result of childhood training, and how many of these are American, possibly as a result of acculturation and culture change.

2. Another point I would like to make is connected with the woman, Subject D, in whose record sexuality was expressed openly. Dr. Richards seemed to have been alarmed by the record as a whole because of the morbidity and chaos associated with sexual expression and enjoyment. I may say I am just as alarmed—but because, as a psychiatrist, I was trained not to be shocked by anything the patient tells you. In this case, shocking the reviewer might very well have been the reason why she answered as she did. However, there is, of course, the possibility that she might be pathological, at least in the psychopathological sense. Offhand, I would not call her psychotic or psychopathic, as such. Maybe the best way to describe her or to classify her is to use Karl Menninger's terms "Neurotic Type—Frustrated Personality."[3]

That brings me to my second proposition, that a possibly pathological case like that should be compared with other pathological cases among the American culture or other subcultures, and not with the successful men and women.[4] It might be, then, a very interesting plan to compare the Chinese neurotics with non-Chinese neurotics, the Chinese psychotics with the non-Chinese psychotics, the Chinese alcoholics with the non-Chinese alcoholics, et cetera. We are hoping someday to accomplish just that.

ADDITIONAL DISCUSSION

DR. HENRY: I would like to ask Dr. Hsu to what extent your field data in Hawaii tend to confirm your Rorschach findings.

[3] Menninger, Karl. A., *The Human Mind*. New York: Alfred A. Knopf, 1949, p. 129.

[4] In this instance, Dr. Wang is applying the term "psychopathology" in a manner which will be difficult to uphold. See F. L. K. Hsu, "Anthropology or Psychiatry," *op. cit.* Editor.

DR. HSU: The field data are still in the process of being systematically written up. At this point I can offer a few impressions. First, the greater importance of form among the Chinese in Hawaii than among white Americans. This is clear in two out of the three comparative charts shown by Dr. Richards, not only in connection with pure F (form), but also with FC. This is consistent with my general impression that the Chinese are more situation-centered[5] in their orientation of life and consequently tend to be more pliable to the restraints of the external world than given to individual predilections.

While responding to the Rorschach test, a number of subjects would ask me for permission to talk about a sex subject. There were other instances in which the subject made no reference to sex in the first place, but when I specifically asked if he or she did not see any sex connotation in certain cards, the subject would say that he or she did think of the sex connotation in several places but did not want to offend me by mentioning it. This is clearly the Chinese way in which sex must be relegated to a specific compartment where it is most appropriate but must not be touched on in general social intercourse such as the testing situation.

However, the usual interpretation of such an observation is that the Chinese control themselves well. Elsewhere I have shown the fallacy of this view,[6] but here in these limited Rorschach results we again find evidence contrary to this popular misconception. For example, in two out of three of the comparative charts shown by Dr. Richards the Chinese in Hawaii exhibit not only lower CF (Color form) or C (Color), indicating more rational approach to emotions, but

---

[5] For a discussion of this concept see Hsu's "Suppression versus Repression." *Psychiatry*, Vol. 12, No. 3, August 1949, pp. 223-242.

[6] "The Chinese of Hawaii: Their Role in American Culture." *Transactions of the New York Academy of Sciences*, Ser. II, Vol. 13, No. 6, April 1951, pp. 243-250.

also lower M (Movement) or FM (Form movement), indicating generally less imaginative activity.

These Rorschach findings, together with the evidences that I presented elsewhere,[7] suggest to me that the Chinese do not in fact have to control themselves more than white Americans in order to appear less turbulent. They have less reasons for control.

Another point that I would like to raise concerns the responses of Subject D, in which "morbidity or chaos" are "associated with sexual expression and enjoyment," which prompted Dr. Wang to observe that the subject might be "neurotic" or at least "pathological." I do not agree with this diagnosis at all. If she were a white American, coming of a Puritan background, I might have somewhat more reason to agree (but by no means fully agree); but since she is a Chinese-American, and reared in a background where repression of sex has never been important, her responses are, I think, probably more indicative of her lack of repression (once she and I established proper rapport) than any alleged "pathology."

A last point concerns anxiety. Dr. Richards thinks the anxiety of these Chinese-Americans is similar to those of white Americans in general. Dr. Wang feels that the differences are greater. My impression from other evidences (life histories, personal contacts, and observations on their social and economic life in general) is that there is relatively little anxiety among the Chinese in Hawaii, in spite of their living in an interracial community where occupational and other discriminations against them are by no means absent. This relative lack of anxiety fits well with my earlier observations that the Chinese are more situation-centered in their life orientation. They are less anxious because they are more pliable to, and less emotionally disturbed by, environmental restrictions.

---

[7] *Ibid.*

V

NORMAL AMERICA IN THE ABNORMAL SETTING

Benjamin Boshes

DELINQUENCY AREA

IN 1938 this essayist had occasion to study the seven surviving members of what had once been a large and typical gang in a Chicago delinquency area—the "42" gang. The opportunity was unique in that it was possible to obtain many of the data at the time when the acts were being perpetrated, and it was further possible to observe the boy in his "native habitat." A brief description of each boy follows.

Case 1. A. S. was a small Italian boy of 134 pounds. Medically he was normal. His father was a laborer from near Naples. This boy had had three mothers. The first died when he was five or six. "She had too many kids. The old man didn't care. Then he met some bum seventeen years old, married her and give her a kid, but she ran away with the kid and the old man's money. So he married my third mother two years later. She had three kids and died in the third childbirth. A year and a half later the old man died, at forty-five. Too much drink."

This boy's delinquencies began in the first grade, truanting, bumming, stealing food from back porches. Later came the cutting out of lead pipe from vacant buildings, "junking," car stealing, stealing from stores, etc. Some acts were retaliative, e.g., breaking into the school, wrecking desks, blackboards, urinating and defecating into the teachers' or principal's drawers.

Arrests and court sentences were no deterrent. He always returned to the gang, to the older leaders with their bankrolls, flashy cars, and girls. Even now, while going "straight," he will roll drunks and go out looking for "Polack" girls for intercourse.

A. S. never got along with his father, as did few of the others with theirs. He was courageous, aggressive, bright, and resourceful, but still a passive person, a follower.

He had some insight into his career in crime. "I'm thinking why criminals come from Italians. The father comes from the old country and never goes to baseball games with his son. You learn English and the old man is just your father. You respected him but you couldn't talk to him; you couldn't bring your troubles. You can't talk Italian. He's here, but his head is in the old country. All he knows is beat you up. The other kids' fathers are the same way."

This was true for the other six descriptions.

Case 2. F. T. was a small Italian boy of 124 pounds, one of seven children of a laborer. Nicknamed "the Cat," or Felix, he was anything but cringing when on a delinquent adventure. He would fight anyone, shoot it out with a policeman, or "steal a broad" from another gang. He was passive, always a follower, without braggadocio, but very loyal. On a "job" there was no one more courageous or resourceful than Felix. His brother, "Benny the Peacemaker," one of the thoughtful members of the gang, was his ideal, and when Benny was killed, Felix settled down. He was studying electrical engineering, working, and using half his salary to send another brother through college. His reflective mind and consistency in behavior portended a good prognosis.

Case 3. A. P. (Hank) was a powerfully built boy of twenty-four who weighed 155 pounds. He was the son of an Italian laborer who previously had been a guide on Mt. Vesuvius. The latter was a drinker and died at forty-three. No English was spoken in the home. Hank was described as having a "good head." He was aggressive, and planned his jobs carefully. His boldness both sexually and otherwise earned him the title of "the Turn," but his pederasty and sodomy while he was incarcerated were "acts of necessity" when girls were not available. Even now he pursues a career on the fringe of crime, rolling drunks, cheating a company for whom he is strike-breaking, or acting as a tipster for a robbery. He is summarized as aggressive and egocentric, a strong, bright, pleasure-loving boy who used his abilities only to gratify these goals.

Case 4. W. B. (Willie), age twenty-three, a small Italian boy of 123 pounds, was born and raised in the area. The family moved away when he was twelve, but Willie always returned. The mother died of a broken neck at the age of twenty-nine. His father, a laborer, originally from near Naples, sold moonshine during Prohibition.

Willie's career started at the age of eight and a half, and he was unusually clever and daring. At great risk to himself he would do things to humiliate the police, e.g., hold them up to take away their stars. He was always "flashy," sexually aggressive, a braggart who loved the sensational. Even now his overdecorated car is used to "collect" the stenographers at the Institute to take them home. He loves attention and prestige.

The next three were studied in the penitentiary.

Case 5. P. V. (Rags) was the son of a tailor; his mother died when he was eight. There was no family supervision and the boy slept in cars, hallways, rarely at home. Then he began to "run" with the gang. He was manually dexterous, and became a skillful automobile thief.

Rags was never a fighter, was always easygoing, modest, humble, and had few enemies. He was intensely loyal. Mentally he was dull as compared with his fellows.

Case 6. I. M. (Chip), Italian, age twenty-three, came from a stable family, but his mother was ill with heart trouble for years and died when he was thirteen. Chip reached tenth grade in high school despite early delinquency. He was described as a "sensible" person whose judgment would keep him out of stupid situations. Chip was placed under the care of a rigid uncle who kept him "locked up." He hated this uncle, and his only family attachment was to a brother who was a "bookie." His adaptability is seen in his having received a gold watch on leaving the boys' reformatory as "the boy most likely to succeed."

Case 7. C. P. (Kutz), Hank's younger brother, aged twenty-three, is described as a quiet, "deadly" type of person who followed the example set by his aggressive brother. Kutz is bright, but passive, and is now "prison-broken," merely marking time.

On examining these case histories, certain common denominators immediately become apparent. All the boys lived in a delinquency area, a zone of low economic status, where there was considerable deterioration of property and where most of the inhabitants were immigrants, chiefly Italian. (It may be added parenthetically that earlier, when the people in this area were successively English, Swedish, and German, the incidence of delinquency was just as high.) In this district many borderline activities like bootlegging and junking were accepted.

The families, recently from southern Italy, did not accept American customs—Italian was spoken in the home. The parents, although residing in America, actually "lived" in Europe. The fathers were confused, beaten down by the economic struggle, and were universally rejected by the sons.

The mothers, usually closer to the boys, were so busy having babies and caring for them that there was little time for the older ones. Of the six mothers, four had died when the boys were quite young. Two fathers died prematurely. Where the father figure was rejected, delinquency started early, even at six to eight years. Chip, from a stable family, started later, at age fourteen, one year after his mother died. He hated and rejected the uncle under whose supervision he had been placed.

Nowhere in the stories is religion mentioned. All the families were Roman Catholic. While the mothers were relatively devout, the fathers had fallen away from the Church. This is in contrast to the practices of these people in their native land, where ties to the Church were paramount for both parents and children. There was no feeling of guilt over violation of the religious or moral code. Siblings of the male sex were more important than parents. These siblings "lived" outside the home, in activities of the pattern of the area, and the boys of the gang had no conflict over leaving the home.

Furthermore, despite their Italian background, these boys had none of the artistic leanings so common in this national group. There was no interest in music or painting. The illiteracy of the parents, their rejection of Americanism, a culture of which they did not feel a part, combined to eliminate any premium on scholastic attainment. Even sports, partly available to all the boys, held no charms. This was not an area where athletics meant much. The parents did not understand sports. Limited facilities and competition did not give these boys an opportunity to learn fair play in the true American sense. Their greatest recreation was delinquency. This offered the greatest outlet emotionally and the greatest material reward. Their attitudes that delinquency was recreation were not new for such areas. Thrasher's gang members had also called these activities "their sport."

All of the factors which make for the usual acceptable social-emotional adjustment were missing: stable family, adequate father figure, family tradition, loyalties, religious and cultural bonds, stabilizing neighborhood patterns, and economic security.

Instead, all around was relative chaos: familial, cultural, sociological and economic deprivation. The boy was essentially a waif. To him, gang life and its blandishments offered the missing elements. The older, sophisticated gang leader became the father figure. The gang itself was almost like a protective mother. It gave him a place to hang out or to sleep, warmth, food, and many actual pleasures. There were women, and there was money to be had. Loyalties were intense when one "belonged." Excitement was high, either in the actual delinquency or in the recounting of exploits. Life in the gang was secure, stimulating, and very gratifying, provided one made the grade.

The point is worthy of reflection. Who made the grade? What was his place in the gang? Certainly these seven boys were no different from any other seven picked in a random sampling. They were all healthy, strong, and with one exception of one relatively dull normal (but of high dexterity —Rags), they were all normal to high in intelligence. The aggressive ones became the leaders; the passive ones the followers; the reflective ones became the planners or "peacemakers." Each one had to qualify for his place by performance, and the standards were high. Even now, Willie is looked down upon by his fellows because he is a braggart. Is the situation different in socially acceptable groups of the nondelinquent area? These boys were different only in that the milieu from which they stemmed lived by different standards. Otherwise they were like any other seven boys of comparable ages.

During the period of study of this gang, the essayist had an opportunity to investigate the make-up of the schoolboys of this area. Through co-operation of the Board of Education of the City of Chicago, permission was granted to examine all the boys in the grammar schools. This examination included medical histories, medical and neurological examinations, anthropometric measurements, and psychological testing. After discarding all questionable cases, incomplete observations, or invalid data, 997 cases became available for analysis. The names were checked against the files of the juvenile court, juvenile detention home, Board of Education records, truant-officer records, police blotter, criminal court, and the special files of Mr. Clifford Shaw and his associates of the Department of Sociology of the Institute for Juvenile Research. None of the examiners in the field had any idea of which boy was delinquent or nondelinquent. Some of the studies were reported by this essayist at the Society for Research in Child Development, in the Biennial Meeting held at the University of Chicago in November 1938. The mass of the study, which included a total of 4,006 cases from three delinquency areas, was in statistical analysis when the advent of the war scattered the workers to various parts of the globe, and the detailed report was never made. However, certain interesting conclusions based on the first 997 boys are worthy of mention. Of this group, 258 (25.9%) were known delinquents.

(1) The delinquent boys had a lower incidence of previous infections, and fewer surgical operations.

(2) Injuries of serious types were few, slightly higher among delinquents.

(3) General nutrition was good in both groups; 76.5% were normal or overweight. More delinquents were underweight, while overweight was equally distributed between the two groups.

(4) Serious organic defects were rare. (This was a culled, healthy school group.) Where pathology existed, e.g., heart diseases, it was usually in a nondelinquent.

(5) Heart-rate and blood-pressure response, used as a

small index of autonomic stability in a stress situation, revealed

(a) The delinquents had a slower heart rate, (b) and lower systolic blood pressure, diastolic blood pressure, and pulse pressure. Delinquents were less "upset" by the test.

(6) Puberty and its precursory state were seen more often in delinquents.

(7) Hernias, inguinal and umbilical, were less common in delinquents.

(8) So-called stigmata of degeneracy, bizarre ears, palates, webbed fingers, etc., adding up to five or more, as in the Lombrosan concept of a criminal type, were seen in only 5% of the total sampling and were found chiefly in the nondelinquents.

(9) Neurological defects, speech defects, and left-handedness were without significance.

(10) Anthropometric conclusions drawn from twenty-six basic measurements, seventeen derived indices, and ten descriptive observations showed little variation of the Caucasoid delinquent. The Negroid delinquents were grouped much closer to the mean than the nondelinquent.

(11) Studies of mental capacity would suggest that among the white boys the delinquents were of slightly lower intelligence rating. Since the tests measure, to some extent, scholastic achievement rather than intellectual power, one would hardly expect truants to keep pace with their fellows. Furthermore, tests of all groups in these blighted areas showed a steadily falling I.Q. as age progressed.

TABLE 1

Mean I.Q. at Different Ages of All Boys Studied

GROUP	AGE IN YEARS		
	7	13	15
White	**98**	**92**	**82**
Negro	**89**	**82**	**73**

Since racial differences in mental ability have never been demonstrated, one must suppose that there is a variation in the social situation between the White and the Negro groups. The falling I.Q. as age goes up reflects a failure of the boys in these areas to keep pace with the demands of the school curriculum. A study of the performance of boys removed from these areas and placed in foster homes would suggest that scholastic stimulation in the family setting is the important factor. The mean I.Q. of the boys removed to nondelinquent areas rises.

This conclusion is reinforced by the findings of a much larger, carefully controlled study in the Chicago area.[1] In the latter study, the delinquent boy is found to be in no way defective; he is not inferior to his nondelinquent fellow, and often is more rugged and disease-resistant. In short, he is "equipped" to carry out the pattern of the area. He is one who "makes the team," which here is the gang, and delinquency is his sphere of activity and gratification.

There is no conflict until he becomes older, more mature and reflective, and learns the larger, more acceptable pattern of society in general. Then he begins to curb his delinquent ways.

FOREIGN ZONE OF COMBAT

From December 1942 until May 1945, this essayist had occasion to study American soldiers in the North African-European Theater of Operations.

The men who underwent this stress were "normal" Americans. Not only had they passed their induction board tests, but they had survived basic and advanced Stateside training. However, despite their apparent normalcy, they were not all equally equipped emotionally, and when the test came, many gave way. Some were neurotically predisposed, but they had managed to cover their symptoms in the training period. Others

[1] Carried out in co-operation with the Board of Education of the City of Chicago and the Department of Sociology of the Institute of Juvenile Research. Some of the findings were reported by the author at the Biennial Meeting of the Society for Research in Child Development held in the University of Chicago in November 1938.

broke only because of the specific stresses of repeated combat experience. The types of reactions may be described in terms of the time of the war at which they were observed: (1) Early, particularly in green troops, (2) later, in combat-hardened troops, and (3) much later, in troops who had had prolonged combat records. Basically, the symptoms of the break in adaptation may be divided into several groups, although there were many variations, much overlapping of groups, and in the course of the disturbance a man might shift from one category to another.

Free-Floating Anxiety States. These were the most frequent. The soldier appeared terror-stricken, mute, tremulous. Speech was difficult, only the stuttering out of an occasional word. Behavior was bizarre, with attitudenizing, or a small stimulus could cause the man to hurl himself across several beds like a human torpedo, his face distorted with fear.

Case 1. C. J., infantryman, age twenty-four. Polish-American extraction. 1-9/12 years' service. His face was blank; most of the time he was mute. Attempted speech was always a stutter. The flickering of the North African electric lights would cause him to hurl himself across the room with: "The Jerries are coming after me!" Parkinsonian-like rhythmic clonic movements of his right arm and leg later proved to be a slit-trench digging maneuver. He had fought from the invasion of Oran through the battle of Kasserine Pass, and was becoming increasingly tense when one day a shell dropped in their chow line, blowing the head off his best friend. On recovery he told the story of a superstitious, "frightening" mother, extreme shyness as a boy, nail-biting, and a strong attachment to a priest to whom he had clung to the exclusion of boys of his own age.

Somatic Regression.

Case 2. F. H. O., private, age twenty-four. 1-5/12 years' service. Swedish Lutheran. Entered withdrawn, confused, resistive. He lay completely covered, head under blanket, body in a fetal attitude. He was mute and had refused food for seven days. On recovery he told the story of a broken home, nervous family, temper tantrums and shyness as a child, low energy drive. He was definitely an immature, happy-go-lucky person.

Other evidences of regression were flexion attitudes with tremor, as in Parkinsonism, astasia-abasia, enuresis, mutism and stuttering.

Psychosomatic Visceral Disturbances. While these appeared in all periods of fighting, we saw them in greatest numbers in the Rome-Arno campaign. The troops were battle-hardened, we had control of the air, and supply was good. The weather was pleasant, and the soldiers' chief concern was the dangers attendant to actual fighting.

The most common symptoms were those referrable to the gastrointestinal tract. Cardiac symptoms, in contrast to World War I, were much less frequent. All systems—genito-urinary with enuresis, nervous systems with headache, vascular with hypertension, etc.—were represented.

The usual disturbance began with anorexia, then pain in the epigastrium, and finally intense gastric distress. The usual complaint was: "I can't eat C rations" (which incidentally were very bland food). Vomiting and diarrhea were common. Many of these men had no anxiety. They were concerned only with their diet and the pain. Some, however, were depressed. Many noncombatant personnel were similarly affected, e.g., combat medical corpsmen.

Fluctuating hypertension with headaches, blurred vision, and dizziness occurred in otherwise calm persons. Enuresis was often brought out by the combat stress as the soldier regressed to infantile patterns. Sometimes the psychosomatic visceral disturbance was the forerunner of a more severe psychiatric disorder, as in civilian life. Here the symptoms assumed the status of a fixed hypochondriacal preoccupation.

Conversion States. Many of these represented actual regressions rather than conversion symptoms in the usual sense, e.g., astasia-abasia and stuttering. Deafness and blindness were defense phenomena against intolerable situations.

> *Case* 3. J. B. W., age thirty, captain in the artillery, 2-8/12 years' service. Entered as a case of "Parkinsonism with flaccid paraplegia." He had a severe wing-beating tremor of the upper extremities, flaccid "paralysis" of the lavers, and total amnesia for battle. His background was that of a broken home; his father died when the officer was thirteen. The captain was smallest in the family, had avoided sports, was enureter to age thirteen, and had had temper tantrums. The family had put him through a military college, where he had broken down in the freshman year. This lasted for three months. He had no anxiety on entrance to the ward, but when the physical symptoms were cleared up he became anxious and developed cardiac, then gastric, and finally depressive symptoms, an example of shifting of the freed libidinous energy.

It may be added at this point that wounds often serve the same function. Just as long as the wound is bad, the soldier is relaxed, "indifferent"; but when the wound heals, then anxiety sets in.

Depressions. These were perhaps more common among commissioned and noncommissioned officers who developed an idea that they had let their fellows down ("old sergeant's syndrome" of Sobel). They were often veterans who had been in continuous combat for as long as 79 days and had a total combat time of over 400 days. They were the "old reliables," with citations, awards, and medals for outstanding courage and devotion to duty. Finally they became tremulous, sweaty, the first to go into a foxhole, the last to leave. They were literally "sweating it out." They "couldn't beat the percentages." Each man was sure that the next shell "had his serial number on it." Ability to make decisions was lost. Finally the sergeant would turn in his stripes, and often his medals, with: "I want to be busted to private; I'm no goddam good." Depression and guilt over alleged failure, letting their comrades down, dominated the picture. The background of these men was usually free from neuropathy. They had been the best soldiers, but they had had too much.

Sometimes the depression came on acutely.

Case 4. P. B., private, age nineteen. Infantry, one month of combat. He was brought in depressed and suicidal. His only verbalizations were, "Buddy, buddy, talk to me, buddy. Forgive me." Tears rolled down his cheeks as he spoke. Otherwise he was uncommunicative, and refused to eat. Under intravenous sodium amytal he revealed that one night, while on guard, he fired in the direction of a noise; investigating this area the next morning, he found the body of his best friend. This boy was exceedingly immature, attached to his family and to his "buddies."

Pseudopsychotic Reactions. This term is used because, while the reactions simulated the picture seen in the psychoses, nosologically they belonged among the psychoneuroses. Often they were mislabeled "schizophrenia" because of the regressive and catatonic features. The reactions were transient and yielded to the various therapies: intravenous sodium pentathal or amytal, or to one or two electroshock treatments. The reactions were of various types.

(1) *Acute Delusional:*

Case 5. D. L., rifleman, age twenty-six, 3-1/12 years' service, one month of combat. He entered the ward, "stuck on battle," yelling for his bazooka. He was noise-sensitive, ducked at the sound of trucks or planes, and tried to awaken other patients, his "squad," to go out on patrol. The ward physician was his commanding officer to whom he reported his forays. He cleared up on one electroshock treatment, and revealed his background of a closely knit family with a very "nervous" mother, on whom he was very dependent. She had died five years before. Like her, he was afraid of water, of thunder, and hid with her in closets during storms. He was enuretic to age fourteen, and had used marijuana on occasion to relieve anxiety. The tension of battle and the sight of blood unnerved him so that he contemplated suicide. Finally he lost all control and was evacuated.

(2) *Epileptoid States:* These are unpredictable, violent explosive outbursts which resemble an epileptic furor.

Case 6. C. B., age twenty-one, private, infantryman. 1-1/12 years' service. His group was apparently engaged in hand-to-hand fighting with the Germans. He knew nothing of this until a citation was read to him. Apparently during the amnesic period he had bayoneted several Germans. Hearing the citation, the patient fainted, and since then he had been having unpredictable dizzy spells with "moods to kill." These were all directed toward officers, and actually he had pounced on several in various hospitals. He was dangerous and his transfer record was marked "homicidal." He cleared on electroshock therapy, and told a very revealing story. Despite an unusually powerful build, he was a passive child, closely attached to his mother. At age fifteen he was put out of the home by his father, who decided that the boy was old enough to be on his own. From then on he hated all father figures, civil and military. Yet he had no overt desire to fight or make trouble, and had "bummed" around the country peacefully until he entered the Army. Here he was submissive until the bayoneting incident, where the unit was sent forward at the point of a gun. He was "unconscious" during the actual hand-to-hand fighting, but the pent-up hostility against the father had been suddenly released, now in its form against all "fathers," any officer. Once, before the successful treatment was carried out, the soldier tried to hang himself because he was so sure that he would kill some innocent officer. When he was quiet, kindness from an officer would disturb him because it could arouse so much guilt about his hostile feelings, hence the suicidal thoughts.

Depressive and Regressive-Catatonic states have already been described. *Schizoid Reactions* were usually of paranoid coloring, but the ego generally retained a hold on reality.

Case 7. Age twenty-four, lieutenant, infantry. Two years' service, one month of combat. He became greatly disturbed when forty-one men in his command were killed. At first he was tense, anxious, depressed, and he stuttered. Later he had ideas of reference, heard noises and felt charges of electricity entering his body. The voices, however, were reassuring. They were those of his mother and grandmother, who told him that he was a good soldier and could now come home. This entire picture cleared spontaneously in several weeks.

Miscellaneous: In passing, it may be mentioned that true fatigue states, true psychoses, and malingering were also encountered, but very infrequently. Despite the long-used term "combat fatigue," actual exhaustion as a prime factor was found in only three to five per cent of cases. Genuine malingering, without some psychiatric deviation in the soldier, was a rarity.

Every man engaged in combat is anxious to a point that would be considered abnormal in a civilian setting. Our studies of these men with the Wechsler-Bellevue test indicated that the pattern of the scatterogram in the so-called "well-adjusted" soldier was almost that of the anxious control of civilian life. Normality must be equated in relationship to the situation in which the reactions arise. In view of the manner in which this generation was reared, it is amazing that more did not break down under the stress of battle. As boys they had been trained to inhibit their hostile aggressive drives, to respect other people and property. Now they were ordered to kill others, to destroy property. The threat of the battle situation to the ego is great; the danger of being killed, maimed, ever present. The release of all these forces, and the body mechanisms concerned, produce feelings of intense anxiety both in the psychological and physical spheres.

Yet these feelings must be contained, and certain factors protect the soldier. He has been trained with a group, and his identification with them gives him a "group ego." We called it the "combat family." Into it are also integrated identification with powerful guns, tanks. In the Air Force, belief in planes —in the Navy, pride and confidence in capital ships—all bolstered the group ego. The persons in this group had a feeling of indestructibility; e.g., the sailors on *HMS Nelson* which sailed from Oran to Malta every week had only scorn for the German Luftwaffe, which was the scourge of the Mediterranean. "They can't sink 'er. 'Er decks are too thick." The reverse was often true of men on the thin-plated LST's, or on our first tanks, the General Grants, when they encountered the German "88." After combat they would rebel against their officers. The ego threat had been too great, and we saw many instances of infantile rage, anger against the sense of impotency.

The group ego may become more important than the individual's own. J. P. Spiegel pointed out in his early report when he described the men as "fighting for their buddies rather than against the Germans."

A good commanding officer is like a strong father figure, and reassures particularly the passive, dependent man. His presence bolsters the ego defenses.

Motivation or goal in fighting is also important. Our soldiers, in contrast to the highly motivated Nazis, were not too sure in the early stages what it was all about.

Sense of invulnerability because of detached attitudes protects for a short while. Bullets and shell fragments are "not intended for me." This sense of detachment disappears as the man becomes combat-wise, and with it is lost another defense against anxiety, as in the "old sergeant" with his fatalistic "the next shell probably has my number."

Another ego defense is mobilization of hostility. In many, the anxious reaction of being shot at is resolved as the soldier fires back. Many men had great difficulty firing at Germans until they saw machine-gunned American prisoners. This released their hostility. In some, however, the hostility and killing actually produced intense anxiety. In noncombatants in combat, e.g., medical corpsmen, fired at by the enemy but without the privilege of firing back, much hostility was aroused with no outlet. Some solved this by the conversion of anxiety and rage into psychosomatic disturbances. Others used the energy by saving a wounded American in a dangerous spot.

The previous personality is also a factor, and the vulnerability of passive, dependent men placed in a dangerous situation has been depicted in the case illustrations. The ego, struggling with the normal anxiety of battle, must also face the infantile rage of this person who feels himself helpless and abandoned, as did the sailors on the LST's after the Sicilian invasion. They turned this rage onto their young officers. Some can take more physical exhaustion than others. In some the passive needs are less than in others, but everyone has his needs, and as the ego defenses are whittled down, everyone reaches a breaking point. The continual pressure of the physical evidences of anxiety—knotted stomach, fast heart, constricted chest, perspiration, aching back; the psychological reminders—anxiety, battle dreams, sleeplessness—keep adding up. The ego loses the ability to discriminate the real from the unreal, and the man gives in. He often mentions that he is losing his grip. A psychosomatic disturbance or a wound is often a means of respite because it allows the channeling of some of the anxiety as long as the symptom lasts; but ultimately the organism must give way to the total pressure and the neurosis becomes full-blown.

SUMMARY

As diverse as are the experiences of the member of the "42" gang and the American soldier in combat abroad, yet there are certain common denominators which determined their adaptability or failure in adjustment.

Fundamentally one must agree that all the men described fall into the broad spectrum of the normal. Granted that they have been placed under stress of one type or another, they have met the challenge with certain adaptive reactions. In war, even the best adaptive mechanism may be strained to the breaking point.

Factors which make for stability are: a solid family with a strong, kind father figure, an understanding, giving mother, strong loyalties to parents and siblings, and adequate ideals or goals.

In the case of the seven boys, all the families but one were disorganized, and even this boy was in the care of an uncle whom he despised. The father figure was confused, inadequate, hence rejected. The mothers were too busy to know what was going on; four or six mothers died when the boys were quite young. There were no loyalties to parents, "whose heads were in the old country;" only to siblings who were already delinquent. The home, disconnected from the Church and cultural ideals, offered no ideal or direction. There was no group ego in the family. But the gang offered everything. It was warm, giving, like a good mother. The hangout was comfortable; there were girls. The gang leader was strong, resourceful. He had a roll of bills, a flashy car. He was a "father" to pattern after. Loyalties were strong, identifications inescapable, and there were goals, rewards of money, thrills, recognition.

In the serviceman the same factors were seen. A good outfit, a good ship, or a good squadron were like a family and a mother. The group provided warmth, food, protection. The good commanding officer was a real father figure; often outfits ran birthday parties with the commanding officer sitting at the head of the table "just like a father." Soldiers came to him with their problems. Loyalties to buddies were intense. It was understandable how one could fight and even die for a buddy in a "good outfit." Members of a "combat family," each group in their own way, sought out their fellows for "bull sessions." An ideal or goal in fighting helped cement the soldiers' fighting front. But a poor outfit, one with an inadequate commanding officer who inspired no confidence, a poor leader—a group which was confused as to what it was fighting for—was likely to have a high psychiatric casualty rate. It lacked the elements for high morale, for emotional stability.

The stress pattern of the man in either the delinquency group or combat group depends on the load placed upon him and his total personality make-up. In the gang setting, Kutz, modeling himself after brother Hank, highly motivated, did well. In prison, with no goal, no motivation, he is "broken" and merely "sweating it out," like the "old sergeant." "There is no future for him; his luck has run out" too. In the ex-gang member too, like the soldier, when the stress is removed and the ego defenses are repaired by rehabilitation or replacement of the shattered elements, much restoration can be accomplished. Felix, devoted to brother Benny "the peacemaker," left the gang when the latter was killed. He started a family of his own, along socially acceptable lines, and is putting a brother through college. C. J.'s attacking of officers in his "moods to kill" was the release of hostilities against a rejecting, cruel father. The battle experiences had broken down his own defenses.

The pattern of behavior of the normal American under stress is, therefore, the result of the dynamic interaction of the total personality against the environmental requirements. A broad multifactor interpretation must be made of these terms. By total personality we mean the person's constitution and its heritage, and all of that individual's experience, conscious and unconscious. By environmental requirements we mean all the stresses, physical and psychological, acting over a period of time.

The individual's adaptations must be continuous, and as we have seen, when one or another factor which makes for stability gives way, various stress patterns of behavior appear. These may be delinquency, battle neurosis, and, in extreme cases, complete personality disintegration.

References

1. Thomas, William I., *The Child in America: Behavior Problems and Progress.* New York: Alfred A. Knopf, 1928.
2. Kardiner, Abraham, *The Individual and His Society.* New York: Columbia University Press, 1944.
3. *Combat Psychiatry,* Vol. IX, supplemental number. *The Bulletin of the U.S. Medical Department,* November 1949:

   (*a*) Ranson, Lt. Col. S. W., "The Normal Battle Reaction: Its Relation to the Pathologic Battle Reaction," p. 3.

   (*b*) Sobel, Maj. R., "The Battalion Surgeon as a Psychiatrist," p. 36. "Anxiety-Depressive Reactions after Prolonged Combat Experience: The 'Old Sergeant's Syndrome,'" p. 137.

   (*c*) Boshes, Lt. Col. B., and Erickson, Lt. Col. C. O., "Pseudopsychotic and Psychotic States Arising in Combat," p. 151.

   (*d*) Halsted, Lt. Col. J. A., "Gastrointestinal Disorders of Psychogenic Origin," p. 163.
4. Boshes, Maj. B., "Battle Neuroses: II. The Electric Shock Treatment of Refractory Cases in the Theater of Operation." *Natousa Medical Bulletin,* April 1944.
5. Grinker, Lt. Col. R. R., and Spiegel, Capt. J. P., *War Neurosis in North Africa. The Tunisian Campaign.* New York: Josiah Mach, Jr. Foundation, September 1943.
6. Grinker, Lt. Col. R. R., and Spiegel, Maj., J. P., *Men Under Stress.* Philadelphia: Blakiston & Co., 1945.
7. Spiegel, J. P., "Psychiatric Observations in the Tunisian Campaign." *American Journal of Orthopsychia,* 14: 381, 1944.
8. Menninger, Brig. Gen. W. C., "Modern Concept of War Neuroses." Ludwig Kant Lecture, *Bulletin of the New York Academy of Medicine, 22,* 1945.

9. BARTEMEIRER, L. H.; KUBIE, L. S.; MENNINGER, K. A.; ROMANO, J., and WHITEHORN, J. C., "Combat Exhaustion." *Journal of Nervous and Mental Diseases,* 104: 358, 489, 1946.

DISCUSSION

Francis L. K. Hsu

THERE IS no question that the factors which Dr. Boshes had outlined were operative in the cases of delinquency he studied: broken home, no father (or father too busy to spend any time with his child), confusion over a succession of mothers (or mother with too many babies to give them individual attention), no religion, no art, no sport, or residence in a low-income area infested with crime and cultural conflict between parents and children. Yet, two questions must be asked: (1) Why is it that not all individuals under these circumstances become delinquent? (2) If subjected to the distresses of similar or other circumstances, would as many individuals in another society become delinquent?

One of the answers to the first question is probably that it depends upon genetic or inherited differences. Being an anthropologist, I feel, however, more competent to dwell on the second. I think the factors outlined by Dr. Boshes are especially serious in a culture like America, where the basic pattern of social relationship is marked by a strong emphasis on self-reliance and emotionality.[2] For example, where the relationship between parents and children is characterized by strong bonds of love, the loss of a parent or the lack of attention by a parent to a child is likely to be much more keenly felt by, or to create a much greater disappointment

[2] See Hsu, Francis L. K., *Americans and Chinese: Two Ways of Life.* New York: Abelard-Schuman, Inc., 1953.

on the part of, the children than if there had been no such strong emphasis on love. It is common sense that the stronger the desire for love the more bitter will be the disappointment over the loss or lack of it.[3]

Self-reliance in its basic form demands freedom from all restraints, and complete equality with one's fellow men. This gives abundant joy to those who have more than others, or are ahead of others, but creates serious misery in those who have less than, or are away behind, others. An American boy who has no father whose exploits he can boast about and who can take him to sports events will feel the lack much more than his counterpart in some other cultures where the pattern of self-reliance is absent and emotionality less intense.

There is, however, a good deal more to the situation than this analysis indicates so far. In America, children are encouraged to develop a sense of independence at an early age. As time goes by they are made to feel that they can accomplish anything they wish, without, however, putting this confidence to the test of reality. For parents are the protectors without letting the young ones realize that they are.

Adolescence is the time when the youngsters are physically big and within range of all adult capabilities, but socially and culturally very naïve, since up to this point they have lived in a sort of unreal world under parental protection. At adolescence or some time before they begin to see that what they have been engaged in so far has given mere illusions of adult grandeur, and they want now to try the real things.

At this juncture they run into a double-barreled difficulty. On the one hand, they know too little of the intricacies of the real adult world, with its hypocrisy, tricks, dishonesty, and what not, and many of them are shocked or disillusioned by the world in general and by their parents in particular.

[3] The opposite extreme to loss or lack of love is overindulgence or overprotection. This also creates very serious problems in America. But this is outside of the scope of the present discussion.

Rejecting parents and being self-reliant only mean great feelings of insecurity. This is the time when the call of the gang is most attractive—in which, as Dr. Boshes pointed out, the youngsters "find warmth and satisfaction."

On the other hand, the youngsters' capacity for real self-reliance threatens their parents with insecurity. For self-reliance means that each new generation ruthlessly replaces the old, so that, once replaced, the old are relegated to the background. Having been *de facto* masters over their children, American parents feel this inherent threat of rejection much more keenly than those in other cultures where parents are not such complete masters of their young children, and where there is no emphasis on self-reliance, so that the old, instead of becoming less important, reach new social and religious prominence.

The American parents' reply to the threat of insecurity is by attempting to hold onto the youngsters at least unil the legal age of twenty-one. Yet many youngsters of sixteen to twenty can do all the things that those who are twenty-one can do. The age of twenty-one is merely an arbitrarily chosen legal barrier which has no physical or mental reference to the growing individual. The American youngsters' reply to their parents' efforts is bigger and more violent rebellion.

All these are not intended as an attempt to discredit the factors outlined by Dr. Boshes, who is supported in this regard by a majority of American sociologists and social workers, but to suggest future lines of inquiry which go beyond the more usually emphasized causes of delinquency.

In regard to Dr. Boshes' analysis of mental breakdown among American soldiers in combat, I have only one point to make. Once again, I have no reason to minimize the factors outlined by him, but wish only to suggest a wider context for them. For example, it seems that relatively few Chinese or Japanese soldiers are known to break down in combat, even in circumstances where all odds are against them. An easy answer to this would of course be that the Chinese and Japanese armed forces have never been equipped with psychiatrists, and therefore the reported high rate of mental casualties in the American forces was merely the result of better means of detection. For the same reasons we cannot compare the rate of mental illness among the general population of the United States with that of the East. But if troubled with overwhelming mental casualties, the Chinese forces probably would not have succeeded in doing as well as they have proven themselves capable of, against decidedly better equipped United Nations forces in Korea, just as the Japanese probably would have surrendered much sooner than they did in World War II.

Insecurity because of self-reliance and strong emotionality drive the American adolescent to his gang. The same forces tend to lead the American soldier to seek a strong object of identification in the person of the commanding officer or in the entire outfit. If he finds this object, he will better survive battle stress than if he did not.

Not having been used to the contradictory forces of self-reliance and strong emotional identifications in the family, but having been accustomed to the idea of mutual dependence with no strong emotional link with parents, the Oriental adolescent has less need for the gang, and the mental sanity of the Oriental soldier in combat tends to depend much less upon the things which are invaluable to the American. The probability is that, under similar stresses, the Oriental soldier is less likely to break down than his American counterpart. At least this should be a possible line of inquiry.

ADDITIONAL DISCUSSION

DR. GILLIN: Are there any figures on the percentage of people who cracked up?

DR. BOSHES: I can answer you first. It all depends on when and where. On the Cassino front the crack-ups were so frequent (sometimes 100 per cent) that the commanding general tried to get all psychiatrists sent home. He was afraid that information on the high rate would get back to the United States and cause unfavorable publicity. The reaction of the troops of different countries is interesting. The British troops just asked for a few days of rest before going back to the front. The Americans said that they had fought hard and long, and desired now to go back home. The French-Mohammedan troops "could not" retreat. Unless they die in battle, they do not go to heaven.

In regard to control factors in the delinquency area, islands of nondelinquency, chiefly Greek and Jewish families, existed. Here were people with strong family ties. These "islands" would frequently move to different zones when the members became more prosperous.

The question of "joining," as related to Americans, is worthy of note. Normal Americans have to join. I knew one group of Americans who were nonjoiners. They were trained as Rangers or shock troops, which are the equivalent of British commandos. They had been trained to destroy, to use every method of fighting and killing possible. The problems we had with these men outside of battle were terrific. After a few drinks their hostility and repressions were often released, and then they caused trouble.

One other point is the story of psychosomatic symptoms which occur in the setting of cultural conflict. There is a tradition among Hopi Indians that if a man steps into the path of a snake, he gets pains in the legs. These pains are normally relieved by treatment from a witch doctor. The young Hopi who is "American"-oriented and who has learned from American doctors that medicine-man treatment is nonscientific still gets pains when he crosses a snake path. However, nothing can be done to relieve him, because these enlightened Indians no longer believe in medicine men. They have no faith in American doctors either, because the latter cannot cure the functional symptoms by medicine or surgery. How can we relieve the Hopi warrior's pain?

Now, to answer a few of Dr. Hsu's questions. His discussion is very interesting and scholarly. It applies accurately to certain situations, but I am afraid that the illustrations are not entirely germane to what I have presented today. I cannot agree that the American parent tries to hold the young, and that the young in turn respond against the parent with bitter rebellion. Actually, in the example of the "gang" boy, the parent did not have any relationship whatsoever with his son, and the latter was in rebellion at home because there was no father figure with whom to identify. He sought a father figure elsewhere and found it in the gang leader. In the "combat family" the soldier selected a father figure in the good commanding officer. Where the father figure and the family setting were adequate, whether at home or abroad, we saw no breakdown. Actually, the American does not break down in his gang, where there are strong bonds of identification, nor does he break down even in war. These are the very factors which give the American strength rather than fostering rebellion and consequent weakness. It has been my experience that the American pattern is characterized by greater individualism and resourcefulness rather than by individual insecurity. The American does well on his own. He loves to be part of a team, but when placed on his own is an extremely ingenious and adaptive person. In the gang setting, the very factors which Dr. Hsu points out as producing breakdown were the factors which held the children from becoming delinquent. In the families with very tight bonds, where there was a strong need for the parent to retain control of the child, as in the Greek and Jewish families, there was no delinquency; instead, we saw islands of socially acceptable behavior.

As regards the question of the Chinese soldier's not breaking down in combat as contrasted with the supposed vulnerability of the American soldier when similarly exposed, I think we shall have to get better documentation of the Chinese soldier and what was expected of him. I am certain that the standards for combat performance are quite different. Behavior which would cause an American officer to send his soldier for psychiatric review might not even draw the attention of the Chinese officer, and if I am to go by some of the reports of General Marshall, General Wedemeyer, and some of the personal observations of some of my friends in the Chinese-Burma-India theater, I think the standard for what is considered acceptable and nonacceptable military behavior is different in the two armies. We are dealing with two altogether dissimilar cultures, and I do not think that we can compare their military aspects. It is not a question of courage. There is no such thing as an uncourageous person. It is only a problem of orientation and motivation. Any well-prepared soldier will fight, and even die, if need be, before breaking down. An example was the no-surrender philosophy of the Japanese. The Japanese did not surrender because they were deeply indoctrinated with the idea that they would be tortured and killed by the United States forces. Statistics, too, have to be carefully validated. For example, when I spoke to a malariologist in Naples about the incidence of this disease in the Italian forces during the Ethiopian War, he said there was practically no malaria whatsoever, but he added quite pointedly, "We had hundreds of thousands of cases of heatstroke. I wonder if you remember that Mussolini issued an edict that there would be no diagnoses of malaria made." From this, some of the statistics in war are derived.

I believe that Dr. Hsu's discussion is of extreme interest because it gives us a picture of another culture. We shall use it as added material for our discussion, but we must not set up comparisons on noncomparable samples.

VI

EMERGING CONCEPTIONS OF NEUROSIS AND NORMALITY

O. H. Mowrer

THE PSYCHIATRIC PERSPECTIVE

IN THE traditional ethical system of Western civilization, the central theme has been: "Be good and you will be happy," i.e., *normal.* Modern psychiatry, following the lead of Freud, has radically revised this formulation to read: "Don't be too good or you will be miserable," i.e., *neurotic.* Let us explore the rationale and the practical results of this revision.

Since Freud was, more than anyone else, the founder of present-day psychiatry, we may fairly take his position as the dominant one in contemporary psychiatric thought. Despite the fact that Freud broke with the earlier emphasis upon constitutional and organic explanations of personality disorders, he very largely retained what may be called the *biological bias* of the medical profession as a whole. In respect to diseases of the body, this bias has been amply validated by the conquest within the past century of most communicable and infectious diseases. But extensions of the same type of thinking into the realm of "mental disease" had left the problem, both from the standpoint of treatment and prevention, almost untouched and has created a perfect quagmire of confusion at the level of theory.

As is now well known, Freud took the position that neurosis arises when *instinctual forces,* notably those of lust and hostility, are prevented from finding satisfactory outlets. Anxiety and depression, two of the core phenomena of neurosis, are supposed to result, respectively, from "repressed sexuality" and "repressed aggression"; and therapeutic effort, in this frame of reference, is bent upon *releasing* these pent-up impulses and thus restoring the afflicted individual to health. Unlike traditional views of the good life, which stressed moral and "spiritual" values, the Freudian approach tends to equate happiness with organic pleasure and enthrones the body (or "flesh") as the ultimate measure of all things. In Freud's own words, "The power of the id (i.e., the reservoir of all instinctual forces) expressed the true purpose of the individual organism's life" and "the holding back of aggressiveness (and lust) is in general unhealthy and leads to illness" (Freud, 1949, p. 19 and p. 22).

Since most physical diseases are due to an invasion of the organism by harmful foreign substances (germs, toxins, or the like) which disrupt normal functioning, "mental disease" is likewise attributed to external influences, but this time to *cultural* or *educational* influences. Out of their own neurotic overrestraint and rigidity, parents and other socializers are assumed to produce inhibitions and fears in children which, though unrealistic and unconfirmed by later experience, blindly persist and render the affected individual neurotic until he is psychoanalyzed.

Among the many paradoxes which this approach creates is the following: If neurosis is due to a learning *excess,* why is not recovery automatic and spontaneous as soon as the individual grows up and escapes the immediate domination of his confused and misguided parents? And why, indeed, if the parents were misled and mistrained in turn by *their* parents, have they not learned *their* way out of these mistaken attitudes and habits by the time they have set up independent households and had children of their own? Despite much ingenious speculation, this problem has not been satisfactorily answered by the proponents of the theory that the neurotic is basically an oversocialized person, one who has been rendered "too good" for his own effective functioning and happiness.

Nothing could today be clearer than the need for—and there is growing clinical evidence which indeed fully justifies—a shift in viewpoint which is as radical and bold in its way as was Freud's original theory. There are many ways of expressing this revision of orthodox psychoanalytic thinking, but one of the simplest and best is to note that for Freud a neurotic symptom was an outcropping or expression of a repressed impulse or desire; whereas the alternative view which seems most clearly indicated is that symptoms represent, not a return of biological drives, but a displaced, or *dislocated,* expression of the self-critical functions which are normally experienced as "pangs of conscience." Clinical researches are showing ever more convincingly that when conscious conflicts are resolved, not constructively, but by means of dissociation (thus laying the basis for neurosis), the part of personality that most commonly "loses the battle" and has to suffer banishment is not the id, as Freud supposed, but the superego or conscience. The reign of the primitive, infantile pleasure-principle is thus preserved, but at the risk of recurrent, seemingly unprovoked "attacks" from the part of the personality which, more than any other, represents the long-term culturally enjoined strategies of integrated conduct called virtue and wisdom. Put a little differently, the Freudian view holds that a neurosis represents the repression of vital instinctual forces by *false fears,* whereas the alternative view is that neurosis represents *real immaturity* which the repression (of conscience) effectively protects.

Freud often confessed to puzzlement over the fact that symptoms are so universally *painful,* rather than enjoyable as one might expect them to be if they really represented surreptitious satisfaction of forbidden impulses. But if we take the position that symptoms are but the "voice of conscience" speaking *out of context,* it is in no way surprising that they are both painful and mysterious. And since by virtue of the dissociation of this part of the personality its effectiveness is neutralized, the infantilism and immaturities of the individual are protected and may persist indefinitely.

That this revision of Freudian premises has far-reaching theoretical implications and leads to innovations in technique which seem to expedite therapy is a thesis which cannot be fully developed here. For fuller elaboration and documentation, the reader must be referred to other works (Mowrer, 1950). But we cannot end this part of our discussion without noting the similarity between this newer point of view and the traditional one against which Freud so vigorously rebelled. The newer view says, in effect, that neurosis is more of a sickness of the "spirit" than it is of the "flesh;" it says that the problem is not so much one of cultural forces overriding biological needs as it is the reverse; and it says that the essential task of therapy is less that of undoing unrealistic learning on the part of the patient than it is of helping him take up once again certain *developmental* tasks which, in the season of his neurosis, he has all but abandoned.[1]

ANTHROPOLOGICAL CONTRIBUTIONS

Anthropology, in its brief but enterprising history, has made two contributions which are invaluable in the understanding and treatment of personality problems. The first of these is the concept of *culture*. It is no accident, I think, that this concept did not emerge until after Darwin had put the theory of organic evolution on a sound scientific footing; for culture, too, presupposes evolution, but evolution of the "mind" rather than that of the body. E. B. Tylor and those who followed him thus gave us a naturalistic way of thinking about the origin of man's "soul," i.e., his distinctive mentality and knowledge, which dispenses with the notion of divine revelation quite as completely as Darwin's work disposed of the notion of a special creation of man in the physical sense.

But more to the point is the fact that the culture concept places a new and relatively great emphasis upon the process of *education*. And it is here, in the resistance of the human animal to the imposition and assimilation of the culture of his group, that the crux of neurosis lies. Freud saw this in a general way, but he made the now seemingly mistaken inference that neurosis represents a

[1] Strictly speaking, the "sickness" of the neurotic lies neither in the "spirit" (superego) nor in the "flesh" (id), but in the self or ego. The real issue, then, is whether a sick, or neurotic, ego is one that has been coerced by the superego into repressing the id (as Freud supposed), or the reverse.

too-great triumph in the part of education, whereas the more justifiable view is that neurosis represents a failure —of the acculturation or socialization process. The simple criminal or psychopath represents the lowest level of socialization; but the neurotic, far from representing an overachievement in this respect, is not greatly removed, falling somewhere *between* the psychopath and the normal.

The second great contribution of anthropology has been the concept or organization, integration, or pattern. Ruth Benedict's *Patterns of Culture* (1934) was a milestone in this respect, and did much to teach us to think dynamically and interrelatedly about societies and the ways in which they function and perpetuate themselves. In psychology we have had the model offered by *Gestalttheorie*, but here the emphasis has been mainly upon perception rather than upon personality in the more inclusive sense. Contemporary conceptions of personality are stressing more and more the phenomenon of organization, integration, pattern, and in this respect there is a distinct parallelism between individual psychology and the thinking of Benedict and many others with respect to what Cattell has usefully called group "syntality." Just as a healthy society is pre-eminently a system, a unity, a synthesis, so likewise is an effective, happy individual; and we are now coming to see more clearly than ever before that it is strain upon, and threat to, this self-system of the individual that generate anxiety and provide the soil from which neurosis may readily spring, just as disharmony and competing trends within a culture provide the setting for social pathology.[2]

[2] This is not to say, of course, that a psychological or social system which is under stress will necessarily react with pathology; it may instead react creatively and develop new strengths and resources.

Many interesting hypotheses follow from an examination of the relationship between personality and group syntality. It is almost axiomatic that a vigorous, effective, well-integrated society cannot be made up exclusively or even predominantly of disorganized individuals. Syntality clearly presupposes organized personality. But the reverse is not necessarily true: while group disorganization makes it harder for an individual to achieve a satisfactory personal synthesis, such an achievement is not altogether impossible, as many historical examples indicate. It is also possible to have a collection of individuals all of whom possess good personality integration but who do not form a society, who do not constitute syntality, for the reason that they do not have a *common* culture, with the result that their attitudes and actions do not interlock and produce a larger synthesis or system. Perhaps the delegates to the United Nations are a good contemporary example of this sort of thing.

In this context, it is also interesting to glance briefly at the relationship between individual therapy and social reform. Some therapists are often criticized for their "conservatism," since they seem to be oblivious to social and economic evils and concerned only with the difficulties and immaturities of individuals. Why, we are asked, do therapists not *do something* about "society," and stop worrying so much about individual neurotics, who, after all, are merely the inevitable products of a bad social system? One can easily get involved here in an infinite philosophical regress, but the therapist need not do so to make his position and purpose sufficiently explicit.

As numerous empirical studies, as well as clinical experience, have shown, virtually every neurotic is a "radical," in the sense of having never come to terms with the problems of *authority* and *responsibility.* The question is: How to help the individual meet and master this conflict? The Freudian approach likewise shuns the task of broad social reform, but instead stresses the bogus character of the neurotic's experience with authority figures (mainly parents) and attempts to provide experience with a more lenient, more permissive, and supposedly more "reasonable" authority, notably the analyst. This approach, as we have already seen, seems not to be giving us either the theoretical answers or the practical assistance which we need in this area. The alternative approach to therapy is to give the patient an experience with an authority figure, or parent person, who is not necessarily more "lenient" or "permissive" but who is wiser, more consistent, more insightful, and thus more successful in helping the patient come to terms with authority, both as represented by conscience and by community, than has heretofore been possible. The difference may seem a trivial one on paper, but in the consulting room it is far from trivial.

All of this is not to say that a proper therapist need necessarily assume that this is "the best of all possible worlds" or that one's particular society might not profit from a little face-lifting now and then. What it does say is (1) that the psychotherapist, by the very nature of his task and training, is prepared to work, *as a psychotherapist,* only at the level of personality, not at the level of group syntality (save insofar as better individuals usually make better citizens);[3] and (2) that most patients,

[3] The psychotherapist may also serve a very useful function by making generally known the conclusions at which he arrives as a result of his work, but in thus communicating his findings to society at large the therapist is no longer functioning as a therapist, strictly speaking; he is now a researcher, a publicist, an advocate.

when they overcome—or, I should prefer to say, when they terminate their neurosis by learning the lessons it is trying to teach them—then do they find that their society is not so absurd or simple-minded as they formerly supposed. I like the comment made by Mark Twain during middle life to the effect that he had been surprised to discover how much *his father* had learned in the last ten years. The neurotic who undergoes successful therapy is likely to have a similar experience with respect to his society and its ways and values. Even Lenin was once prompted to observe that "the curse of every revolutionary movement is the number of adolescent mentalities it attracts." Although not every revolutionary necessarily has an "adolescent mentality," yet a lot of persons, if they attend to the challenge of growing up emotionally and morally and of becoming more responsible and better integrated as individuals, discover a remarkable store of accumulated wisdom where they had formerly seen only folly and malevolence. That Freud sometimes thought of human culture as little better than a necessary evil—necessary for the survival of groups but evil in the sense that it stands constantly between the individual and the fullest possible attainment of instinctual pleasure—is suggested in *Civilization and Its Discontents* and in many other places. It should hardly surprise us that this thought pattern, for all its naturalism, has failed to guide us either to a sounder conception of mental hygiene or to a highly efficient form of individual treatment.

Finally, I want to say a word about something of a disservice which anthropology has sometimes rendered with respect to the field of personality theory and psychotherapy. While the tendency is lessening, there are a goodly number of anthropologists who still see it as their main mission in life to spread the doctrine of cultural relativity. In some ways this has indeed been a useful thing to do. It has served to point up the social, i.e., the pragmatic and historical, origins of culture and to undercut ethnocentricism and absolutistic conceptions of human nature. And in still another, perhaps more subtle, way the relativity emphasis has been salutary. Whenever psychologists or others have attempted to derive measures of personal normality or abnormality which were based upon narrow social modalities or norms of behavior, anthropologists have been quick, and quite correct, in pointing out that such measures do not mean much since the inventory of specific behaviors expected of an individual is so very different as one goes from society to society, and even as one goes from class to class or caste to caste within a single society. There is thus no generality in the normality of concept; and hence the slogan that everything is culturally relevant.

Moreover, in the minds of many anthropologists there seems to be the implicit premise that there never can be any kind of generally applicable conception or criterion of personality order or disorder. This assumption is unwarranted.[4] From a dynamic standpoint, psychopathology is

[4] Hsu, in his paper "Anthropology or Psychiatry—a definition of objectives and their implications" (1952), has stressed "the differences in objectives between anthropology and psychiatry" (p. 13) and has taken sharp issue with the view that "absolute criteria for mental abnormality will forever be impossible (and) that psychopathology is invariably relative to culture, that what is abnormal in one culture may be normal in another" (p. 18). Dr. Hsu goes on to indicate the differences "... a psychopathic person, in his attempts to escape from the conflict-producing situation, will usually cling to or fall back onto his past, ... but a normal, functioning person is one who will face the tension-producing situation, and attempts and succeeds in solving it in some presently practical or culturally accepted way." Granted that the presence or absence of dissociative trends may sometimes be hard to demonstrate in practice, yet *in principle* this is a perfectly explicit, technically de-

the same in one society as in any other, in one social subclass as in another, and, so far as one can gather, in all historical periods. As already indicated, the essence of neurosis is this, that in attempting to deal with what is at first an entirely conscious conflict individuals sometimes, when other expedients seem not to work, resort to the strategy of dissociation, or partial self-destruction, as a means of re-establishing inner tranquility. However successful this strategy may be for a time, it hardly ever proves successful in the long run, because of the "will to health" or inherent integrative trends within the personality which keep trying to bring the separated pieces of personality back together. And it is this struggle between the dissociative and associative, the repressive and expressive, between the divisive and cohesive trends, that constitutes the core of neurosis, regardless of time, place, or person.

Freud thought that it was always forces of the id that get fissioned off from the rest of the personality, whereas my own studies suggest that far more commonly, perhaps quite generally, it is the superego that is denied and pushed aside. But important as this issue is for certain purposes, it should be noted that in either case we still have a completely universal, culturally nonrelative view of the essential nature of psychopathology.

This point may be clarified by referring to a paper which Clyde Kluckhohn and I wrote a few years ago (Kluckhohn and Mowrer, 1944). In it we distinguished between four components, or levels, of personality. These

---

fensive, and universally applicable criterion. Needless to say, differences in the *degree* to which dissociation has been adopted as a strategy for dealing with conflict by different persons will have to be taken into account in determining how much social freedom and accountability they are granted, yet, for conceptual purposes, we may say that as soon as a person *begins* to use dissociation he is "abnormal," psychologically "diseased," and headed for trouble.

we termed the *universal* (panhuman) component, the *societal* (society-wide) component, the *role* (largely occupational and status) component, and the *idiosyncratic* (unique-to-the-individual) component. To date anthropologists have been mainly interested in the second and third of these, i.e., in the components of personality that are determined by virtue of membership in a particular society and by performance, either on an ascribed or an acquired basis, of a particular role or combination of roles. The psychotherapist, by contrast, is concerned with these two personality components hardly at all. It is his assumption that, at least in this and most societies, there is considerable latitude in terms of what one may be occupationally, and one can even change his nationality if he wishes. By their very nature these are things which are done *publicly* (save in the exceptional case of the imposter or the spy) and rarely do they have a basic clinical significance.

But there is no option (short of suicide) with respect to being a human being and no option (short of psychosis) with respect to being an individual. *As a human being* a person must face certain basic issues with respect to consistency and responsibility which human beings have to face everywhere; and *as an individual* a person has to cope with the problem of keeping his impulses and experiences co-ordinated, else he will suffer from anxiety and the danger of neurosis. For these reasons the psychotherapist works almost entirely with the universal and the idiosyncratic components of personality. Thus, what anthropologists say about the relativity of cultures with respect to the second and third components is, from one standpoint, of no more interest to the therapist than what psychologists say from the opposite point of view about normality or abnormality in the basis of culture-bound tests or personality inventories. In order for his art and science to serve the intended purpose, the therapist must, in his thinking and his practice, be international, interracial, intercultural, and able to help members of any particular nationality or race without respect to their particular vocational, political, religious, or other special roles within the larger group.

References

1. Benedict, Ruth, *Patterns of Culture.* Boston: Houghton Mifflin, 1934.
2. Freud, Sigmund, *Civilization and Its Discontents.* London: Hogarth Press, Ltd., 1930.
3. Freud, Sigmund, *An Outline of Psychoanalysis.* New York: W. W. Norton & Co., 1949.
4. Hsu, F. L. K., "Anthropology or Psychiatry—a definition of objectives and their implications." *Southwestern Journal of Anthropology,* Vol. 8, No. 2, Summer 1952.
5. Kluckhohn, C., and Mowrer, O. H., "Culture and personality: a conceptual scheme." *American Anthropologist,* Vol. 46, 1944, pp. 1-29.
6. Lewis, O., and Mowrer, O. H., "The public-private and overt-covert dimensions of behavior." Unpublished.
7. Mowrer, O. H., *Learning Theory and Personality Dynamics.* New York: Ronald Press Co., 1950.

DISCUSSION

George Saslow

Dr. Mowrer has presented to us for discussion a presumed cross-culturally valid definition of psychoneurosis. As I understand his position, he has certain general grounds for rejecting Freud's views on the matters he had discussed. First, Mowrer believes that Freud's explanation of self-defeating, self-perpetuating behavior in terms of an excessively strong superego is not tenable, because behavioral responses become extinguished in the absence of the reinforcing agents (in this instance, the parents). Second, Freud's general philosophical view of life, which implies that primary drives are always good and that socialization is inherently difficult or bad or both, is unacceptable. Third, therapy which proceeds along the lines of Freud's conception has proven difficult, long, and often unsuccessful.

The following comments upon the above general statements appear to be in order. First, Mowrer gives no weight to the capacity of verbal cues to act as highly potent reinforcing agents, channeling the responses to primary and learned drives in ways indistinguishable from those associated with the physically present initial reinforcing persons. This subject, obviously of great importance, is ably presented by Dollard and Miller in their book *Personality and Psychotherapy*. Second, the history of the acceptance and rejection of theories in various branches of science gives us little encouragement to decide upon the merit of one of several alternative theories in a given field in terms of a philosophic view of life prevalent at a given time. What Mowrer seems to be saying is that socialization is not only, in a certain sense, part of the definition of man as a species, and hence an inescapable part of an individual's life, but also that it has certain positive aspects. Thus socialization in itself is a source of important individual satisfactions, and, in addition, when it becomes automatic, frees the individual for the pursuit of other satisfactions: in the same sense that learning to walk, or talk, or ice-skate automatically, could be regarded as yielding similar satisfactions. Even though it seems correct that Freud's keen awareness of the evil effects of overinhibition of emotional expression upon personality development led him to overemphasize the importance of free expression of primary drives, and even though I personally see no way of escaping the conclusion that socialization has both necessary and highly important positive aspects, I do not see how juxtaposition of these statements allows us to choose undersocialization as a general theory of the source of individual maladjustment rather than overinhibition. Data bearing upon overinhibition and underlearning which came from the careful study of maladjusted individuals would appear to be more relevant to such a choice. Third, it is an ancient, well-documented fallacy in medicine that a treatment which cures a patient of a malady necessarily tells us something about the nature of the malady. A treatment which fails to cure a patient may tell us equally little about the nature of his malady. In general, the problem of evaluation of psychotherapy is in such an early stage that the results of psychotherapy by different methods cannot be compared at the present time; hence, apart from the fallacy above mentioned, no evidence is available which could support Mowrer's position, nor does he himself present any at this time.

Mowrer thus proposes that Freud's general views of neurosis be rejected on certain broad grounds (to which, as I have indicated, serious exceptions may be taken), and that we accept, instead, on those grounds, Mowrer's general views of neurosis. Current research on the psychotherapeutic process, such as it is, appears to indicate that both undersocialization (or learning deficit) and overinhibition (or learning excess) are of great importance in individual maladjustments; and that a central feature of the therapeutic process is what Franklin Shaw has called a minimizing of the ego-involvement of the subject, so that the subject is able to delay his well-practiced responses to the old cues while considering the consequences (both short-term and long-term) of alternative responses, thus becoming free for the first time to block an old response, to try a new one, and to practice it until it suits him. Such views of the therapeutic process imply a conception of personality formation and of individual maladjustment which does not necessarily depend exclusively upon any single one of the current bitterly disputed theories. Mowrer's views may thus be seen more as correction of the unavoidable overemphasis which is frequently part of the contributions of genius than as a revolutionary change in fundamental Freudian concepts.

Consider now Mowrer's major positive contribution, that neurosis is to be regarded as learning deficit in relation to dissociation (which itself is to be viewed as partial self-destruction). How would the kind of individual maladjustment described by Arnold Green, in his paper "Culture, Normality, and Personality Conflict" (*American Anthropologist,* Vol. 50, 1948) be regarded within Mowrer's conceptual framework? Green describes the following situation involving men of the Ojibwa Indian tribe in Southeast Ontario, Canada. The man tries to attain his two supreme goals, safety and prestige, which have been thoroughly inculcated in him as he has grown up, by becoming a successful warrior and hunter. Yet if a man succeeds in becoming unusually successful as a warrior and hunter, other men fear him and direct their power of sorcery against him, thus threatening his safety. It would appear that he is forced to dissociate in some way if he is to maintain his equilibrium. It is noticed that the men are very frequently severely anxious while fulfilling their cultural expectations to excess. Can this situation be regarded as a matter of learning deficit? Can it be regarded as an estrangement of an individual from his society? Or could it be looked at otherwise? Green proposes, in view of anxiety having this sort of origin in various cultures, a theory of individual maladjustment which appears in fact to have cross-cultural validity: this is that mutally inconsistent roles, or goals, or self-conceptions, can be viewed as the source of conflict and symptoms. It is difficult to see how Mowrer's conception can cover a number of the types of individual maladjustment described briefly by Green.

We come now to a more detailed consideration of "dissociation" as a criterion of neurosis. Mowrer indicates that any degree of dissociation is to be taken as indicative of neurosis. In view of the fact, frequently commented upon by many observers, that in any individual's perception of the world, and in any society's interlocking ways of perceiving the world, there is always some degree of distortion (which observers from our own society consider to be very marked in some other societies), it is quite unlikely that dissociation can be regarded in the all-or-none manner which is crucial to Mowrer's view. One must raise the question when dissociation has reached the extent which warrants labeling the person showing it as sick. How is one to define the degree of dissociation, the intensity of dissociation, the "extensity" (in the sense of the number of areas of life activity involved) of dissociation which individuals in diverse cultures show? To these questions Mowrer gives no answer except the all-or-none one which is difficult to utilize. One may still, therefore, mention the probability that definable patterns of symptoms or of dysfunctions are better criteria of "sickness" than dissociation in the sense indicated but not clearly defined by Mowrer.

Finally, the question must be raised of the place of what we call biological factors in a theory based upon the conception of learning deficit. In this connection, the following items may be mentioned:

1. The highly individual responses to frustration of infants during their first ten days of life, as reported by D. P. Marquis (*Journal of Experimental Psychology*, Vol. 32, p. 123, 1943).

2. The individual, familially loaded, patterns of autonomic response to stress of children of various ages, studied at the Fels Research Institute.

3. The significant differences, as observed by Malmo and co-workers (*Science*, Vol. 112, 1950, p. 325) in the electromyographic patterns of response to a sound stimulus of no symbolic significance, between anxiety neurotics, on the one hand, and

control subjects on the other. These differences represent differences in neurophysiological functioning very difficult to relate to the conception of learning deficit as basic. Of a similar nature are the observations of Malmo and others on the prolonged and excessive blood-pressure responses of anxiety neurotics to such a nonspecific stimulus as immersion of an extremity in water at 0° C. as compared with control subjects (presented at meetings of the American Psychiatric Association, May 1951).

4. The effects of certain substances which, in quite small amounts, produce marked and complex changes in human behavior, are not likely to be explained in terms of learning deficit. Among these substances are ACTH, mescaline, lysergic acid, and niacin. ACTH, for example, when given to persons with rheumatoid arthritis, has been observed to produce all of the following effects (at different times) in the same person: decrease in number of dreams recalled over a given period; increase in submissiveness to equals or superiors; increase in assertive behavior toward equals, inferiors, and superiors. It would seem that even very complex kinds of behavior may simply be reflections of the biological state of the organism (for in a number of these experiments the subjects never knew when they were receiving the potent drug), rather than matters dependent upon learning. One is forced, therefore, to consider the possibility that equally complex behaviors may originally have become well established in the organism at times of altered biological state.

5. The behavior manifestations of "organic" origin are extremely difficult to distinguish from those of personality or social origin. This statement is true, for example, of controlled experiments in which there has been vitamin deprivation, of patients with pellagra, of patients with brucellosis who suffer interference with their highest functions, of patients with rheumatic brain disease, of patients with brain tumor, etc.

Items 4 and 5 raise the question whether we must consider

individual maladjustments to be of two types of origin, (a) "organic" and (b) learning-deficit origin, or of a single origin. In the absence of conclusive evidence at the present time, the simpler hypothesis is certainly that behavior disturbance (among which neurosis is to be included) is of one kind. It does not seem likely that the learning deficit hypothesis will cover all the types of behavior disturbance which one must consider in a general theory of maladjustment.

6. One may even raise the question whether conflict, discomfort, or pain is necessary for personality disorganization, maladjustment, or neurosis (since Mowrer postulates dissociation as occurring in relation to conflict). From an example in Hebb's book *The Organization of Behavior,* it seems clear that intense fear may occur in a young chimpanzee, not in relation to discomfort or conflict, but in a situation involving the interference of one complex brain process with another. Neither of the interfering processes involved was in the least unpleasant, but the necessity of acting upon both at once, or choosing between them, resulted in the disorganization observed.

7. Here also it should be mentioned that the cessation of patterns of sensory impulses and of related nervous system activity to which the subject has become habituated may be associated with intense anxiety. Experiments of this kind have been undertaken in human subjects in connection with the blotting out of auditory stimulation.

If one wishes to put all of the relevant observations together in order to arrive at some hypothesis about maladjustment in general, and wishes to utilize the smallest possible number of concepts, one could proceed along the following lines:

a. There are genetically, biologically, and culturally vulnerable individuals.

b. All individual maladjustment (neurosis and psychosis included) occurs in relation to sudden or repeated disruption of patterns of brain-cell activity.

c. Such disruptions need not be unpleasant, conflictual, or painful at first; they may be metabolic, pharmacologic, or toxic in origin; they may result from sudden cessation of habitual patterns of nervous activity; they may occur at times of mutually incompatible actions neither of which is unpleasant; they may occur when an individual needs to carry out mutually incompatible roles, or act toward the attainment of mutually incompatible goals, or act upon mutually incompatible self-conceptions.

d. Learning deficit undoubtedly plays a role in the maladjustment of individuals, but that it is an adequate explanation for all of the relevant phenomena is open to serious question.

VII

THE PROBLEM OF INVARIANCE IN THE FIELD OF PERSONALITY AND CULTURE

Jules Henry

THE FOLLOWING observations of mother-baby interaction in the immediate post-partum[1] were made in a maternity ward:

Female. Post-partum day 7. Bottle-fed. 1 *p.m. nursing, March* 19, 1951.

Mother says, "You burp first; we don't want you spitting up like this morning.... Aren't you going to burp?" M (other) patted B(aby), and B burped. M says, "There you go."

At 1:50[2] milk leaked from B's mouth and M withdrew the nipple, saying, "You're supposed to drink it and not spit it out."

Nipple in at 3:38. B sucks from 3:38 to 4:05, still wheezing. M jiggles nipple. B sucks from 4:10 to 4:20, and M says, "Come on, just got a little more to go." Milk leaks in a stream

---

[1] Joan Whitehorn Boggs, observer.

[2] This means one minute and fifty seconds after feeding was initiated.

from B's mouth, and M says, "How sloppy can one person get? How sloppy can one person get? . . . Come on, burp! . . . Come on, hey, hey. . . . You're hopeless! . . . Boy, you'd think she'd burp. Mommy's going to give up on you. . . . Okay, if you're going to be that way about it. . . ."

At 7:25 M pried B's lips apart and inserted nipple, but removed it immediately, saying, "No?" B burped. "Oh," says M, "you burped lying down. . . . You'd better drink your formula or they won't give you any more."

Male. Post-partum day 3. Bottle-fed. 1 p.m. nursing, February 26, 1951.

M comments to observer, "All he wants to do is sleep." Nipple in at 1:00. M says to B, "Come on and show off for the lady . . . come on and get both eyes open."

He started to suck again at 4:37. M asked, "Why don't you get your eyes open, huh?"

M looked at milk level in bottle, saying, "He took quite a bit." At 23:15 M moved B over on her hand and patted his back. B burped. M says, "Come on and get some more." B burps again. M says, "Hmmm" in a pleased tone; kisses B on the head.

Nipple in at 24:05. B chokes and M takes nipple out, saying, "Oh, oh." Moves B up over her arm at 24:06, says, "I'm not going to make you take any more."

When the mother says, "You burp first; we don't want you spitting up like this morning," it is clear that the mother is (*a*) constraining the baby—by withholding food until the burp is produced; (*b*) entering into a bargaining relationship with baby—food in exchange for burp. When milk leaks from baby's mouth, mother says, "You're supposed to drink it and not spit it out." Here mother communicates the notion of "waste not, want not," and acts to constrain the baby not to waste. When mother says, "Come on, just got a little more to go," she is urging the baby on to the mother's own goals—finishing the allotted number of ounces. When the milk again flows out of the baby's mouth, the mother comments on baby's sloppiness, thus emphasizing our cultural preoccupation with neatness and saving. When she finally says, "You're hopeless... Mommy's going to give up on you," she emphasizes the importance of failure and its devastating accompaniment, loss of maternal love.

The emphasis on quantity, achievement, failure, and constraint runs through both these exceedingly short extracts.[3] We perceive also a vital distinction between what baby wants and what mother wants. Baby often wishes to sleep, but mother wishes to feed it; baby often wishes to spit out milk, but mother wants baby to swallow it and to "show off." Thus *in the immediate post-partum the culture as communicated by the mother envelops the individual—the baby.* It impinges upon baby at the most elemental biological level—the level of satisfaction of elementary needs; the level at which its mother ministers to it. Now, although the culture does not impinge upon the young organism in the same way as it impinges on the adult, yet we must recognize that both adult and infant have culturally determined problems of achievement and constraint, even though these may be qualitatively different. We see also that it is not quite correct to assert either that the individual is distinct from his culture, or that the individual and the culture are the same.[4] The

[3] Mrs. Boggs studied eighteen babies and mothers, with two observational periods for each.

[4] "This conception of culture and the individual as two aspects of the same process or event is... a recent deviation from the... pattern of thought about society and the individual.... Today we... see culture and the individual much as we conceive a gas as an electron." Frank, L. K., "Cultural Coercism and Individual Distortion." *Psychiatry* 2: 1939, pp. 11-27.

culture is expressed through forms of behavior that are re-emphasized daily to the individual through traditional communications and activity, and we see these forms expressed as the activity of individuals.

We are thus at a point where it is necessary to develop a general formulation that will cover two systems of research in such a way as to bring them under a single comprehensive theory. In other words, to develop a set of invariants.[5] I believe the way to this has been suggested by the brief analysis of mother-child interaction in the immediate post-partum, where we saw that in the first instants of its life the infant, in its interaction with its mother, is confronted by situations that also have concrete institutional expressions, and which are abroad in the land as cultural shibboleths that are thundered at the adult from the means of communication and in the task at which he works every day. These situations include those involving success and failure, constraint and free choice, reward and punishment, bargaining relations, quantitative considerations of various kinds, neatness, waste, threats, and so on.

Now, if individuals have specific experiences, such as those of success and failure, of constraint and free choice, punishment and reward, and so on, and if cultures, through their institutions and means of communication, state and provide certain general conditions under which such experiences may be expected to take place, then we may say that there are certain types of conditions that hold for society as a whole and also for individuals.

In the paragraphs that follow, I shall be concerned

[5] A full exposition of my position is to be found in my paper "Toward a System of Socio-Psychiatric Invariants, a Work Paper." *Journal of Social Psychology,* Vol. 37, 1953, pp. 133-161.

only with two of the factors that are present in all cultures and which can serve as a starting point for the development of a system of invariants that will have meaning both within the system of society and the system of the individual. The invariant relationships will be stated by means of equations. These have three purposes: (*a*) to sharpen definition; (*b*) to facilitate manipulation of ideas; (*c*) to suggest possible quantitative expression of the factors examined. The possibility of quantitative expression is stated last because it is the most difficult possibility of all, and the one on which the most work is still to be done. Yet I believe quantification is a very real possibility, and an eventual goal at which this theory is aimed.

REWARD AND PUNISHMENT

Definitions: (*a*) *Reward* is used in the sense of recognition, and by it I mean a special material or symbolic increment accruing to a person. Thus, salary for work performed would not be reward in the sense in which I use it here, but a medal for work well done *would* be. (*b*) By *punishment* is meant the administration of pain to a person by another person or group as a consequence of the performance or nonperformance of a given act. Such punishments may range from having people merely look at one, to capital punishment. (*c*) By *conformity* is meant the expression in attitude or action of mores. (*d*) By *nonconformity* is meant the failure to express the mores or to go contrary to them in attitude or action. (*e*) The vague expression *aware of the imminence of social punishment* refers to the feeling or the belief that one is in danger of punishment for nonconformity.

If I assert that in all societies there is reward for conformity and punishment for nonconformity, I can then urge that the extent to which people in a society are aware of the imminence of social punishment is a function of the relationship between the totality of rewards and punishments provided by the society. Stated symbolically:

Equation 1:

$$AP = f\left(\frac{P}{R}\right).$$

Here P stands for possibility of social punishment, R stands for possibility of social reward, and AP stands for "sense of social punishment." The equation states that in societies where the possibilities for social reward for conformity are small and the possibilities for social punishment for nonconformity are great, the individuals in the society will tend to have a great sense of social punishment, i.e., to feel that they are in imminent danger of being punished for nonconformity.[6] The equation states also that in societies offering many opportunities for reward, but providing relatively few opportunities for punishment, the sense of social punishment will be small. It is important to bear in mind that the equation makes clear that the sense of social punishment is not alone a function of the situation with respect to punishment, but that it depends also on the situation with respect to social reward. Thus the equation implies that in societies offering many opportunities for social reward the individuals in

[6] Obviously any attempt to give this equation mathematical expression would have to take into account not only frequency of occurrence but also the quality of the punishment.

the society might have a high tolerance for social punishment.

If we turn our attention now to the reward (recognition) system of our culture, we shall see that, search its laws as we may, we find no reward provided for the individual who conducts his business fairly, or conforms in any other of the myriad ways the culture demands. Hence we see a culture with a gigantic institutional structure of punishments but none of rewards (recognition). Thus P is greater than R, and we may expect AP to be very large *in the society as a whole.* If, now, we want to know the value of AP for any individual, we must study his *particular life.*

Equation 1 suggests that where the value of P is high in relation to R, an individual will try to divest himself of AP. One way in which he may be able to do this is by overconforming, and thus reducing the possibility of social punishment (value of P). R will then appear extraordinarily large.

Another way in which a person may attempt to reduce AP is by striving to increase the value of R for himself, by trying hard to acquire whatever rewards the society affords. Thus one kind of person who is outstanding because of the way he fights for recognition is one who is acutely conscious of the imminence of social punishment. Hence we may find in one person overconformity and struggle for recognition.[7]

A consideration of Alor, Kwoma, and Pilagá cultures

---

[7] Other obvious ways of reducing the value of AP is by developing techniques of avoiding punishment by: flight, deception, secretiveness. This is documented by the Kwoma data. (See Whiting, J., *Becoming a Kwoma.* New Haven: Yale University Press, 1941, pp. 56-57.) There we may note also important differences in the value of P for different age levels.

indicates that the type of relationships we have been discussing can be discovered where the culture has been well enough described.

In Alor, one-sided emphasis on punishment as a sanction for conformity and the almost total absence of rewards in childhood and adolescence[8] have resulted in struggle for prestige and running away from the village, especially by children, to escape punishment. Of the Alor struggle for prestige, Kardiner has the following to say:

> It is the answer to the question "What do I think of myself?" that can supply us with some information about the source from which the quest for prestige derives its motive power. The wish to be equal to, or better than, another, is really a reflection of an internal need to think well of oneself. In this regard the Alorese quest for prestige has a very strong internal function, since at no time in the life cycle of the individual does he have the opportunity to think highly of himself.[9]

One may well understand why, in a culture where there is an "almost complete lack of reward systems,"[10] the individual, far from thinking well of himself, should be constantly impressed with the imminence of punishment, and hence seek surcease by struggling to get the few rewards the culture does have to offer.

This appears in the analysis of the autobiography of Kolmani the Seeress:[11]

> . . . She tried to get the most out of those around her. From Kolmani's dreams it is also quite apparent that her

---

[8] Dubois, C., *The People of Alor.* Minneapolis: The University of Minnesota Press, 1944, pp. 39, 51, 54, 57, 61, 62, 64, 65, 135, 136, 179, 185.

[9] *Ibid.,* p. 188.

[10] *Ibid.,* p. 179.

[11] *Ibid.,* pp. 542, 543.

> fears of being mistreated were compensated for by her claims to supernatural powers.

and also of Mangma[12] the genealogist, who boasts "about trivialities." In Mangma we have in addition a complementary process—"exaggerating . . . injuries and wrongs . . . suffered at the hands of others;" for it would appear that P and R can be psychically inseparably linked as direct functions of each other: if one phantasies excessive rewards, then one must phantasy excessive punishment to make the rewards inwardly acceptable; and if one phantasies excessive punishment, one must phantasy excessive reward to make the punishment acceptable. Mangma also "never has the courage [*sic!*] to acknowledge his wrongdoings . . ." I would suggest that Mangma's tendency to blame others for his own "wrongdoing" has nothing to do with our notion of "courage," but rather with the internal balance between P and R, wherein P must be repeatedly denied in order to reduce the value of AP.

In the woman Kolangkalieta, on the other hand, we seem to have an overconforming person. Kardiner says that "her dreams about gardening are a way of proclaiming her endless occupation with her maternal activities and therefore a protestation to the effect that she is a very 'good girl.' "

We have a similar situation among the Kwoma, where "The only technique used by Kwoma teachers which does not depend upon pain or fear is that of inciting."[13] Whiting explains Kwoma striving for prestige as follows: praise is used most frequently

> when a pupil has performed an unexpectedly "good" re-

[12] *Ibid.*, p. 228.

[13] Whiting, *loc. cit.*, pp. 191-192.

> sponse rather than merely a right one. Kwoma pupils are thus reinforced for excelling . . . and this may explain in part why Kwoma individuals strive for superiority and prestige.[14]

Actually in view of the great predominance of P in Kwoma, whatever R does appear is *overvalued*. This, "in part" also, serves to account for striving among the Kwoma. We can see that a by-product of our analysis is the discovery that *a simple learning theory is not adequate to explain behavior.*

One may observe among the Pilagá a situation that is in some ways quite similar to what is seen among the Kwoma and the Alor: children are not rewarded (i.e., recognized) for conformity, but are punished bitterly, largely by insult and deprivation, for nonconformity. On the other hand, episodes like the following are characteristic of male children in the four-to-six-year age group:

> The boys and girls of from four to eight years were playing together and the girls scratched the boys' faces. Then Yorodaikolik, age four years, and Darotoyi, about the same age, came to Mrs. Henry and proudly displayed their faces, saying "Look, I was scratched, but never did I cry." After the playing continued a while longer their faces were very red and Mrs. H. suggested that they stop playing, remarking, "It will hurt later, maybe you will stop now." However, Yorodaikolik said, "I'll never cry, for I'm a powerful fellow!" He continued playing, and kept saying to Mrs. H. every once in awhile, "Never do I cry."

> Nakinak, male, age six years, says, "I am a great copulator."

> Yorodaikolik comes in where J. Henry, Mrs. Henry, Kalachiyoli (female, age forty-five to fifty years) and a number of the little girls and boys are. He holds up his penis with a smile and then runs out.

---

[14] *Ibid.*, p. 199.

> Wet'el, age six years, and Nakinak, take their penises from under their G-strings and show them to JH.

> Darotoyi with erect penis calls the attention of Soroi, female, age seven years, to it, saying: "Look, I take hold of my penis."

Bragging about strength and the power to resist pain and other forms of physically taxing stimuli are characteristic of Pilagá. The culture lays stress on the importance of being *wanyeraikolík,* strong, enduring. Stress on maleness is also great. One can thus come to understand why these children, who are practically never given recognition for conformity, but are bitterly punished for the reverse, should eagerly seek some form of recognition in terms of cultural shibboleths.

The mechanism of compensation is, of course, well recognized. Hence, the data presented here reveal nothing unexpected. But this is not the purpose of the presentation. Rather it is to show that when general statements are made about the relationship between reward and punishment *in a society as a whole,* one can expect to find specific kinds of reflection of this in the lives of *individuals* and in predictable directions. This is the essence of invariance, for it makes possible a comprehensive understanding of society and the individual in terms of a single equation.

It is not the purpose of this discussion to prove that all striving for prestige is compensation for excessive punishment, for it seems likely that striving for prestige might arise on a different basis. Nor is it our purpose to prove that wherever there is excessive punishment in childhood there will be striving for prestige, for such striving depends on at least two other factors, so it seems to me: (*1*) the more general configuration of the society and the role prestigeful activities play in it; (2) the presence of some reward. I would urge that where there is practically no experience of recognition in childhood, as is the case among the Pilagá, the striving for it will tend to disappear in adults. I would suggest that this is why prestigeful activities are at such a low ebb among the Pilagá; and I believe that the presence of such activities among the Kwoma is to be explained—always "in part"—by the fact that there *is* praise for outstanding performance. This would make more understandable also the striving for prestige in Alor, for in spite of the emphasis by Kardiner and Dubois on the absence of reward systems in that culture, Kardiner appears to contradict himself in his discussion of the autobiography of Fantan:

> . . . early in Fantan's life his parents fostered his self-esteem and encouraged him in performing exploits. For example, when he is about eight years old his father sends him to fetch a moko. He is dressed appropriately, and when he accomplishes his errand his father praises him and calls him a rich man. His father sends him to fetch a pig from a relative for a new house that his father has completed. Although the pig is almost as big as he is, he finishes the task much to his own satisfaction. *Such an occurrence is not unique, but the telling of it in an autobiography is rare.* [Italics supplied.][15]

Thus in spite of the frequency and severity of punishment in Alor, there is enough reward to provide the basic ex-

[15] Dubois, *op. cit.*, pp. 391-392. While it is true that it is emphasized that Fantan is unusual in the extent to which his parents "fostered his self-esteem," the last sentence of the quotation makes it clear that in Alor, the placing of the child in situations where he could find "satisfaction" in task completion, was "not unique," even though the appearance of such an incident "in an autobiography is rare." In regard to the pig, it is to be noted that when Fantan returned with it, his father said, "He is already a rich man; he doesn't travel empty-handed." *Op. cit.*, p. 351.

perience that makes pursuit of prestige intelligible: that make it emerge as a compensation for punishment.

COMMITMENTS AND FULFILLMENTS

Definitions: (*a*) By a *commitment* is meant a statement, embodied in tradition and expressed in the customary modes of communication, to the effect that individuals in a given society may expect to receive certain goods by virtue of being members of that society. (*b*) By *fulfillment* is meant any act or acts occurring in the society that bring to realization the expectations outlined in (*a*). By the vague expression "sense of satisfaction" is meant a state in which the individual feels that he is getting what he desires and has relatively little grounds for complaint. (*c*) By *powers* is meant the natural resources and culture traits available to a society for carrying out its commitments. The culture traits include technology and forms of social organization.

In our society one is led, among other things, to expect equality of treatment from his fellows and a relatively high standard of living. A Pilagá Indian is led to expect that all people will share their food with him. These expectations I call *commitments,* and the realization of these I call the *fulfillments*. The socio-economic organizations of the United States and the Pilagá are *powers* these societies have through which they may presumably fulfill their commitments.

The relationship between fulfillments and commitments is stated symbolically in

Equation 2:

$$S = f\left(\frac{C}{F}\right),$$

where C stands for commitments, F for fulfillments, and S for "sense of satisfaction." The equation implies that societies that make few commitments and many fulfillments of them tend to be relatively "satisfied societies;" while societies that do the opposite are relatively "dissatisfied societies."[16]

The full discussion of these hypotheses involves examination of the relationship between powers and commitments. The relationship is given in

Equation 3:

$$S = f\left(\frac{Pw}{C}\right),$$

where Pw stands for powers to fulfill commitments. It will be seen from the equation that a society that commits itself to many things it simply does not have the powers to fulfill is bound to be one with a low sense of satisfaction. It is better by far that a society commit itself to little but bend every effort to expanding its powers to fulfill the little it does promise. Purely speculatively, one might wonder whether the optimum condition in a society is not one in which powers are always somewhat in excess of commitments, so that the society may always be in a position to commit itself to new promises which it may then quickly fulfill. This might be called the condition of "radiant hope," and might be said to have characterized American society before the disappearance of the frontier. Societies may be committed to many grand things but lack the powers to fulfill them. Our own society, for example, is committed to the granting of equality to all, yet under

[16] This does not imply that I believe the commitment-fulfillment ratio is the only key to understanding satisfaction. There are, of course, many roads to satisfaction.

the present conditions, it does not have the powers to fulfill this ideal. The major commitment of Pilagá society is that each shall receive food from all. But this is impossible,[17] because there simply is not enough to go around. The result is that although the Pilagá strives to meet the commitments to which he is obligated by tradition, he receives less than he gives away, and gives away to more people than he receives from. He must make up the deficit by retaining some of his goods for himself; but since the culture commits him to share with all, he finds no ease in retention. Pilagá culture is one with a very weak "sense of satisfaction."

The relationship of C to F is most important for any society, yet few indeed are the anthropological monographs in which the relationship is examined. Thus neither the Alor nor Kwoma monographs examine it; although Dubois does give some attention to the relationship between promises and deception in the lives of the Alorese children:

> Very rarely is a reward for being good promised to a child, and more rarely still is the promise kept.[18]

> I have seen youths in their late teens and early twenties send boys on fool's errands and deceive them with false promises of rewards for services, and then guffaw with laughter when the crestfallen child returned.[19]

If, now, we assume the existence of an individual with weak S, then we may suppose that he may behave in one or more of the following ways: (a) Attempt to increase F by trying to get as much out of the society as possible in terms of what its commitments are. (b) Diminish C by

---

[17] See Henry, J., "The Economics of Pilagá Food Distribution." *American Anthropologist* 53: 1951, pp. 187-219.

[18] Dubois, *op. cit.*, p. 51.

[19] *Ibid.*, p. 65.

lowering his expectations; declaring to himself that he is not entitled to anything or that he never expects anything from anyone. (c) Attempt to increase his powers.

Among the Pilagá the exceedingly weak S is expressed in adults by poaching on the food supplies of babies and young children, for the adults dare not face ridicule and insult by scrounging on other adults.[20]

Ethnologists send some biscuits to the women next door, using Yorodaikolik as a messenger.[21] Saradaik is given a little piece, and when only he has his left, Nenarchi holds out her hand to him, saying, "Share it with me." The baby puts his piece of biscuit into Nenarchi's mouth.

Ethnologists give Deniki a small piece of biscuit. He immediately turns away from their tent and heads for home. Nenarchi, Nagete and Arana are sitting outside and immediately hold out their hands, saying, "Share it with me." Deniki does not give up his food.

Yorodaikolik is eating a small piece of pheasant. Nagete repeats and repeats to him, "I want you to share it with me," until he gives up what he is eating. Although there

---

[20] Weak S is not the only reason for this, but such poaching is certainly in part an expression of weak S, deriving from the asymmetrical relationship between F and C.

[21] Table of approximate age and sex of individuals in the Pilagá examples:

NAME	SEX	APPROXIMATE AGE
Yorodaikolik	M	4-5 years
Saradaik	M	First year of life
Nenarchi	F	20-25 years
Deniki	M	Second year of life
Nagete	F	40-45 years
Arana	F	20-25 years
Sidinki	M	50-55 years
Katinorodi	M	10 years

> is goat meat in camp, it is taboo to Yorodaikolik, but not to Nagete, who is also getting some meat from Sidinki.
>
> Sidinki takes Katinorodi's small piece of fish away from him.

As can be seen from the third example, poaching takes place regardless of the condition of the larder.

In the Alorese Mangma the Genealogist we have an individual who in the effort to increase S has taken the path of denying that he expects anything from anyone –C=O.

> Mangma's attitude of expecting nobody to do anything for him and his fear of being exploited lead to extreme touchiness and vindictiveness. His low self-esteem, based on this original constellation, must express itself in compensatory activities that take the form of pride, lying, boasting about trivialities, profound avarice, and envy of what other people have–upon which he unconsciously has persistent designs.[22]

Thus Mangma is a person who shows the expected characteristics of one who feels the society has committed itself to much that he is not getting. Pride, lying, and covetousness (increase of F) are not alone the expression of one who has low self-esteem–nothing in human behavior is ever the expression of *one* factor; they also are compensations for one who has been at first led to believe that society had something to offer and has then discovered that it had little or nothing for *him*.

PSYCHOGENIC NEEDS

Had space permitted, I would have examined other situations such as those involving "The Permitted and the Forbidden," "Choice and Constraint," "Gratification and Pain," and "Success and Failure" with the help of more

[22] Dubois, *op. cit.*, p. 228.

symbolic equations.[23] But even the limited material presented so far seems adequate toward clarification of certain basic points. For example, if what has been said in the preceding pages is true about the direction behavior and feeling will take in the presence of changes in magnitude in the factors involved, we have, I believe, an approach to the problem of psychogenic needs that may be fruitful. If a person has a strong sense of social punishment, it follows from our reasoning that under certain conditions he will develop a "need for recognition." Since the types of experience involved in the generation of all these needs are social, it is seen that psychogenic needs evolve out of the field of forces in which a person lives, and are not inborn or "instinctive." Thus, psychogenic needs are seen to develop out of interpersonal relations, not the other way around. Once the need is developed, of course, it then enters with its own dynamic into interpersonal relations and conditions them.

I think it will be seen at once that this theory of need simply applies to "normal" needs the theory of "compensation" developed by psychiatry for the understanding of "abnormal" needs. There is implicit in psychiatric theory a mathematical model of the abnormal person. He is one who strives "too much" for recognition; who wants "too much" to be free; who hungers "too much" after novelty; and who tries "too hard" to achieve. This "too muchness" is believed, generally, to arise out of experiences of "too much" punishment, failure, and so on. If this is correct, then there is nothing left but to conclude that just the

[23] For an additional seventeen of these equations, see my paper "Toward a System of Socio-Psychiatric Invariants, etc.," *op. cit.*

"right amount" of punishment, failure, and so on, must account for the "right amount" of striving, search for new experience, struggle for achievement, and hunger after freedom.

THE NORMAL PERSONALITY

Expressions like "excessive generosity," "overconforming," "underassertive," are relatively loose, intuitive evaluations of personality. They indicate that in our minds there is an ideal type of person who will give, conform, assert, in "just the right amount." This would mean, for example, that in the "normal" person (not "overgenerous"), the ratio between the number of things he kept for himself and the number of things he gave to others would have a certain socially accepted, or ideal, value.[24]

Symbolically expressed:

$$P^1 = f\left(\frac{K}{G}\right),$$

where K stands for keeping, G for giving, and P^1 for the "psychic ratio" developing out of the relative values of K and G. Practically all our conceptions of the characteristics of normal and abnormal personality turn on these culturally determined notions of "more" and "less." For conformity we could establish a similar ratio (P^2), for assertiveness another (P^3), and so on up to P^n, encompassing in this way all the personality traits we recog-

[24] While the assumption here is that conceptions of normality are culturally determined, this implies nothing in regard to the "most efficient" or "biologically best" kind of personality. These are very different problems.

nize in our culture.[25] For the "normal" person each P would have a value P^1, P^2, P^3, . . . P^n. Hence "normal" (N) could be represented by the mathematical model

$$N = f(P^1_N + P^2_N + P^3_N \ldots P^n_N),$$

where "normality" is expressed as a function of the summated "psychic ratios" rather than by the simple sum, because a personality is not just a summation of culturally selected traits, but also a certain kind of integration of them.[26]

All of this indicates that we have not progressed much beyond the Aristotelian concept of the "middle-class" man, the "continent" man, who has and does everything "in proportion" or "in a mean." Where we have progressed beyond him is in recognizing that the definition of "middle class" or "continent" is cultural; and that whether a man turns out to be "incontinent" or in an extreme is determined by the way specific culturally defined circumstances impinge on him. The proportions of Aristotle, we now recognize, are the result of culturally determined exposures to success, failure, reward, punishment, commitments, fulfillments, gratifications, deprivations, and so on. Perhaps at this point all that a mathematical model of the "normal" personality does is to clear away the brush and enable us to see the underlying mathematical matrix of our thinking.

[25] Not all cultures recognize the existence of all the personality characteristics we do. The Pilagá, for example, while they talk much of angry persons, stingy persons, stupid persons, never speak of people who blame others rather than themselves or of persons who habitually overestimate themselves. It does not seem that they give attention to such matters.

[26] But, in our culture, we face the paradoxical fact that where N is "too large" we think the person is "abnormal." This would seem to be an entirely unique definition of abnormality.

SUMMARY AND CONCLUSIONS

What is the difference between culture and the individual? There is no doubt that they are not the same, for it is clear that when patient faces therapist, the "culture" is not in the room. Nor when mother and new-born infant interact is the "culture" at work. The "culture" is out in the traffic, in the churches, in the libraries, in the armies, in courts of law, and the buildings and policies of governmental institutions, where individuals, groups, and institutions, all interact. Patient, therapist, and mother have learned the ways in which individuals, groups, and institutions may be expected to interact, and the baby is being prepared by its mother to interact in the expected ways, but mother and baby, patient and therapist, are not the culture. The culture is the *summation* of the integrated interactional systems of individuals, groups, and institutions. Thus the individual and culture are related to one another somewhat as the molecule is to the total volume of the gas of which it is a part: the culture as a whole has properties that the individual *alone* lacks; the behavior of the individual cannot be understood apart from the culture of which he is part, and the culture cannot be understood without an understanding of the individuals in it.

It is by such reasoning that the way is paved for the assumption of certain generalities that hold for both culture and the individual, but in different ways. A culture may be said to administer certain rewards and punishments to individuals. But it is inaccurate to say that cultures can be "frustrated," have "feelings of inadequacy," or "overreact." Only individuals can do these things: they are processes whereby individuals adjust to culture. Individuals adjust to certain cultural circumstances, such as punishments and rewards, opportunities for success and failure, promises made and promises fulfilled, and so on. The *culture,* through fixed systems of interaction that have become traditional, provides the basic conditions in terms of which individuals shall experience reward and punishment, success and failure, gratification and pain, and so on. Hence a single system of equations can be used to describe the conditions provided by the culture and the experiences of the individual. The advantage of such a system is that it makes clear at once what the relationship is between culture and individual, that is states the relationship concisely, that it facilitates manipulaton of ideas, and, finally, that it shows the direction in which we may eventually move toward quantitative descriptions.

The construction of mathematical models of personality process simply constitutes graphic statement of the assumptions that are unexpressed in all personality theory. If we say that a mother rejects her child, we simply mean that she performs more acts of repudiation than she does of acceptance. If we say that an individual has feelings of inadequacy, we mean that there are more occasions on which he feels inadequate to a situation than occasions on which he feels adequate. If we say that an individual represses his feelings, we generally mean that he more often conceals them than gives them overt expression or recognizes them. Much of our thinking about personality turns upon such notions of "more" or "less." The contribution of this paper, as I see it, is that it takes this underlying pattern of assumptions and puts it together into a single theory with the social circumstances from which personality emerges.

DISCUSSION

Jules H. Masserman

IN AN effort to establish "closer working collaboration of social scientists and psychiatrists," Dr. Henry offers us a number of "invariant equations" which, in simple algebraic terms, deal with concepts common to both fields and therefore promise to be heuristically valuable. Instead of discussing each equation separately, I should like to deal with the basic assumptions common to all, and for this purpose we may, for convenience and simplicity, select the first of the series. You will remember that Henry's Equation 1 reads

$$AP = f\left(\frac{P}{R}\right),$$

which, when translated according to his own equivalents, states essentially the following proposition:

"The sense (or apprehension?) of social punishment is a direct function of the possibilities of social punishment and an inverse function of the possibilities of social reward."

Let us now examine this formulation for a moment. To begin with, the transliteration of the formula, however general its terms, seems rather more meaningful than the ostensibly exact algebraic expression which preceded it. Indeed, it might be contended by some mathematicians that the algebraic form of the statement is in some ways deceptive and unjustified. Even in Boolian symbolic logic, for instance, it is required (1) that the terms of a derived proposition must be (*a*) quantitative rather than qualitative, except in those rare instances in which the former can be translated into the latter, and (*b*) that the manipulations implied must be operationally meaningful. To give a trite example, apples can be multiplied or squared as apples, but can never be divided by, say, bananas to give, say, a measure of musical appreciation. Unfortunately,

Henry's Equation 1 violates both of these criteria, inasmuch as (*a*) there are no consistent units of measurement for "sense of social punishment" and (*b*) the (=f) sign implies a transposition of concepts and not an equation of values. Similarly, the right-hand term of the equation postulates a division of rewards (signifying cultural prestige) into the number of punishments (defined as inflicted pain), an operation equivalent to dividing the number of symbolic diplomas awarded a person by the number of colds or toothaches he suffers, to obtain an inverse measure of his sense of social security. Actually, the equation would in this respect have more nearly approached validity if R (or reward) represented anticipated satisfaction of bodily needs, and P (or pain) their frustration or violation, but even then the formula would have given only an exceedingly rough index of the momentary hedonic balance of concurrent physioadaptive processes, each still different from the others in function, intensity and meaning. We thus return to a somewhat obscure restatement of the old concept of pleasure-pain balance—a development which, valid or not, I do not think Dr. Henry meant to imply.

But suppose we disregard such logical strictures as mere sophistries (an escape from hard thinking frequently practiced by psychiatrists as well as anthropologists), and concentrate our attention less on Dr. Henry's excursions into cryptography and more on the intent and purport of his dialectic formulations. This brings us to the nub of the question: can "motivations," "senses," "values," and other such semantic bugbears be defined culturally, or do they have truly operational meaning only with reference to particular individuals with unique histories in that culture? If the former is true, then sociology is the matrix not only of psychiatry but of all sciences of human behavior; if, however, cociometric terms can be derived only from individual psychology, we shall have to put up with the highly contingent nature of psychologic abstractions and psychiatric formulations for yet a while. Perhaps I can illustrate this dilemma by attempting to fit Dr. Henry's first equation to two clinical examples.

Consider first the case of a highly successful criminal lawyer who consulted me several years ago. This man had acquired great prestige in his field, had earned a sizable fortune, and was in a position of considerable power and professional influence. In effect, society as a whole had burdened him with almost no serious deprivations or punishment; on the contrary, in addition to his already rich and varied rewards he was about to be appointed to a federal judgeship guaranteeing a lifetime of financial and social security. Now let us fit this case to Dr. Henry's first equation. In this instance, P for punishment apparently approaches zero, and R for honors (even neglecting honorariums) is certainly very high, so that our patient's sense of social anxiety should have been infinitesimal. And yet, to return to the facts, this man applied to me for treatment with the complaint that for years he had been troubled by a sense of failure, futility, and isolation, and that his anxieties had reached the intensity of impending panic precisely when he had been proffered the culminating reward of the judicial appointment. How, then, can we explain this exact antithesis of what would be predicted by Dr. Henry's formula?

As is almost invariably the case, only a re-evaluation of the situation from the patient's standpoint could lead to the answer. Thus, in exploring the patient's personal history it developed that he had been raised by immigrant parents in a metropolitan fringe area assigned to a lowest-income minority group, and had suffered deprivations and stresses encountered under such circumstances. As is not unusual, he had rebelled against what he considered his social oppression by becoming an active member of a closely knit gang of vagrant and partially delinquent youths organized to commit petty thefts and other minor crimes for their mutual glory and profit. By good fortune he himself had avoided punishment and a police record; instead, he had used his precocious experiences, his material spoils, and his exceptional intelligence and other capabilities, to achieve success in school, to secure scholarships, and later to work his way through the law college of a university. But this presented him with a great personal dilemma. He could no longer openly identify with the young delinquents through whose peculiar friendship he had experienced the only security he had known in his formative years; nor, on the other hand, could he feel part of a larger society which to him had always seemed, like his parents, forbidding, threatening, or even overtly hostile. His compromise was to become a defender of those he considered downtrodden and handicapped, and even to protect those who had rebelled violently against the larger social order. With such identification and sympathies directing the use of his great talents, he quickly became a famous criminal lawyer, successful in everything but his search for personal peace (Dr. Henry's S?)—a state denied him as long as he vacillated precariously between incompatible social roles. And now that he was offered a judicial post in which he would be forced not only to dissociate himself from, but to condemn and punish, criminal surrogates of himself, he could regard this not as a reward but only as an intolerable irony on the part of a society that was still unconsciously regarded as his enemy. Ergo, his panic, and his pathetic flight to a therapist who he hoped would be understanding, friendly, and helpful—an exception in the ranks of a social order that, whatever its hard-won material rewards, to him still seemed inimical.

Now let us turn even more briefly to another typical instance—that of a petty criminal with a long record of incarcerations in various institutions whimsically named penitentiaries or reformatories. The history of this man is apropos as a social control on our first example because he, too, had been raised in poverty; indeed, after somehow surviving abject squalor for four years, he had been doubly orphaned when his parents finally managed to kill each other in a drunken brawl. After this he was placed by a public agency in a Catholic orphanage—only to find (*a*) that he was neither as bright nor as strong as other children his age, and (*b*) that he continued to be neglected unless he managed in some way to get into so obviously pathetic a position of helplessness and martyrdom that the sympathies of the Sisters or someone else in authority would finally be stirred and he would be succored and protected. Unfortunately, the second of these discoveries, bolstered and rendered urgent by the first, quickly became ingrained in his life patterns; in effect, the boy began to cultivate responses of immaturity, failure, and clinging dependency as solutions to his problems. After leaving the orphanage, he demanded further indulgences, protected work apprenticeships and other special favors, and for a period secured them by his ostensibly sincere but pathetically futile attempts to help himself. Inevitably, however, his demands became more insistent, his failures more obvious, and his friends fewer, until in his twenties his behavior had come to follow an almost predictable pattern: begging, arrest for vagrancy, a sentence to a house of "correction," sympathetic help for a time by some religious or social agency, exhaustion of the agency's patience, vagrancy with or without commission of some misdemeanor public enough to invite arrest, another period of incarceration, and so on through a stereotyped cycle, unconsciously designed to express and re-enact the patient's regressively demanding social phantasies. Superficially evaluated, this man's P (for social punishment) was large, and his R (for visible rewards) small, yet, far from being anxious about his fate, he was gentle, placid, and as exasperatingly serene as any other ne'er-do-well who, according to his own lights, has found a moderately successful way of coping with our restless and competitive culture. Once again, then, AP could be said to equal P/R only if the right half of the equation became socially paradoxical, i.e., punishment by imprisonment and other apparent deprivations really represented the rewards of relatively carefree dependence, whereas R (for rewards and honors for successful effort) meant the painful threat of emancipation and self-support. As Henry proposes, then "the equation states that the sense of social punishment is not alone a function of the situation with respect to punishment alone, but that it depends on the situation with respect to social reward." This is true in a sense, but each of the terms in this statement may have a quite unexpected meaning.

There is, I believe, no need to multiply such examples to illustrate the main burden of the argument, namely, that motivations, symbolic evaluations, patterns of social interaction, and other such categorical abstractions of behavior have an almost infinite range of variability in any culture, and that their interrelationships acquire meaning and significance only when studied from the standpoint of the individual subject as he developed uniquely, according to his own endowments and experiences, within some special sector of his social order. Indeed, I took occasion over a decade ago to embody this thesis in the first two of four principles of behavior which I somewhat sententiously called the Principles of Biodynamics. Briefly stated, the first of these principles holds that the behavior of any organism is actuated by its special and current configurations of needs; the second principle modifies this contingency even further by proposing that behavior is adaptive not to some extraneously conceived environment or culture, but to a milieu uniquely conceived and structured by the special preceptive, mnemonic, and reactive capacities of the developing organism. Limiting this general law of behavioral relativity to the special field of human conduct, it may be said that each of us, however culturally bound, sees his universe according to his own lights, and responds to his own interpretations of its actual and symbolic threats and values by uniquely characteristic patterns of behavior that vary extremely widely in any society—be it Pilagá, Peoria, or Park Forest.

Unfortunately, this pronouncement applies to nearly all of Dr. Henry's other dialectical-mathematical formulations, since in all of them he uses terms as protean in meaning as "commitment," "fulfillment," and so on. Obviously, these terms are too impalpable and interrelated to be isolated as independent variables; certainly, while their complex configurations might possibly be approached by vector analysis, their juxtaposition as postulated "invariants" in simple ratios subject to equation and substitution is, by any useful standard, an untenable and possibly seriously misleading oversimplification, open to question by mathematicians and perhaps by most sociologists and psychiatrists.

Possibly this critique could be modified if Dr. Henry's equations followed the more individualized pattern of one of Dr. Adolf Meyer's famous aphorisms, expressible symbolically as

$$H = f\left(\frac{G}{W}\right).$$

In trenchant English, this simply states that a person's happiness is a function of the ratio between what he's got and what he wants. Be it noted that, although once again none of the terms of the equation is defined, the statement is still operationally cogent precisely because all the terms refer to the wishes, deprivations, and value-systems—however fantastic or deviant—of a particular human being. Parenthetically also, it might be best to use different symbols for the f-sign in each of Dr. Henry's equations, since the functional relationships implied have little or no relationship to each other.

Dr. Henry may well wish to point out that sociologists deal with larger issues, whereas psychiatrists are always quoting cases—and one can always quote a case to prove or disprove anything. With this I can agree, although it must be added that anthropologists, historians, and sociologists, too, deal ultimately with cases—en masse—and can set up ranges of so-called norms (to reverse the usual figure) only in relation to the number and extent of individual variations from such modal concepts. Indeed, even when a whole society or culture "deviates"—as one which shares its women, prefers guns to butter, or eats its enemies—that society is (*a*) understandable only in terms of the predominant motivations, stresses, and behavioral adaptations of the greater or lesser majority of individuals within it, and (*b*) unique only in relation to a preponderance of contrasts elsewhere. Certainly, no one can be averse to thoughtful and courageous attempts like Dr. Henry's to work comprehensively within the organon of the sciences of behavior—an organon which should comprise not only sociology and psychiatry but anthropology, history, theology, and many other orientations and disciplines. Obviously, we should all enlarge our conceptual framework, use a broader and more meaningful terminology, and perhaps develop a calculus toward which Dr. Henry's formulations may be a first tentative step.

ADDITIONAL DISCUSSION

JULES HENRY: Dr. Masserman criticizes me severely because, so it seems to him, I have not followed the rules of Boolian logic. It appears to me, however, as it must to any student of science, that every logic, like every dog, has its day, and that none is sacred—or immortal. Even so, it is no problem to reduce some of my qualitative statements to quantitative ones. Thus:

SCALE FOR COMBINED RATING OF P:
SEVERITY AND FREQUENCY OF PUNISHMENT

(Quality of punishment: *1. severe* *2. moderate* *3. mild*
Frequency of punishment: *A. often* *B. sometimes* *C. seldom)*

Combinations	Rating Values
1A	9
1B	8
1C	7
2A	6
2B	5
2C	4
3A	3
3B	2
3C	1

In this way we can start with nine rating values for P, which we could compare with a similar system for R.

The real problem for me, however, is not to answer Dr. Masserman's attack on this score, but rather to understand why he chose to examine my crude paving bricks with a microscope; for I have clearly indicated that the last thing I hope to do is to reduce my formulations to quantitative statements, and that I present them as preliminary rough formulations.

Dr. Masserman attacks the division suggested in Equation 1. The implication is that there is no *general* relationship between reward and punishment in the make-up of human beings, but that in a conceptual scheme punishments may be balanced against rewards only if it can be shown at once that one bears some very *specific* kind of systematic relationship to the other. Hence Dr. Masserman's criticisms about apples versus bananas and diplomas versus toothaches. Against this I would urge, first, that the inner system of the human organism has, through complex learning experiences, the remarkable faculty for transmuting bananas into apples, and diplomas into headaches and social security; and, second, that the aims sought in the construction of a conceptual model are (*a*) to state the hypothesis as succinctly as possible, and (*b*) to point the direction in which research must move. It would seem to me unwise to destroy a model because one cannot immediately perceive where to find the material with which to make it a reality. Meanwhile there is an honorable tradition of dividing apples by bananas in the more exact sciences, as in physics, where the equation that expresses Ohm's law, for example, is

$$\text{Amps} = \frac{\text{Volts}}{\text{Ohms}}.$$

As far as "consistent units" for the measurement of the "sense of social punishment" is concerned, these are probably more easily constructed than many other measures that have been used successfully in the social sciences. Questionnaires, sentence completion tests, and other devices can be used to get the basic data for the establishment of simple indexes for the measurement of this factor.

Dr. Masserman has chosen two cases he has handled in psychotherapy to disprove the correctness of my formulations. However, not only is it always easy, as Dr. Masserman himself says, to cite cases to prove or disprove whatever one wishes, but it is also easy, in such a method, to fall into the unconscious error of revealing just as much of them as one pleases. Furthermore, I nowhere suggest, as Dr. Masserman seems to think, that AP or any other factor can be derived *only* from the relationships I discuss. With regard to the lawyer that Dr. Masserman had in therapy, I would hesitate to force this case into the matrix of Equation 1, for it is transparently one where an authoritarian punitive parent makes success a frightening prospect to the child. Dr. Masserman, however, interprets the neurosis as arising from a disparity between the successful lawyer's mature achievements and the goals of the beloved companions of his youth. Because of this, according to Dr. Masserman, the lawyer could not accept the rewards of the larger society. However, in this way R, in my formulation, becomes zero, and the sense of social punishment maximizes. Meanwhile, it should be noted that since Dr. Masserman's patient is not described by him as suffering from a sense of social punishment as I define it, there seems to be no real relevance of the case to my thesis!

There is no room to go further into detail. I do not imply that what happens in the individual is the product of a standardized system of outer events that exercises an ineluctable standard imprint on everyone in a given culture. This kind of Meadian[27] reasoning I definitely eschew. Whatever the outer stresses, each individual experiences them in his own unique way. But that he shall experience them at all is determined by his culture: *culture provides the conditions in terms of which each person shall experience life stress.* Hence the same system of equations can be used to describe the culture and the individual.

The crucial error in Dr. Masserman's criticism is not in making excessive demands on what is an initial attempt at the formulation of a range of problems, but in what Kingsley Davis has called "psychologism," a term Davis has applied to the mental hygiene approach that locks all the individual's troubles up inside of him and leaves out the social dimension.

---

[27] Margaret Mead.

VIII

THE NATURE OF MAN

G. K. Yacorzynski

AS THE TWO preceding papers of the present discussion imply, in speaking of personality development one must take into consideration the original nature of the child as the material which the impact of the environment structures into a definite personality. It is the source of these ideas which I wish to examine.

During the Renaissance, concepts about the original nature of man and the effect of the environment upon him were introduced which in effect broke with some of the traditions of the past. Roughly speaking, within this ideology the original nature of man is endowed with all the characteristics of goodness. The child is born with all the qualities which within our culture are socially acceptable. In this ideology the good is within the individual. The evil is in the outside world, and soon the child is thrown into contact with the cruel, evil external world. The evil consists of the lust for power, for personal aggrandizement in wealth and fame—and the lust of the body—those natural biological appetites and the drive for their satisfaction. What is good? It consists, first of all, of the absence of evil in the child, but in the adult it is more positive. It is the regard for one's fellow men—pity, humanitarianism, consideration, kindness, and, in addition, self-abjection.

It is with the awakening of the Renaissance that these ideas were incorporated within the religious framework of our time. The goodness of man resided within him. The evil was outside, personified in the devil. There was a constant struggle between good and evil. Whichever side won in this perpetual struggle depended not only upon the power of the devil, but also the free will of the originally good man. There was also a neutral mediator—a referee, so to speak. He was God, who passed judgment. Unlike the devil, who strove actively to involve the originally good man in evil, God was an observer. He had made man in His own image and sat passively in judgment of His handiwork.

This viewpoint which characterized Christianity until recent times had Rousseau as one of its chief exponents. If man was left in his original state of goodness without the impact of the external world, he would not acquire the evils of the world. He would rather be the God-like figure of the ideal man. It should be pointed out here that this viewpoint, although incorporated into the Christian beliefs of our time, broke with some of the traditions of the past. The earlier beliefs endowed man with original sin, so that the evil actually resided within him.[1]

---

[1] I am addressing this footnote to my colleagues at the symposium. In the light of our discussion at that time, I am taking the liberty of modifying the statement that the ideas introduced during the Renaissance were characteristic of the earlier Christian viewpoints. They were, however, incorporated within our religious beliefs and have persisted until the present. I cite as authority for this statement the Very Reverend Alden Drew Kelley, Dean of the Seabury-Western Theological Seminary. Within recent times there has been a reversal of the present trend toward the earlier beliefs. The slight modification in my argument here in no way invalidates what I am to say later. As a matter of fact, it even points up the argument that psychoanalysis is culturally bound to very early religious beliefs in considering the original nature of man.

The very end of the nineteenth century and the beginning of the present century introduced a viewpoint which seemed to be a complete rejection of the idyllic conception of the original goodness of the nature of man. Rather than the original nature being endowed with goodness, the child was conceived as an egotist who thought only of himself. He had a lust for power and recognition, with a hatred of those siblings who threatened his status. Verily, he was an individual with all the lusts of the body, and Freud and others emphasized the early sexuality of the child, with rivalry for love of the parents—a rivalry whose intensity could be equaled only by the jealous adult. In order to emphasize these basic (formerly considered base) qualities, even purely physiological concepts were introduced to name the various states of development of the child, such as anal, oral, sexual. The idyllic child now became the idy child.[2] The evil was within him, the good outside. It was only through the socializing forces of the external environment that he repressed those antisocial cravings and in time became considerate of others, altruistic, and self-effacing. Again the struggle between good and evil was present. The mediating God in this case was the ego—a sort of neutral but perpetual sentinel. The free will of the child and the struggle to fight off the forces of evil disappeared in this systematology. Since the evil was within, it had to be repressed, and this repression came about through contact with the external environment. The forces of evil were always there, although repressed and unconscious, but perpetually ready to spring to the fore at the least opportunity, even though they might appear in

[2] I find no adjective for the word *id,* and so am taking the liberty of creating one.

some distorted and symbolic behavior, and, at times, be of such a nature as to lead to psychopathology.

The change in viewpoint introduced at the beginning of this century could undoubtedly be understood within the cultural setting of the time. It is revealing that Commager, in *The American Mind*, in tracing the vast upheaval in all spheres in America, places the date of its beginning as 1890.

> In a general way it could be said that the two generations after 1890 witnessed a transition from certainty to uncertainty, from faith to doubt, from security to insecurity, from seeming order to ostentatious disorder, but the generalization was too loose to cover adequately the American mind and too tentative to justify dogmatic conclusions.

And again:

> Yet, that changes so profound in the mechanics of living and in the intellectual climate should produce modifications of character was all but inevitable. To suggest that the modifications were either for better or for worse implies the existence of a moral standard; all that can be said with assurance is that the modifications were, in important respects, departures from what had seemed the nineteenth-century norm. Some of the changes were in the realm of ideas, some in habits and practices, some in morals.

The changes were profound and rapid in all fields. Within these forces the old ideologies were either disregarded or rudely uprooted by the new. It was a fertile ground for the inception of the new ideas advanced by Freud and others.

But every fresh viewpoint does not completely break with the cultural past. It is based upon the cultural antecedents, and the frame of reference is not too far removed from it. Was the trend in thought which is now labeled as dynamic or Freudian far removed from the viewpoint which we have labeled Christian? Far from it. There was the same dichotomy between good and evil. There was a constant struggle between these opposing forces. There was the mediator who acted as a sentinel or referee between this perpetual struggle. In some cases the good triumphed, but the evil was always there to nag the conscience of the individual or even to affect his behavior. Sometimes the bad triumphed. The goodness, or the conscience, or the superego, of the individual suffered when that was true. In many such cases, unless the good and evil were in some way resolved, the individual was damned—whether by spending his after-life in hell, or by becoming possessed by a demon, which resulted in irrational and abnormal behavior.

There were differences between the two viewpoints, to be sure. One of the differences was the more scientific approach in the collection of data in the new systematology. The differences, however, were ones of emphasis. In the Christian viewpoint of the Renaissance the good resided within the individual, the evil outside. In the present-day psychoanalytic attitude the evil is within the individual and the good comes from the environmental influences. It is true that in both cases the individual was denied control over the evil—in one case the perpetrator being the devil, and in the other, the id. However, the dynamic viewpoint abrogated much of man's free will. Since the evil was within the individual it could not be consciously tolerated. There were, therefore, strong unconscious urges which dominated man's behavior. It is the postulation of the unconscious factors which Freud believed was largely responsible for the strong antagonism originally expressed toward psychoanalysis. Man could not admit that he was the Charlie McCarthy of strong hidden urges over which he had little control.[3] However, the Freudian ideas may be more fundamental than this. If his viewpoints had been completely divorced from the Christian ethics of the time he might have created little furor. He accepted these ethics, but in doing so he controverted them in such a way that they were no longer compatible with the accepted system. He was dealing with ego-involved ideas which were so dear to man. He showed them that their dearest self-esteem—that of being Christian—was a chimera, a bauble to be exploded. It was a Nietzschean anti-Christ. Nietzsche, it must be remembered, was a profoundly religious man who could not think on a plane different from the Christian ethics. Freud and psychoanalysis followed the same pathway. In speaking of Freud, Erich Fromm as recently as 1950 states in his *Psychoanalysis and Religion,* "Slowly he [Freud] became aware that he had gone far beyond the realm of medicine and had resumed a tradition in which psychology as the study of the soul of man was the theoretical basis for the art of living, for achieving happiness. Freud's method, psychoanalysis, made possible the most minute and intimate study of the soul." And again, "If we thus define the function of the psychoanalyst we find that at present two professional

[3] Dean Alden Drew Kelley would be in agreement with the present interpretation, since he has drawn the writer's attention to the Biblical passages from Romans, Chapter VII, verses 15 to 24, which substantially express similar ideas to the notion of repression of the psychoanalytic school. Thus psychoanalysis does not violate traditional religious ideas. It does disagree with more recent interpretations advanced during the Renaissance. Some of these Biblical passages state: "For I know that in me (that is, in my flesh) dwelleth no good thing: for to will is present with me; but *how* to perform that which is good I find not. . . . For the good that I would I do not; but the evil which I would not, that I do. . . . I find then a law, that, when I would do good, evil is present with me."

groups are concerned with the soul: the priest and the psychoanalyst."

That viewpoints which were not directly iconoclastic toward the Christian morality did not suffer the general repudiation of the Freudian school, is evidence that Freud triggered that which was dearest to man. I am now referring to the general viewpoint which has been labeled as mechanistic or behavioristic. This viewpoint developed separately from, but concomitantly with, that of the dynamic school. Since man is not endowed with native goodness, since he is a product of the environment, it is evident —so the school postulated—that he starts as a bundle of reflexes which are then modified through the process of association in various ways into the adult personality. There are no forces either for good or evil driving man on. He is simply a plastic recipient with certain inherent potentialities and with the capacity of being modified in various ways by his environment. As one wag put it, psychology first of all lost its soul, then its conscience, and finally its mind.

This viewpoint embraced the more acceptable doctrine of the day in that it followed the tenets of the scientific thought of the other disciplines. It did not challenge directly the Christian ethics of the period. It disregarded them. It is of interest that the dynamic school focused its criticism against this viewpoint—evidence of the strong repressive forces against admitting that their viewpoints were the disguised Christian ethics: a sheep in wolf's clothing, if we may reverse the aphorism.

It is also not possible to summarize the vast theoretical systems which have been postulated to explain the development and structure of personality. I would like, however, to dwell only on a minor point in this whole field, one which I consider important and which has not received the recognition which it should.

I believe that the consensus of scientific opinion at present as well as the viewpoints of a nonscientific nature of the past consider man as endowed with certain desires, whether or not these are at the time taken to be culturally good or bad: a striving which in its active endeavor runs into many situations which frustrate these desires. Man is an actor, not a reactor. He strives to attain in the face of various barriers to such striving.

Why does man strive? It has been answered in many ways. He strives because he has the biological needs of sex, hunger, thirst, and so on, to satisfy. He strives because he is endowed with natural goodness which must be expressed to clear his conscience. He strives because he has strong, ungovernable appetites which must be expressed, even if sublimated. He strives because of an all-prevailing sexuality. He strives because he has developed certain social needs as an early conditioning in satisfying his more basic and biological desires.

I would like to postulate the hypothesis that man strives to attain goals because he is specifically endowed with a creative urge. It is a basic desire for self-expression—for creativity. He strives because he obtains an esthetic experience from the process of striving itself. It feels good to him—it is an esthetic experience by itself to attain and to achieve.

Is there any direction for this striving? Are there any other causes behind it? The striving for creativity is neither "good" nor "bad." It is simply a matter of self-expression. It is fundamental within the individual and is due neither to strong, destructive urges, biological needs, nor the inherent goodness. It is true that such striving meets many frustrations of an environmental nature or due to shortcomings within the individual. In such cases the urge can be directed and expressed in various ways and with many tools. The frustrations of the creative urge can also bring about many forms of aggressive behavior, regressions, flight into unreality, and so on, which in its exaggeration leads to psychopathology.

The evidence for the belief that creativity—the desire for self-expression—is the all-prevalent urge for man's behavior is limitless in scope.

In all of man's acts this tendency is present. In clinical parlance we talk about adjustment or homeostasis, meaning by that that man is capable of integrating to the demands made upon him by the environment. Adjustment to the environment, however, does not explain the changes which man brings about in his environment. Political and economic ideas, social mores, art, literature, and science all show a perpetual change in response to the creative urge of man for such change. It is true that man must adjust to his environment. But such adjustment is necessary only so that man will have more freedom to express his creative urge.

This creative urge is the predominant behavior pattern expressed by the child. Children are constantly striving to attain self-expression. It is this desire which allows them to grasp their environment on an intellectual basis. It is of interest that Gesell, on the basis of all his tests of the young child's behavior, is unable to predict what the eventual intellectual development of the child will be. He states that clinical impression is often more valuable than test results. He does not tell us what the clinical impression consists of. It is difficult of verbalization. It is not what the child does. It is what he wants to do—expressed in such terms as interest, responsiveness to the environment, and so on. It is this creative urge which leads finally to intellectual comprehension. Again, Mowrer in his *Learning Theory and Personality Dynamics* tells us that children develop language because "words *sound good to them.*" It is the esthetic experience they obtain from performance. Again, teachers in the field of art invariably insist that the paintings and drawings of young children are artistic, and it is only with age that this ability is lost. Now, good artists may know nothing of child psychology. They can, however, judge paintings. What they are in essence saying is that the young child is inwardly creative; and any person in contact with young children knows that they love to draw and paint just for the sake of doing it. There is evidently not only an urge to do this, but it is done in an esthetically pleasing manner.

When one peruses the reports of students of various cultures, one is impressed by the time and effort devoted to the study of their arts. Is the cultural anthropologist capable of understanding a culture better if he considers largely that form of behavior which allows much self-expression, such as carving, drawing, painting, song, and poetry? I do not know the answer to this question. I suspect it is so. Certainly that is true of present clinical techniques. Ambiguous stimulus situations such as ink-blots, painting and drawing, verbal rambling in history-taking, play therapy with children—yes, and even non-directive therapy—all emphasize the necessity for self-expression of one's own creativity in diagnosis and therapy.

DISCUSSION

Oscar Lewis

I MUST confess to some difficulty in responding to this paper, which, as Dr. Yacorzynski explained, was somewhat rambling. He has offered us what a psychologist might call free association on two very interesting but quite unrelated problems: (1) the changing notions of the original nature of the child in the history of Western civilization and some of the cultural factors related to these changes; (2) a suggestion for a theory of motivation in terms of the proposition of a "creative urge." I should like briefly to touch upon both of these points.

Dr. Yacorzynski has raised the important general question as to the relationship between ideology (be it that of science) and culture. He asks what is the relationship between our theories of human nature and the cultural milieu in which these theories arise and are propagated. This is a fascinating but difficult question. The answer proposed by Dr. Yacorzynski represents a great oversimplification and contains some questionable interpretations of historical fact.

He attributes to Catholicism and Christianity the notion that the child is born good and that the evil is in the outside world. But does this not contradict the well-known Christian concept of original sin? Moreover, there were many competing views of human nature in the Renaissance in Europe, as reflected, for example, in the bitter theological arguments on this point between the various religious sects.

Similarly, the interpretation of the role of God as a mediator in the struggle between man and the devil seems hardly to jibe with the more popular interpretation in which God and the devil represent the forces of good and evil, respectively, and each is struggling to win man to his side. It is also difficult to reconcile Dr. Yacorzynski's indentification of Rousseau as an exponent of the Church or Christian viewpoint on the original nature of man, with the fact that Rousseau directed his attack against the Church view of original sin.

The interpretation of Freud is also questionable. The emphasis in Freud's thinking and writing was not that evil was within the child at birth. Rather, the evil resulted from the repressions and societal frustrations of inner drives. The drives in themselves are neither good nor bad. The emphasis in Freud is upon the evil wrought by society, by civilization, and not the evil of the individual per se. In this sense Freud and other late nineteenth-century thinkers represented a break with the old Christian tradition rather than its continuity.

The second point of Dr. Yacorzynski, concerning the creative urge inherent in individuals, appears to me to be a kind of word magic which may give one psychological satisfaction (like all magical procedures) and a feeling of accomplishment, but explains little that we do not already know. How would one measure individual "creativity" cross-culturally?

ADDITIONAL DISCUSSION

DR. THOMPSON: I would certainly agree with Dr. Lewis for, having been brought up in a very religious Baptist family, I was taught from my earliest years that I was very evil and only by the grace of God could I live to be good. The fact that Catholic and Episcopal faiths insist that the child be baptized before death confirms this.

DR. YACORZYNSKI: I am only too willing to admit that I can be very much in error on any question of theology. The questions raised by Dr. Lewis and Dr. Thompson show that, although we have a number of disciplines represented in this symposium, yet it is not as representative as it should be, since we should have a theologian to answer the questions that Dr. Lewis and Dr. Thompson raised. Even if the early Christian viewpoint maintains that the evil resides within the individual, and it was only during the Renaissance that this idea changed and was later incorporated into religious beliefs, the general argument which I present is in no way invalidated. (As a matter of fact, following this discussion I took the liberty of consulting the Very Reverend Alden Drew Kelley, Dean of the Seabury-Western Seminary, to inform me upon whether my general interpretation was correct or not. I have been guided by his statements and have incorporated a few changes in the manuscript so as not to violate theological philosophy. Actually, the idea that the individual is born originally in sin and is thus endowed with evil brings psychoanalysis in much closer relationship to the religious viewpoint than if we consider that the individual is endowed with goodness and that the evil resides in the external environment.)

DR. WANG: In the same connection, perhaps you would like to hear what Confucius had to say: "Human nature is good to begin with, but through training men gradually get to be wide apart." Translated into the language of modern anthropology, you might say: "Only through the process of acculturation some men become good, some become bad." This may not sound like what you used to hear about what Confucius says, and it is a wonder that Dr. Hsu never passed it on to Dr. Yacorzynski.

As to the question "Why does man strive?" here is one of the answers given by a modern psychoanalyst. According to Harry Stack Sullivan, all human behavior or interpersonal phenomena may be classified into two categories; the purpose of the one set of activities is the pursuit of satisfaction, and that of the other, the pursuit of security. Included in the first group are such activities as the seeking of food, drink, sleep or rest, lust, et cetera; that is, the needs are primarily biological. It is interesting that he used the word "lust" to denote what we usually call "sex." Included under the second category are things such as seeking the good feeling of your fellow men; that is, these are cultural and not merely biological. Sullivan even said, "By 'cultural' I mean what the anthropologist means—all that which is man-made." Here is a theory that is much closer to present-day anthropological thinking and is something yet to be tested through experimental research, just as the Freudian theory should be subjected to the same sort of critical examination.

DR. BOYER: I appreciate Dr. Wang's bringing these things up. I don't know where the concept that sex is so envelopingly important in the writings of Freud arises exactly. This has not been my understanding of his writings. There is nothing which Sullivan said that Freud had not written long ago.

DR. THOMPSON: It seems to me it illustrates how we get lost in who said what when. Is or isn't that important?

IX

WHAT WE KNOW AND WHAT WE DON'T

Ralph Linton

THE TITLE which has been assigned to me, "What We Do and Do Not Know About Society, Culture and the Individual," raises a semantic question at the very outset. What do we mean by "know"? Scientists today feel that they actually know, in the sense of being sure of, exceedingly little. As recently as the days in which I received my own scientific training, they conceived of a universe of clear-cut realities, called facts, and dynamic interrelations, called laws. It was the task of the scientist to discover these, and it was anticipated that when he had done so he would be able to predict and ultimately to control future events of any order. At present, scientists have ceased to deal in absolutes. I believe that most of them would concur in the definition of a fact as "the consensus of opinion among persons who should be in a position to know," and the definition of a law, even a law of mathematics, as "an expression of a probability." As our understanding of phenomena of all sorts has increased, we have become increasingly conscious of the complexity of even the simplest phenomena, and of the importance of configurations in contrast to the distinct elements into which they can be logically analyzed. Each time our unit of study has been expanded to take in a new series of factors, we have found that some of the generalizations which we made before no longer hold good. The contrast between present and recent scientific attitudes can be summed up in two verses. A great poet of the eighteenth century, age of enlightenment and optimism, wrote:

Nature and nature's laws lay hid in night
God said, "Let Newton be," and all was light.

To this a minor poet of the twentieth century, age of disillusionment, has added:

Angles were right and Newton's theorems true,
God said, "Let Einstein be," and all's askew.

The study of society, culture, and the individual involves an almost infinite number of variables. Perhaps the most that can be said for workers in this particular field is that we now have enough information about our subject material to establish something like adequate frames for further investigations. We have succeeded in organizing certain small areas within the field, and are able to see certain interrelations, but at the present time we do not have any neat, all-encompassing conceptual pattern into which all the various phenomena can be fitted. Although numerous attempts have been made along this line, none of them have proved adequate, and the various schools based upon them soon reached a point in their development where they limited research instead of aiding it. We now know enough about particular societies, cultures, and individuals to be able to carry on comparative studies by the methods common to all sciences. This makes it unnecessary for us to continue reasoning about these phenomena from faulty analogy. It also makes us realize what a curious *tour de force* in terms of general evolutionary trends human societies and cultures constitute. Within the vertebrate order, the all-over evolutionary trend has been toward increasing complexity in the organization of the nervous system and with it the substitution of learning ability for automatic responses, i.e., instinctual behavior. By the time one reaches the primate level, automatic responses have dwindled to those unconscious reactions which are controlled by the autonomic nervous system. As far as we can determine, human beings have no instincts in the sense that this term is used by the students of animal behavior. At the same time, they have acquired a great capacity to learn and to integrate their experience. Since individual experience is inevitably idiosyncratic in numerous respects, with this ability goes unparalleled potentialities for individuation. Potentially, adult experienced human beings are more unlike each other than the members of any other species. That a species with these characteristics should not only turn to gregarious living but should have developed a type of highly organized society with specialized division of labor is something that no one could have foretold in terms of general evolutionary trends. As I have said elsewhere, human beings are anthropoid apes attempting to live like termites, and, as I think we all will agree, not doing too well at it. The elaborate, formalized patterns of cooperation and interaction required for life in a highly organized society can be controlled by instincts much better than by any type of learning.

As I said previously, our increased understanding of societies, derived from our current ability to study them comparatively, makes it unnecessary to reason from analogy regarding them. As a matter of fact, all the analogies used in the past have been faulty at certain points. Thus, from the earliest times societies have been compared to biological organisms. There is, for instance, a familiar story of the revolt of the Roman plebs being quelled by a patrician who explained to them that, as the human body contained many organs, each of which had its function, so also did the body politic contain numerous classes, each of which contributed to the survival of the whole. We can see now that the main fallacy in such biological analogies is that they ignore the relative looseness of integration of the individuals who compose human society and, in particular, the irreducible factor of their free will. The persons who make up a society are integrated not at the physiological but at the behavioral and psychological levels.

The involvement of psychological factors makes it equally fallacious to attempt to understand human societies by a comparison with insect societies which depend for their successful functioning on the instinctive behavior of their members and their complete and automatic integration into the community. There are, as far as we know, no rebel ants or bees.

At the present time we are acquiring an increasingly good understanding of the way in which societies can be organized and of the factors which hold them together. The latter presented no problem for the sociologist of a few generations ago who blithely posited a human gregarious instinct. While the findings of modern psychologists have made this idea untenable, they have provided a quite adequate substitute: one which makes the universality of the human gregarious tendency quite understandable. We know that all human beings spend the first few years of their lives in a state of extreme dependency. They must elicit response from older individuals if they are to survive. As a result, they come to associate all patterns of security and comfort with the presence of other individuals. They also, due to their extreme development of learning ability, have the capacity to form strong individual attachments. The persons who form a society at any point in time are not held together simply by their formal patterns of cultural participation and by the mutual interdependence arising from their divergent social roles. They are united even more strongly by the common understandings and values which derive from the culture which they share and by their subcultural patterns of habitual association and emotional attachments.

In order to explain the existence of societies, it is unnecessary to posit, as did the eighteenth-century philosophers, a social contract. Such a contract, in so far as it exists at all, can only be a rationalization after the fact. It is also fallacious to think of societies as dependent upon the development of patterns for establishing and maintaining social solidarity. This belief seems to be implicit in the thinking of the school of French sociologists who stem from Durkheim, and in that of several members of the British functionalist group. It seems to me that this concept can best be explained as a reflection of the urban conditioning of such social scientists. It is perfectly true that in a modern urban society largely composed of individuals who have been more or less accidentally brought together as adults, the individual is likely to suffer from a sense of isolation, and if the society is to function efficiently it is necessary for it to develop patterns for social integration at the adult level and for emphasizing its own solidarity. However, in the small face-to-face communities in which most human beings have lived throughout most of human history, the development of social solidarity is taken care of by the unconscious learning of a common culture and by the gradual accumulation of personal ties. Every element of culture, by providing a common area of understanding among a society's members, contributes to social solidarity, but very few culture elements have this as their primary function.

The existence of any society is dependent upon two factors: a group of individuals in more or less continuous association, and a system of organization regulating the interrelations and activities of the group's members. The first provides a society with its personnel; the second makes it possible for this personnel to function as a unit. The system of organization may be termed the society's structure.

The structure of a society persists through time, and normally survives even a complete change in the society's personnel. One of its most important functions is to serve as a guide to the training of young individuals. There are certain positions in any social system which can be predicted for any normal member of the society simply on the basis of sex, kin ties, or class affiliations. The potential occupants of such ascribed statuses can be accurately trained to perform the associated roles.

In its relation to the individual, the social system may be regarded as a substitute for the instinctual equipment which makes possible the functioning of complex insect societies. The social system maintains the form of the society generation after generation and assures the performance of the activities necessary to its survival. The strong cohesiveness of human aggregates (already discussed) makes it possible to organize such groups in a number of different ways simultaneously. Each member of society normally has a place assigned in each of these simultaneous systems. In general, the individual's statuses in each system are determined by a different set of factors, and the roles associated with these statuses are usually functionally related to different sets of social needs. Every society apparently has simultaneous systems of organization based upon: (1) age and sex; (2) kinship; (3) voluntary association as in work groups, secret societies, etc.; (4) specialized occupational groups; (5) the ordering of individuals, or the categories of individuals established by any one of these systems, into a prestige series. Particular societies may have additional systems, but the foregoing seems to represent the irreducible minimum. While the positions of any individual in the various systems in which he participates are not necessarily closely interrelated, in all those cases in which a particular set of statuses deriving from different systems normally converge upon the same individuals, considerable adjustment between the various roles involved will have been worked out. Thus, the role of adult female in any society will not conflict at any important point with the role of mother, or the role of doctor with that of family head.

One of the most interesting problems which still remains to be solved is that of how the individual succeeds in relating to his diverse roles and performing first in terms of one, and then in terms of another, without apparent psychological conflict. It seems that it is entirely possible for the average individual to operate in terms of a whole series of statuses as long as the role requirements of his various statuses are clearly defined. When, as a result of changing cultural and social conditions, this clarity of definition is lost and the individual is required to make numerous decisions between alternative roles, the psychological results are likely to be disastrous.

Investigations of social structure have now been under way for many years, but, curiously enough, only one of the multiple systems has been studied with anything approaching adequacy. This is the system based on kinship. The initial choice of kinship as a field for specialized study was probably due in part to the nineteenth-century British obsession with everything relating to sex and the family, and partly to the striking, and from the European point of view, frequently bizarre, forms assumed by kin terminology and kin obligations in various "primitive" societies. For many years, all field ethnologists have felt it incumbent upon them to collect data on kinship terminology and on the roles prescribed for the various statuses within kin groups. In this way a vast amount of data has been accumulated, and the first steps have been taken toward the development of an adequate classification of kinship systems, and the determination of fairly constant correlations.[1]

Outside the area covered by kinship organization, our information is probably most extensive with regard to the voluntary associations involved in religious and economic

[1] Among the modern workers in this field, most important contributions have been made by various members of the British functionalist school working with African and Melanesian societies, and by George P. Murdock, whose recently published *Social Structure* is a first step in the direction of a genuinely scientific approach to kin phenomena through statistical methods.

activities, but even here there are many lacunae in our data, and, so far as I know, no adequate taxonomic system has been developed. We know still less about the organization and functioning of the other systems normally involved in social structure. There are very few societies for which we possess even the terminology of the age-sex categories which they recognize, still less any account of the roles assigned to the various categories and their functional relations to the society as a whole. Lastly, the structuring of prestige, with its closely related factors of power and social control, is almost *terra incognita.*

While human societies present certain resemblances to the life patterns of other gregarious mammals and, at the operational level, show even closer parallels with the life patterns of communal insects, human culture bears only the most tenuous relations to any nonhuman phenomenon. A culture is the accumulation of learned behavior, using that term in the widest sense to include not only patterns of overt behavior, but also value-attitude systems and conditioned emotional responses, which are transmitted from generation to generation within a society. This close and continuous relationship has led to frequent confusion in thinking and to a regrettable tendency to use the two terms interchangeably. A society is an organized aggregate of individuals; a culture is an organized aggregate of ideas, habits, and conditioned emotional responses which is implemented and transmitted by the members of a particular society. At this point, some notice should be taken of a matter of terminology which has been responsible for considerable confusion. The term *culture* has been used with the meaning here given it since the very beginnings of the sciences of anthropology and sociology. The attempts which have been made by one modern functional school to eliminate the term and to substitute for it *social system* seems to me to do much more to confuse than to clarify the issue. A social system, according to long-established usage, is the collection of statuses and roles in terms of which a society's members are organized. As such, it is a component of the total culture. It represents the solutions which have been developed for meeting certain problems inherent in social living just as another sector of the culture provides a solution to the problem of economic production, and as still another, that of religion and magic, is a response to the individual's feelings of insecurity and inadequacy in the face of situations which he is unable to control.

Cultures as wholes are carried and transmitted by societies as wholes. The culture bears somewhat the same relation to the total society that the personality bears to the individual. It is important to recognize in this connection that no one individual is ever familiar with the total content of his society's culture. In all cultures, there is a central core of value-attitude systems, generalized knowledge, and basic role anticipations which is shared by all normal adult members of the society. In addition to this, there are a considerable number of specialized attitudes, behavior patterns, and items of knowledge which are related to particular statuses. Thanks to the co-operative nature of societies, occupants of other statuses do not need to share these. These two series of culture elements are in constant interaction, and are mutually adjusted to form a congruous functioning whole. Lastly, every culture includes a series of attitudes and behavior patterns which may be mutually inconsistent and may even involve duplication in their primary functions. These constitute the growth zone of the culture. They are never shared by the entire personnel of the society. New culture elements which are in process of adoption and integration fall into this class, as do old culture elements which are on their way out. A good example of this segment of culture would be the current situation in our society with respect to sex mores, where we recognize that there is a very considerable range of attitudes and behavior patterns. It seems safe to assume that the present rather incoherent situation is transitory, and that it will be followed in due course of time by the general acceptance of certain values and behavior patterns relating to sex.

Although we realize that cultures are integrated wholes, we still know comparatively little about their structure, and have not as yet developed any satisfactory system for classifying them on this basis. The familiar culture-area classification, depending as it does upon a combination of cultural geographical factors, is by no means satisfactory as a basis for most comparative studies. Functionalists, especially Malinowski and his followers, have made various suggestions as to the interrelations of culture elements, but, due to lack of adequate data for comparative study, only the simplest and most obvious of these interrelations can be demonstrated. We have a somewhat better knowledge of the processes of culture growth and change, thanks largely to the older generation of American anthropologists, especially Boas, Wissler, and Kroeber. Here there is enough information to make the use of comparative studies possible, although those made to date have been extremely one-sided. They have dealt mainly with the diffusion of particular elements of culture and the development of various techniques of historic reconstruction based on distributions. As a result of this focus of interest, we still know surprisingly little of the dynamics involved in the acceptance and integration, or the rejection, of new culture elements by societies. There is urgent need for more descriptive studies of such episodes.

It is already evident that the tacit assumption of the earlier diffusionists that new elements of culture needed only to be presented to societies in order to be accepted is quite untenable. There is plenty of evidence that the process of acceptance is highly selective, and it is unfortunate that we do not know more about the factors involved. The only generalizations which can be made regarding these processes are: (1) The less the disturbance in pre-existing culture patterns involved in the acceptance of the new culture element, the more likely it is to be accepted. (2) New culture elements which are congruous with the existing value-attitude system of a society will be accepted much more readily than those which are not congruous with it. Both the above generalizations should be qualified by "other things being equal." (3) The transmission of culture elements from one society to another takes place primarily at an overt objective level. The receiving society borrows culture elements as it perceives them, without anything like a full comprehension of the meanings and associations which attach to them in the donor culture. In fact, it is virtually impossible to transfer these, due to semantic difficulties. The assignment of meanings and associations by the receiving society is one of the most important processes involved in the integration of new elements into any culture.

While our studies of the dynamics of culture change are still in their infancy, I believe that they have already succeeded in throwing considerable light on a problem which has intrigued social philosophers for centuries:

whether the individual's role in culture change is simply that of an agent of his society, or whether he is a free agent to the extent of being able to influence significantly the future course of culture development. It has often been noted that inventions tend to appear in a singularly pat fashion when a society needs and is therefore ready to accept them. No one can question that inventions must originate with an inventor, or at most with a small group of inventors who pool their abilities to solve a particular problem. Also, since the inventor must operate from a foundation provided by the pre-existing content of his culture, it is quite natural that several inventors who are intrigued by the same problems will find very similar solutions. However, the fundamental question seems to be whether the pat appearance of particular inventions is a real phenomenon or only an apparent one. There is abundant evidence that innumerable inventions have been made in response to quite individual interests and not as responses to needs of which the society was conscious. An excellent example of this would be the many ingenious devices recorded in the notebooks of Leonardo da Vinci, but never used by his contemporaries. The successful invention is not simply one that will work. It is primarily one which is accepted by a society and integrated into its culture. Inventions which are not accepted by the society are stillborn, and in nonliterate cultures, or even in literate ones in pre-patent days, are doomed to be forgotten. Although the evidence is not definitive, it seems probable that inventions along all lines are constantly being made as a result of personal and often atypical interests, and that the inventor becomes an agent of his society only when the society feels the need for and is ready to accept these particular inventions.

The human individual, like the human society and culture, is a phenomenon which has no close parallels. As has been said before, man is the culmination of an evolutionary trend toward increased learning ability and consequently increased potentialities for individuation. At the same time, he has to be shaped to a high degree of behavioral conformity if he is to perform his social roles successfully. The extreme teachability of humans is matched only by the numbers and complexity of the things which their societies require them to learn. In order to live as a member of society, the individual has to acquire both patterns of overt behavior and value-attitude systems. The first are easily learned and extinguished, and the mechanisms involved in both these processes are fairly well understood. The problems set by them can be dealt with experimentally, and many of the results obtained from the study of animals are directly transferrable to humans.

The processes involved in the learning and extinction of value-attitude systems are by no means as well understood. Most of these systems appear to be established in childhood, and are exceedingly difficult to extinguish as a result of later experience. Although we cannot say this with certainty, it seems probable that these difficulties are linked with the fact that such systems represent generalized responses which tend to become incorporated into a number of more specific response patterns. As a result, the value-attitude systems are constantly being rewarded in some contexts, even though they may be unrewarded or even punished in others.

Even in the learning of overt behavior patterns, the individuation of human beings is evident. Although it is possible to define the statuses and roles which constitute a particular social system, no two persons perform the same social role in exactly the same way. The role, like all culturally patterned behaviors, is not a fixed point but a limited range of variation within which the individual's behavior will be effective. In describing such a pattern, the anthropologist commonly takes the mode of this range as representative of the whole. Very few studies have been made of the actual ranges involved in such cases, and this would seem to offer an exceedingly valuable field for further research. The individual in learning his role selects, consciously or otherwise, the point within the pattern range which is most congenial to his abilities and personal value-attitude systems. As the situations evoking role performance repeat themselves, this response becomes automatized. Such a personalized version of an individual's social role may be called his *interpretation* of it. The systematic deviations from the pattern mode shown in the individual's interpretation of a series of roles may be called, for lack of a better term, the individual's *style*. In the absence of more exact techniques, it is from the observation of the style factors that we deduce the qualities of the individual's personality. This procedure is in constant use in everyday life, and it is upon it that we base such characterizations as generous or stingy, courageous or cowardly, and so forth.

In any discussion of the individual, the term personality is certain to come in sooner or later. I believe that there is a general understanding as to its meaning, although little agreement as to the exact limits of the configuration of phenomena to which it should be applied. In practice, it seems to be used with respect to the more or less generalized responses which characterize the individual rather than to the automatized behavior involved in specific responses of limited applicability. Perhaps a general agreement on what is and is not to be subsumed under this term will have to be a preliminary to the development of anything like an adequate system for the classification of personality types. Even in psychiatry, where the extreme nature of many of the symptoms of personality disorder would seem to make classification easier, there is lack of agreement. The study of neurotic and "normal" personalities is still the concern of numerous divergent schools, frequently dominated by messianic founders, whose members often seem to be more interested in imposing their particular vocabulary upon the emergent science than in furthering its growth by sound research. Anyone who has even a superficial knowledge of the literature will be daunted and puzzled by the number of terms used to label closely similar if not identical phenomena. In spite of the conceptual uncertainties which hamper research in personality formation, certain things seem fairly clear. Each individual is born with a unique configuration of physical and psychological potentialities, and from the moment of birth finds himself in interaction with his environment. The process of personality development is one of the continual assimilation and organization of the experiences which he derives from this interaction. As each new item of experience is integrated it becomes a factor in later interactions with the environment, and consequently in the production of new experience. This approach makes the old dichotomy between nature and nurture in the development of personality largely meaningless. There is no technique known to us by which the results of these two sets of factors can be differentiated.

One closely related problem, which has numerous practical connotations, is that of the age at which the basic personality patterns of the individual become established. This can be solved only by observation through time, but several institutions are carrying on such research and should be able to provide the answers. Closely linked with this is the question as to how far it is possible to change these basic configurations in later life; also, if they can be changed, what are the periods in the life continuum when such changes are easiest or most difficult to make; and, lastly, what techniques will be most effective. The practical connotations of these problems are obvious. Studies carried on on a cross-cultural basis are likely to be useful here. We know that in most societies the roles of the individual as a member of different age categories differ tremendously and would seem to call for different personality configurations for their really effective performance. To take a very simple and familiar example, the role of the "good boy" in our own society—obedient, nonaggressive, and considerate of others, in fact the perfect Sunday school scholar—would seem to require personality characteristics quite different from those needed for the successful businessman. Nevertheless, it is a fact that the average individual in all societies makes such status transition without serious personality derangement. In most societies, the most important role changes come at adolescence with the individual's transition from child to adult status, but there are a number of primitive societies in which the changes are as drastic in the individual's transition from adult to old age. Case studies carried on in these societies might do much to solve certain problems which are becoming increasingly pressing for our own society.

There are, however, unsolved problems in the field of personality dynamics. For example, what is the actual role of primary drives in personality formation? Laboratory experiments have provided much information on the role of these drives in animal learning, but it is questionable how far these results are applicable to humans living under normal social conditions. Culture is very largely a mechanism for satisfying the primary drives of the individual before they rise to compulsive intensity. It is only in highly atypical situations, such as concentration camps or lost lifeboats, that hunger and thirst reach a level at which their satisfaction becomes more important than any other consideration. Also, attempts to apply conclusions based on animal experiment to humans seem to me to overlook one exceedingly important factor. Humans, if they are not unique in their sense of future events and their ability to anticipate them, at least possess this quality to an extent only slightly approached by any animal. The result of this is that they can anticipate future tensions even when these tensions are not currently present. At the low level at which cultures serve to keep most drives, such anticipated tensions are nearly as powerful motives for action as current tensions. The result is that, in devising a behavioral response to any situation, humans are always operating in terms of a number of simultaneous drives, and their behavior represents a compromise between their various behaviors which might provide complete satisfaction for single drives. So far as I know, this situation, which is basic to all human behavior, cannot be reproduced successfully in animal experiments. It is easy to present an animal with a choice between lines of action leading to the satisfaction of different drives. For example, a rat which is both hungry and sexually unsatisfied can be given a choice between food and a female. However, in the absence of the ability for anticipation, he cannot be confronted with a situation which will call for the sort of compromise response, say inviting a lady to dinner, which is the essence of nearly all human behavior.

The relation of culture to the development of personality offers a whole series of unsolved problems. The influence of culture on the formation of overt behavior patterns in adults is obvious. A more significant problem is that of the effects of cultural patterns of infant and early childhood care in establishing fundamental personality configurations. Studies in basic personality, to be discussed presently, seem to indicate that these patterns do have some influence but that their importance should not be exaggerated. Even more significant than the formal patterns may be the emotional atmosphere associated with their performance. Two parents may adhere to the same culturally delimited forms of behavior, but one of them uses it as an expression of sadistic aggression toward the child while the other employs it with affectionate accompaniments. Another important problem in this connection is that of the role of patterns of child care in the formation of the individual's self-evaluations. The extreme importance of the individual's conception of himself as important or unimportant, adequate or inadequate, loved or hated, has been pointed out by numerous psychoanalysts, especially the late Harry Stack Sullivan and his associates. Do patterns of infant care such as swaddling or strict toilet training in themselves have the effect of making the child feel that he is helpless or persecuted, with the result that such attitudes become an integral part of his later personality?

Cultural factors may be important in still another way. I find in the psychoanalytic literature few references to the child's ability to compare the treatment which he receives with that of other children in his own society, although anyone who has been a parent has had the reality of such comparisons forcibly brought home to him. I believe it to be highly probable that the effect of frequent beatings upon the personality will be quite different in a society where all children are normally beaten, and in one in which such treatment is exceptional. In these two cases, the symbolic value of the same treatment would be quite different.

The basic problem with which we are dealing is that of whether the culture patterns themselves, or the individual's deviant experience with respect to these culture patterns, are of more importance as personality determinants. The fact that psychoanalytic studies have been carried on almost entirely within the frame of European culture, so that a whole series of cultural factors which may influence personality formation have been quite unconsciously taken for granted, may have resulted in a disproportionate stress upon the individual's culturally deviant experiences. The recently developed collaboration between psychoanalysts and anthropologists, with the consequent opening up to study of whole new fields of personality and culture interaction, may very well result in a too extensive swing in the opposite direction.

A consideration of the influence of culture patterns upon personality brings us at once to another area of research, one in which a rather limited group of psychoanalysts and anthropologists now find themselves involved. This is the current studies of basic personality and national character. Although these two concepts are frequently confused, the studies of each have been carried on by different groups of research workers employing markedly different techniques. Basic personality studies have been made upon small, relatively well integrated groups, either "primitive" tribes or rural communities. National character studies have been directed toward modern nations.

The term "basic personality" refers to those elements of personality which are found to be common to a great majority of the adult members of a particular society. It represents a common substratum of attitudes and generalized responses which are assumed as normal by the society's members, upon which the personality characteristics implied by membership in the various statuses in the social structure are superimposed. These studies have been carried on by a combination of techniques.

1. Psychoanalysts in their studies of our own society have found certain rather consistent linkages between particular types of childhood experience and particular features of adult personality. It is possible on the basis of these clinical findings to hazard a guess as to what sort of individual a particular tribal pattern of child-rearing might be expected to produce.

2. An informal analysis of any culture will indicate rather clearly the type of personality which would be able to function in such a milieu with a minimum of frustration or other internal stress.

3. A number of techniques have been developed for diagnosing personalities through the use of projective tests such as the Rorschach, T.A.T., Zande, and so forth. Although the individual's reaction to these tests is unquestionably influenced by his cultural background, when given in combination they can provide a good deal of information on his personal characteristics.

4. Life histories, when the investigator is able to establish friendly rapport with native subjects and has time to obtain them in extended form, are exceedingly valuable

as guides both to the personality of the informant and to the particular experiences which have contributed to the formation of personality.

A small number of "primitive" cultures have been investigated with the aid of all these techniques. The various techniques were, as far as possible, kept separate. Thus, for the interpretations of objective tests, the individuals who were selected did not know the results of the other lines of investigation. Although the results of the various approaches in every case showed certain inconsistencies, they were sufficiently similar to confirm the belief that there is such a phenomenon as basic personality. The members of each of the groups investigated showed a wide range of individual personality variation, and it seems probable that, given a sufficiently large population, it would be possible to discover in any society examples of any personality configurations to be found in other societies. Nevertheless, the frequency of particular personality types varies tremendously from one society to another. Thus a personality configuration which is numerically dominant in one society may be so rare in another as to be regarded as psychopathic by confreres.

It should be urged emphatically that these results apply only to small, relatively homogeneous groups. In this respect, the concept of basic personality differs from that of national character, which is an attempt to apply the same concepts to modern national groups. Unfortunately, although the concepts have been transferred from their original context, the techniques upon the use of which the concepts were based have not been similarly transferred. The studies of national character which have been made to date have been carried on almost exclusively upon an intuitional basis. No attempt has so far been made to do adequate sampling in terms of life histories or projective tests for any national population. Moreover, the cultural data which have been used as a basis for investigators' analyses have been derived largely from national literatures which do not necessarily reflect the actual values and behavior patterns of the groups involved. To understand how considerable the difference between the literary culture and the real culture may be, one has only to contrast the picture of American life given in the more or less romantic aristocratic literature of our own Civil War period with the realities of American life at the time. A modern nation is a political entity composed of numerous subsocieties and subcultures. The national character of any people would have to represent the common denominator of personality both for the members of various regional groups and for various classes. For instance, the British national character would have to represent the common denominators of personality for such groups as the English, the Scots, the Welsh, and the North Irish, and for such social strata as the aristocratic English country family, the upper middle-class banker and merchant, the small shopkeeper, the peasant, the trade-unionist, and the Cockney coster. One questions whether the common denominator of such diverse groupings would differ very much from the common denominator of human personalities generally.

In summary, on reviewing our present knowledge of society, culture, and personality, it is apparent that many problems remain to be answered. At the same time, anyone whose memory extends over the last thirty years of investigations in these fields must be impressed by the tremendous advances which have been made within that time, and especially by the development of adequate tools for research. Although we really know very little today, we are in a much better position than we ever have been to find out.

DISCUSSION

Franz Alexander

Most authors—as Dr. Linton does here—agree that there is an intimate relationship between psychiatry and anthropology. The disagreement is not that there is a relationship, but what is the nature of this relationship. Almost everybody who writes or speaks about this subject has a somewhat different opinion. The relationship can, however, be empirically proved if you pick up a modern treatise on anthropology. Most of them—or many of the recent ones—could be called "Studies in Psychoanalysis," applied to personality development in different cultures. They consist, very often, of the study of early parental influences upon the child; of the formative, early influences about which Dr. Linton talked. These early parental attitudes and influences have undoubtedly a decisive role in personality formation. Some of these influences have been tested experimentally.

I would like to differ with Professor Linton concerning his views about the importance of infancy experiences on the formation of personality. Animal experiments show, beautifully, that early experiences have a very decisive influence upon later characteristics of these creatures. Rats which are, in the early months of their life, exposed to deprivation, will develop a hoarding instinct[2] to a much higher degree than those rats

[2] Dr. Alexander is probably using the term "instinct" loosely here to denote any characteristic behavior. Editor.

that were not deprived in their infancy. What is even more interesting, however, is that this deprivation has a lasting effect upon the maturing organism only if it occurs in a certain phase of development. Such an observation alone probably makes less ridiculous such statements as we hear about swaddling customs. I was not born in Russia, but would not be surprised if it were to become an established scientific fact that similar early experiences may have a very important influence upon personality formation.

I am, however, in complete agreement with Professor Linton that it would be extremely difficult to single out one individual influence, since its effects can be neutralized by some other experiences. It is a very complex phenomenon, and the organism is an extremely sensitive instrument. I also agree that, not so much singular experiences in themselves, but consistent exposure to certain types of experiences—which one could call "parental attitudes"—are more important than the various physical techniques in child-rearing. But there is very little disagreement that parental attitudes are largely responsible for what type of adult the child will become. The step-by-step study of environmental influences upon personality development is a problem which belongs to psychiatry. Therefore, I often become a little impatient when I read these excellent anthropological studies in personality development, no matter how instructive they may be. I become impatient because the questions which we psychiatrists would expect from the anthropologists, and from the social sciences in general, very often are not even treated in these books.

I am referring to the question of the origin of the parental attitudes themselves. They are often treated as given phenomena which do not need any further explanation. But from where do these different parental attitudes come? To take them for granted, or, as the old philosophers called it, as *causa sui,* is not satisfactory for the scientifically curious mind.

Of course, the so-called functional school of anthropologists have something to say about it. This functional theory maintains that these parental attitudes are not accidental, but they are functional adaptations to the total social configuration, or the total social structure, in which these parents, so to speak, live and grow up. These parental attitudes which are transmitted through tradition, from generation to generation, do make sense if one looks upon them from the perspective of the larger configuration; they have sociological significance. They have a functional value. They are not only adaptations of that member of the society to that social configuration, but they are necessary for the survival of the society.

The total social configuration, again, has its own history. The social configuration must be derived and understood from a number of factors, such as historical, geological, geographical factors. Whether it is a peaceful nation, whether it is surrounded by enemies, will all account for the parental attitude, which will be of a kind suitable to produce either peaceful peasants or warriors, according to the existing needs of the society in question. The total problem becomes, in this perspective, rather complicated. We have, at first, the whole society with all its institutions, its economic structure, which itself is determined by the history of the society. The genesis of this social configuration is being studied by the social sciences through not yet too-well-developed methods. This social configuration produces certain attitudes—among them parental attitudes, child-rearing practices, a philosophy of education—which in turn influence and determine the orientation of the group members.

The concept of the basic personality is certainly a sound one if we speak of homogeneous groups. If the parental attitudes are similar in a group, we can expect that the products—the personalities who are exposed to these influences—will also show certain similarities. This is not the case in a complex industrialized nation; there the parental attitudes are *not homogeneous*. Maybe certain basic attitudes are common, or almost common; possibly one could find a common denominator, but this is yet to be demonstrated.

We conclude that the understanding of the total picture—the social group and the personality of its members—requires the co-operation of at least three disciplines: (1) History should give us an explanation of how the social structure developed. (2) Sociology should tell us how the total social structure determines parental attitudes. (3) Psychiatry, again, can explain to us how parental attitudes influence the development of the personality of the child.

It is important to note that this type of study does not exist as yet; it is still the music of the future. One of the reasons, I think, is that anthropology, up to this date, primarily dealt with the so-called primitive civilizations, the history of which is not known. When I discuss this matter with my anthropological friends, their usual answer is: "Well, we don't know anything about how these customs developed. We can only describe them." And because the historical genesis of the social constellation cannot be studied in primitive cultures by the anthropologists, the anthropologists study what can be studied, namely, how these customs and child-rearing practices influence personality development, a topic which really requires psychiatric method. If I took the privilege and the opportunity to talk about topics about which I know very little, history and sociology, I also listened patiently to my anthropological friends discussing the complicated phenomenon of personality development.

I would like to add here only one remark, if I may. After World War II, when interest in psychiatry and sociology became so acute, when we began to discover that we know so little about the facts and laws of social life—although we know so much about nature and animal nature—we came to the conclusion that now we should develop the knowledge of man and society in order to protect ourselves against too much natural science, particularly against its so dangerous applications in the technology of destruction. Being so ignorant about society, we are really in the position of children who have a very dangerous weapon in their hands, and do not know how to use it. We have technology, but we somehow cannot utilize it for the improvement of social relationships, national or international. The expectation is quite natural that perhaps psychiatrists, anthropologists, or sociologists ultimately would develop a knowledge which can be applied to the improvement of social conditions. And we psychiatrists, particularly, are on the spot, in the face of the World War II's extensive destruction. The challenge is: "Well, you psychiatrists must tell us how to produce more peaceful human beings."

And we psychiatrists must refuse this task, because we are not prepared for it. It is possible that suitable child-rearing practices, how to educate and to bring about peaceful individuals, can be worked out very neatly among psychiatrists and anthropologists. Parental attitudes, however, are not determined by scientific insight, but by the needs of the total social configurations.

We played with the idea, for example, of democratizing the Germans; we had long conferences on how to introduce new national characteristics into Germany. We had had enough of Prussian militarism, we said. We know how it is inculcated in the children; well, let us change their educational philosophy. Those of us who psychoanalyzed Germans know in all details how these militaristic tendencies are inculcated from generation to generation through parental influences in the children. So, let us now educate the German children differently.

But who will educate them? German parents! And German parents' attitudes will depend upon the total configuration of Germany and Europe. If the present international situation persists, it will continue to give the Germans the conviction that only if they are good soldiers can they survive. No social science could change their child-rearing practices unless every

German child were to be taken over by American parents—and what kind of a hybrid product would come out of such an experiment it is hard to predict!

Therefore I want to emphasize that we must begin to think in this field much more comprehensively and realistically. You can't impose upon a nation, or upon a group, a kind of new philosophy, as you can an overcoat. National mentality is an organic part of the total Gestalt represented by a nation or a social group.

We can't even implant a gland from one animal into another species. Similarly, we can't implant psychological attitudes which we develop in one cultural setting into another cultural setting, for which this other cultural setting is not receptive.

DISCUSSION

Louis Schneider

PROFESSOR Linton has graciously given me my cue in his final comment to the effect that "although we really know very little today, we are in a much better position than we ever have been to find out." I should like to carry forward somewhat from this point (although in part traversing again in my own way some of the ground that has been covered) and consider how we might "find out" more than we do, and what pitfalls we might avoid in the drive to know more. An approach to these matters may be made by emphasizing what I shall call the values of unrelenting juxtaposition, the values of a self-critical methodology, and the values of self-knowledge.

1. THE VALUES OF UNRELENTING JUXTAPOSITION.

The very spirit of this symposium is interdisciplinary and it may appear superfluous to advocate in this place the constant juxtaposition of findings from related disciplines or areas of study. Yet there is a certain justification for the comment of two recent critics of "the culture-personality approach" to the effect that "the interdisciplinary nature of the approach is often stressed but it is, in actual fact, sharply limited."[3] Indeed, from time to time there occur failures of juxtaposition that are rather astonishing.

A single example of this kind of failure will suffice. Professor Linton has referred to national character studies. At the same time as national character studies have been pursued, more especially in the past decade, there has been going on study of what may conveniently be called the deferred-gratification pattern. This refers, most briefly, to a pattern of delaying gratification that increasingly appears to be class-typed or class-correlated. In the sexual sphere, for example, according to the data assembled by Kinsey and his co-workers, there is much more marked deferment of sexual gratification through intercourse at "higher" than at "lower" social levels.[4] Much the same differentiation, with the deferred-gratification pattern again relatively less marked at the "lower" class levels, has been noted for Southern town Negroes by Allison Davis, and John Dollard in their *Children of Bondage*.[5] The deferred-gratification pattern extends beyond the sexual sphere. It is evident, for example, in the enterprise of prolonged education, in which monetary rewards for work are deferred until relatively late in the career-line, of course on the presumption that the rewards in the end will be appreciably greater than if the roundaboutness of education had been avoided.[6] Davis and

---

[3] Lindesmith, A. R., and Strauss, A.L., "A Critique of Culture-Personality Writings." *American Sociological Review*, XV, 1950, p. 587.

[4] Kinsey, A. C., Pomeroy, W. B., Martin, C. E., *Sexual Behavior in the Human Male*. Philadelphia: 1948, Chapter X.

[5] Published by American Council on Education, Washington, D. C.: 1940.

[3] Lindesmith, A. R., and Strauss, A. L., "A Critique of Culture-Personality rewards at the "lower" class levels is well set out in A. B. Hollingshead, *Elmtown's Youth*, New York: 1949, Chapter XIV.

Dollard made the pattern a very important part of a general contrast between "lower" and "middle-class" ways of life, in which, *inter alia,* they noted for the members of the "middle" class a relative distaste for violence, a certain inhibition of sexuality, marked pursuit of education, a relatively high aspiration level, etc.

Other investigators have worked on similar lines, and their work reinforces the notion that the deferred-gratification pattern is relatively absent among the "lower" class groups. This is true, for instance, of Cayton and Drake's *Black Metropolis,* which rather impressively sets out data bearing on the deferred-gratification pattern among Chicago Negroes; of Whyte's *Street Corner Society;* of Hollingshead's *Elmtown's Youth;* of some of the work of Warner and his associates. This work is certainly not beyond criticism. But it is important, rather, for the present purpose, to note the sheer fact that it is going on, and perhaps to add that it is being pursued by increasingly refined techniques.

As far as I am aware, not a single serious or systematic effort has been made to relate the work on the deferred-gratification pattern to national character studies. There are some adumbrations and hints on appropriate lines in Fromm's *Escape from Freedom,* but little more. Yet the relevance of this work to study of national character must be entirely obvious. Critics skeptical of the work of national-character theorists constantly point to class differences, among others, as indeed Professor Linton has done. If we were to engage in some pertinent investigation of, let us say, a limited number of Western nations, would the deferred-gratification pattern, or other cognate patterns, stand out as so overwhelmingly important cross-culturally that it would be clear that class differences virtually obliterate presumed national differences? Or would the deferred-gratification pattern, while present cross-culturally, fade into the background in virtue of the prominence of national differences? These are only two of a number of questions that might be asked. Answers to them, plainly, that could now be given would have to be crude and highly speculative. But it is quite clear that to allow two areas of study of the kind under consideration—national-character study on the one hand, and deferred-gratification-pattern study on the other—to go on in isolation from one another, as if each were quite irrelevant to the other, is rather absurd.

But this example of failure of juxtaposition can be further exploited. In terms of one of the central problems in the tradition of sociological theory, the problem of "order,"[7] the deferred-gratification pattern may well turn out to be of crucial significance. If there is training in deferment of gratification, and the rewards that have been held out for such deferment are not forthcoming, is the psychological outcome relevant to "order"? Who becomes "revolutionary" under these circumstances and who does not? Is there in the relative absence of the deferred-gratification pattern in the "lower" class groups a special source of conservatism, in that expectation levels are accordantly very low?

These questions, difficult though they are to answer, are certainly highly pertinent within the framework of attempted integration of "culture and personality," or at least of "social structure and personality." Yet, again, such questions seem to have remained quite largely outside the purview of those whose names are now conventionally associated with "culture-personality" study. Admittedly there are men who are exceptions, and one may hope that their number will increase.

It is well worth remarking, incidentally, that social scientists not especially identified with "culture-personality" study may in their turn overlook important leads that that type of study might suggest to them in their own research. Thus, it is of interest to be given descriptive material that indicates that high school officials, blocked in the enforcement of rules they

[7] See Parsons, Talcott, *The Structure of Social Action*. New York: 1937, index, on "order."

seek to impose on both "upper" and "lower" class children as far as the "uppers" are concerned, turn upon the "lowers" and enforce the rules more rigidly for the latter.[8] This is of "interest," as said, but its "interest" could be very considerably enhanced if the occasion were taken to relate events of this kind explicitly to the hypothesis of displaced aggression. Small-scale, "manageable," potentially experimental investigation of ambitious theories of displaced aggression (for example, to the effect that French-Canadian anti-Semitism has its roots in anti-English sentiment)[9] in contexts such as this would be extremely valuable.

It will be recalled that our emphasis is on *unrelenting* juxtaposition. It may be acknowledged again that there are social scientists whose work reveals a quite inadequate sensitization to the types of juxtapositions here suggested. But the object is to propagandize for more sensitization of this kind. Accordingly, it may not be amiss to suggest that anthropologists, for example, could hardly lose by paying closer attention, in "culture-personality" work, to certain well-known aspects of the anthropological tradition itself, more especially the "functionalism" of Malinowski, Radcliffe-Brown, Durkheim, and others. The study of "culture and personality" does at least occasionally present us with rather aimless, discursive bits of work, characterized precisely by "an interest in 'culture and personality.'" Such aimlessness, such discursiveness, could be considerably diminished by the relating of work to the anthropological tradition mentioned, which is also a significant sociological tradition in process of further development.[10] Fortunately we have some fine precedents in this connection.

---

[8] Cf. Hollingshead, *op. cit.*, Chapter VIII.

[9] Cf. Hughes, E. C., *French Canada in Transition.* Chicago: 1943, Chapter XIX.

[10] Cf. especially Merton, R. K., *Social Theory and Social Structure.* Glencoe, Illinois: 1949, Chapter I.

and accordant character of humans in the West and off the coast of New Guinea.[14]

Perhaps I have propagandized sufficiently on these lines. And if I have "overpropagandized," it has at least been done in the conviction that the paths above indicated can help us to "know more."

2. THE VALUES OF A SELF-CRITICAL METHODOLOGY.

There are certain methodological difficulties that come up time and time again in the "culture-personality" field that would appear to call for unwearying tirade.

One of the best known of these difficulties is that of what I may call the "psychoanalyzing analogy."[15] Alfred Adler once suggested that those who cry excessively in childhood are especially given to fits of depression in later life. This is a good enough illustration of the form the psychoanalyzing analogy tends to take. Of course, as long as all that is intended by such a statement as this is that limited clinical observation

---

[14] The theme here suggested would certainly be worth independent pursuit. Perhaps especially intriguing in this connection would be the analysis of universal and particular elements in cognition and perception. It may simply be noted here that, again, the same Malinowski who could argue on the assumption of universal elements in human nature could also claim the existence of important cognitive differences (and it is not implied that this is self-contradiction): "We must realize that the cardinal dogma of God the Father and God the Son, the sacrifice of the only Son and the filial love of man to his Maker would completely miss fire in a matrilineal society . . . where all family obligations are associated with mother-line." *The Sexual Life of Savages,* New York: 1929, pp. 186-187. So also Kardiner, who believes in the universal operation of certain psychoanalytic "mechanism," can claim that, in view of frustrating maternal behavior, "it is inconceivable that the Christian concept of the Madonna should make any appeal to an Alorese, and no less inconceivable that he should be able to invent such an idea or representation." *The Psychological Frontiers of Society,* p. 233.

[15] This is suggested by Sullivan's term (evidently after Adolf Meyer), "neurologizing tautology." Sullivan, H. S., *Conceptions of Modern Psychiatry.* Washington: 1945, p. 3.

suggests the connection pointed to, there is nothing to quarrel about. But a frequently occurring and uncritical kind of acceptance of statements like this rest simply on connection through congruity. Depression, after all, bears plausible resemblance to crying. The idea, moreover, has a certain ingenuity. Yes, it must be so: what more natural than that those who cry excessively should later be much given to depression?

This "argument," obviously, does not rest upon evidence. The argument nevertheless appears repeatedly, and, to mention a single instance of a "culture-personality" student addicted to it, Mr. Gorer engages in it quite frequently and casually.[16] Wonderful things can be achieved by use of the psychoanalyzing analogy, and in the "culture-personality" field one need only fill in the proper cultural terms to make the analogy "apply."

I may suggest that the close critical watch for this particular type of argument is highly salutary and bound to have a chastening effect. A pertinent enterprise, tedious but quite possibly very illuminating, would be to examine a number of the "culture-personality" studies sufficiently widely recognized as "outstanding" contributions to the field, excise from them all growths with a foundation in the psychoanalyzing analogy, and see what is left over. It is not implied that nothing would be left over, but the psychoanalyzing analogy has so long and so insidiously substituted for hard thinking in this field that it is justified to call attention to it in the most dramatic ways possible.

The problem just touched upon suggests another. If we undertake to "bring together" the study of culture or social structure on the one hand, and that of personality on the other, we must really *bring them together*. A common, too

[16] Cf. the appropriate quotation and comment of F. L. K. Hsu, "Anthropology or Psychiatry," *Southwestern Journal of Anthropology,* Vol. 8, No. 2, Summer 1952; and Irving Goldman, "Psychiatric Interpretation of Russian History: A Reply to Geoffrey Gorer," *The American Slavic and East European Review, IX,* 1950, pp. 151-161.

common, procedure in this field runs as follows: One announces that one is going to "relate" at least certain aspects of culture and personality. There follows some initial discussion of how the variables of personality and culture may bear on one another. Next comes a prolonged enterprise of writing in which the twain never meet, or in which, at best, the treatment of one set of variables is no more than irritatingly allusive with regard to the other set.

We have to be "hard" on ourselves here. Chatty talk about culture on the one hand and personality on the other is no substitute for the difficult work of "interrelating." We are brought full swing back to a previous suggestion in regard to aimlessness and discursiveness. The functional mode of analysis can again be of the utmost help. That mode of analysis, as currently pursued in social science, is itself already sufficiently near to the field of personality so that it will serve to direct theoretical formulations and research to fairly definite problems in the interrelations of personality and culture or social structure.[17]

There is a third methodological problem that may be touched briefly. It is not incumbent on the student of personality and

---

[17] A pertinent theoretical study of my own in some of the relations of personality elements to elements of social structure, guided by a functional mode of analysis, is contained in "Some Psychiatric Views of 'Freedom' and the Theory of Social Systems," *Psychiatry,* XIII, 1949, pp. 251-264. None of the foregoing is intended to imply that major questions about interrelationships of personality and culture are likely to be easily resolved, or that a sensitization to functional analysis will quickly obviate large difficulties. Our most competent social scientists have a keen sense of the complexity of this whole area. See, for example, the comments of Talcott Parsons in "The Prospects of Sociological Theory," in *American Sociological Review,* XV, 1950, pp. 9-10, and A. L. Kroeber, "The Concept of Culture in Science," *Journal of General Education,* III, 1949, p. 194. And we may well be warned by Professor Linton's comment early in his paper that, in the study of society, culture, and the individual, "at the present time we do not have any neat, all-encompassing conceptual pattern into which all the various phenomena can be fitted." Nevertheless, as prizefighters say, when you step into the ring you're supposed to be able to take it. If we announce we are going to "integrate" or "interrelate," it is not unreasonable that we should be expected to make an appreciable effort to do so.

culture to explain "everything." When so complex an entity as a nation is investigated, it is fairly obvious that even the best endowed researcher will need the aid of historian, economist, political scientist, perhaps others. Social scientists have been aware that there is such a thing as "psychologizing" social phenomena, "reducing" them entirely to the psychological level and thereby effecting, not simplification, but an egregious oversimplification that misses a great deal of what it purports to "reduce." To be armed with a subtle and penetrating knowledge of the ways of repression, displacement, and rationalization plainly has its advantages, but such knowledge is certainly no substitute for a familiarity with history and with institutional forms where these are pertinent. There is a mode of "psychologizing"—and in this case the reference is particularly to the bringing in of special psychological considerations where they are not needed—that may be singled out for emphasis. Where the student of personality and culture falls into this mode of "psychologizing" he courts altogether unnecessary trouble: his tasks are in any case difficult enough.

To indicate what is here meant it will be helpful to make use of the phrase "logic of the situation,"[18] and convenient to refer to the procedure of the historian. Assume that Caesar is aware that he has enemies. Given the knowledge that he has, he can defeat his enemies by expedient A or expedient B or expedient C. Expedient A, even if it works, will gain him new and more powerful enemies; expedient B, if it works, will cost him everything he has gained to date (e.g., political influence, prestige, etc.); expedient C will work without any adverse consequences as far as he can see. The "logic of the situation" therefore in this case virtually pushes Caesar in the direction of emphasizing expedient C. At least implicitly, the historian has to use such models unless he is not to write history. All this does not assume that Caesar is not—let us say

[18] Cf. Popper, Karl R., *The Open Society and Its Enemies.* Princeton: 1950, Chapter IV, esp. p. 289.

—neurotic. It only assumes that he is sufficiently nonalienated to be able to act in accordance with his objective interest. To act in accordance with objective interest in this way is compatible with very *diverse* psychological make-ups. Psychological make-up can therefore vary almost indefinitely if not quite at random, and objective interest still be followed. No special psychological considerations need be adduced to explain Caesar's course of action.

Undoubtedly, the study of culture and personality has at times been unnecessarily "ambitious," in a sense that the foregoing implies. Much of the "contradictory" behavior of the Nazis of which Richard Brickner speaks is susceptible of situational explanation without recourse to Brickner's special assumptions about the existence of a German paranoia, just as much recent Russian endeavor in the technological sphere is situationally comprehensible without recourse to assumptions about distinctive Russian psychological characteristics.[19]

Much can be gained in regard to these particular methodological difficulties. To strip off fruitless analogizing, to cease engaging in easy pretenses about "interrelating," and to spare ourselves certain distinctive, unnecessary troubles—all around, these would constitute a considerable achievement.

3. THE VALUES OF SELF-KNOWLEDGE.

Under this last caption, it is worth emphasizing that in the areas of concern of this symposium the opposition of belletristic and scientific approaches is marked and troublesome. Four disciplines are here represented, those of anthropology, psychiatry, psychology, and sociology. To an appreciable extent, in each of these disciplines we have a peculiar and exasperating lack of cumulation of work. We have a situation not unlike that found in such eminently "cultural" enterprises as the writing of novels. A Dostoievski, a Tolstoi, and a Stendhal do their work

[19] Cf. Brickner, Richard M., *Is Germany Incurable?* Boston: 1943, and Goldman, Irving, *loc. cit.*, p. 161.

and pass from the scene. It is not that other novelists are not edified or aided by this work, but they cannot build directly and definitely upon it, carrying on from where the masters stopped. It is plainly doubtful whether any steady "advance" can be discerned in an area such as this. So also, a great psychiatrist may be looked upon as a marvel. He is likely to have developed penetrating insights, but insights not readily acquirable by specific and rigorous methods. Rather, these insights are attained, if at all, through experiences difficult to define with precision and through elusive sensitivities. Again, the influence of the psychiatrist need not be lost. It can ramify through the persons and practices of his students. But it, too, fails markedly to cumulate. An occasional student may attain the stature of the master, but this is not the same as the steady and reliable cumulation of knowledge.

Since, in Mr. Anthony Standen's vivid phrasing, "science is a sacred cow," we have all, perforce, to be scientific: nothing else will do. Hence, typically, the furor that arises over such an item as Mr. Gorer's *The American People*. This could well be looked upon as a pleasant little book, mildly and at least to some—not uncongenially psychoanalytical, and at times rather perceptive. But insist upon regarding products of this sort as "scientific," and difficulties are bound to ensue. It is as well to be honest. The word "science" will presumably allow a certain amount of stretching, but not an indefinite amount. If we wish to write in a literary vein on the "topic" of personality and culture, no harm is done if we are clear about what we are doing. The results may be charming, even very revealing, although they may have rather little to do with "science." A rigorous, genuinely scientific enterprise has its own distinctive merits and is certainly not the same as this kind of belletristic endeavor. I happen to think that there is an intermediate category of "analytical" endeavor, but for present purposes it is well to rest with the duality of the belletristic and scientific.

The representatives of our several disciplines are well aware that we find ourselves constantly confronted by these unhappy alternatives: greatly insightful and perceptive work tends to be difficult to check and difficult to build upon; on the other hand, work that is methodologically rigorous tends to lose significant problems and bog down in trivialities. Even in this form, this is perhaps too absolutely stated, but it sets out a dilemma familiar to all of us. It is in connection with this dilemma that I am eager to stress the values of an honest self-knowledge. Spurious claims to being "scientific," and scientistic rejections of significant problems, can be avoided only if we first recognize them fully and cleanly for what they are. I would submit that if we scrutinize our work carefully and represent its character accurately to ourselves and others, we will at least have a chance to create more satisfying alternatives than the "literary"-without-proof or the "scientific"-without-importance.

We would all presumably agree that it is desirable to "know more." The above may be regarded as a set of tentative suggestions designed to be of aid in just that direction, and perhaps especially inspired by the familiar notion that a first step toward increase of knowledge is awareness of ignorance.

X

EVALUATION FROM FOUR POINTS OF VIEW

Robert F. Winch

SOCIAL PSYCHOLOGY

THE CHAIRMAN has asked me to make some comments in an effort to evaluate this symposium in the light of those things which I think it might have—or may have—accomplished. In view of the nature of my assignment I shall have to forego the pleasure of commenting separately on each of the excellent contributions.

I should like to begin by expressing my discomfiture with the title of the symposium: Anthropology and Psychiatry.[1] Perhaps my discomfiture springs only from an unconscious feeling that as a sociologist I am a rejected poor relative from across the tracks, that sociologists—and psychologists too—are really intruding here. But if that be the case, I do think that I can phrase my rationalization in reasonably presentable form. We have not been concerned with all of anthropology, but only with that part of it which bears on personality and its study in a

[1] See Prologue.

cultural setting. We have almost completely ignored a good deal of general psychiatry. Shock therapy and psychosurgery have not been central to our deliberations. We have focused our discussion on personality, its processes and its development as these are determined by culture and as these in turn influence culture. Although the phrase "culture and personality" is hackneyed and timeworn, it seems to me that our focus may have become slightly blurred by failing to use that phrase.

My agenda for what I had hoped we might accomplish is as follows:

1. What really are the central issues which need to be clarified in order to advance our theory (or theories) of personality?

2. What is the best way to state such issues in order to be able to get on with finding some answers? A thorough consideration of the first point would, I am confident, reveal that some issues are not issues but circular statements; that others are definitional in character and hence need not concern us. This would leave us with those issues which are contingent propositions—which, in other words, are researchable.

3. Having arrived at a body of researchable propositions, we might then have paused to see whether or not anybody had any answers to such questions—to find out, in other words, whether or not such questions had already been researched.

4. This would leave us with unstudied but researchable propositions. The next question is "how?" What techniques of observation are available, on what kind of subjects, with what experimental design?

5. It was my feeling that after some time spent on the

level of the previous four points we should have become somewhat short of breath in the rarefied atmosphere of such high-level abstractions. I felt, therefore, that it would be well to include one or two empirical studies with concrete data in order to provide some solid ground on which to try out our methodological ideas.

Now how does the performance compare with the agenda which I have outlined? Some issues were posed in the paper by Dr. Mowrer and in the discussion by Dr. Saslow. Some interesting methodological problems were raised in the papers of Drs. Gillin and Henry and in the discussions of Drs. French and Masserman. And there were informative reports of empirical studies by Drs. Kuhn, Boshes, and Richards. It is my feeling, however, that we did not get a set of issues into sufficient focus in order to proceed with the agenda which I have outlined. Perhaps the reason is that as a group we have been insufficiently aggressive and that we have been too respectful of the feelings and defenses of others and of ourselves. Perhaps we have been too inhibited by the inexorable movement of the clock. Perhaps we could not possibly have covered the agenda in the allotted time. Perhaps the reason is that I am the only one who has regarded this to be the appropriate agenda.

Now, although we did not get through the agenda which I proposed, some progress was made. At the outset John Gillin proposed the establishment of a postulational system for a science of human behavior. And, as you will recall, Dr. French was critical of the proposal, as well as of Gillin's suggestion for a research organization. It is unfortunate, in my judgment, that this difference was inadequately developed. When a science is in its infancy, it must operate on the level of description and classification. I believe that at this stage it is premature to try to operate deductively from a postulational system. The question then arises: In the science of human behavior are we now at a sufficiently advanced stage of development where the use of a postulational system would be fruitful? Or possibly the question should be phrased: Which areas in the field are sufficiently developed for the employment of such a method? It is clear that this method enables us to fit together bits of knowledge and fragments of research into a coherent system. But, as Dr. French pointed out, if we adopt the system too soon, we may shut out more light than we let in. Perhaps a consideration of the fruits of Hull's theory would have enlightened us on this point.

We have engaged in some good-natured chiding of one another's fields. In general, this chiding has been on the basis of method and techniques. If you will accept the kind of investigations done as an index of a field's development, the disciplines represented here show quite a spread in the stages to which they have evolved—from the almost poetically written descriptions of certain literary anthropologists to the tersely written, statistics-studded reports of "brass-instrument" and "rat" psychologists. No doubt this mutual chiding enables each of us to see how his field looks from the critical view of the outsider; it provides us with an opportunity, moreover, to explain to our critics the difficulties of doing otherwise than we do.

Now, I would like just to pause to give an example of the sort of thing it seems to me we might have done in the light of the points which I have suggested for the agenda. I am not sure that the example which I shall suggest is necessarily the best or the most fruitful we might have considered, but I think it will do as an example.

In the various theories of personality, it seems to me quite clear that there is a very gross disagreement concerning the importance of the period of early childhood for the ultimate determination of the adult personality. Some say that the personality is completely set, or nearly so, by the end of the infantile period; others, such as Gordon Allport, assert that it is really never set; and Horney takes the position that it may be set by the fifth birthday, maybe not at all.

To me, at least, it would have been very interesting for us to undertake the analysis of questions such as that, to see, among other things:

What do we mean by the idea that personality or character is really determined or set at any given age?

From what kinds of behaviors do we draw this kind of inference?

Do we really disagree as to the facts, as to what the behaviors are, or is the disagreement on such a level that it really doesn't make a great deal of difference?

Is there any research we can point to that is in any way crucial in helping us to arrive at any conclusions in this kind of question?

I should have felt it extremely helpful, at least in my own thinking, for us to have discussed a question of this sort in order: (*a*) to see how we could have stated the issue, and (*b*) to determine whether or not it might ultimately be researchable.

While on the subject of methodological difficulties in our various fields, I wish that we might have had time to discuss the logical impasse involved in working with the individual case, and possible ways of circumventing this impasse. This problem is particularly evident in psychoanalysis and in cultural anthropology. (In the latter field, of course, the individual case is the individual culture.) Since students in these disciplines generally work on a case-by-case basis, their findings, when judged by the conventional standards of scientific method, can never have the status of generalizations, but only of hypotheses. Even when more than the single case is involved in a study, moreover, the *post hoc* interpretation of the clinical method involves us in another difficulty. For example, there were many "passive-dependent" men among the soldiers whom Dr. Boshes treated. It appeared from his paper that this type of man might be particularly predisposed to a breakdown under the stress of combat. Before we can be sure of such a conclusion, however, we must know that the proportion of "passive-dependent" men who crack up under combat is significantly higher than the proportions of men of other types. This is the kind of information which is so crucial and so scarce.

Yesterday Dr. Mowrer pointed out to me why it is very difficult to assess the accomplishments of such a conference as this. One of the most lasting values, perhaps the most important value, he said, inheres in the individual participant's preparation for the conference, and in the modifications in his thinking and operating after he gets back home. I have enjoyed the discussions in which we have engaged and trust that we shall all be more fruitful scholars for having participated in them.

Adamson Hoebel

ANTHROPOLOGY

I AM in the position of presuming to speak for the anthropologists present. Of course, I actually present only one anthropologist's reaction to our undertakings here.

It is quite obvious that the basic principle that underlies all our discussions is that mental phenomena are not really separable from social affairs; and, correlatively, cultural phenomena are not separable from mental processes. We also recognize that overt recognition of what today seems to be an obvious fact has come late in the development of our two sciences. As a result, most of our interdisciplinary work in the area of personality and culture is still to a large extent concerned with the formulation of hypotheses and working concepts.

Although the last decade and a half has seen a great number of specific empirical studies of real worth that have been directed to the recording of data providing sound raw materials, the impression is strong that more type has gone into the publication of theoretical material than into the recording of new findings.

By title, seven of the papers presented at this conference indicate theoretical and methodological discussions, while four are clearly field or clinical reports. In content, the quantitative impression derived from title classification was validated by assessment of the contents as delivered. Now, this strikes me as not unrepresentative of the orientation of the personality and culture movement at large up to the present. We ask the question: Is it or is it not a healthy condition? I raise the question as an anthropologist who is wholly receptive and sympathetic to the movement but who, at the same time, does not center his main research interests in the area that permits me to be labeled a personality and culture specialist.

Since I am what my colleagues at New York University used to call a "primitive lawyer," I am more of a receiver than an initiator in this field that is represented here in the conference. However, I should also like to identify myself as a propagator of what I receive from you creators, for I have been teaching your results in a personality and culture course for some ten years, and I have done special lecturing as what you might call an adjunct member of the faculties of the psychiatric departments of the medical school of New York University, and presently at the University of Utah. I cite this fact because it should put me in a position of one who is aware of what is going on and who, at the same time, is detached enough to be able to look at it more or less from the outside.

There can be no challenging the statement that personality and culture theory has reoriented anthropology. It is true that there are a few anthropologists who have resisted reorientation, but the bulk of our colleagues have had their directions changed in the last fifteen or twenty years. Anthropological interests and theory prior to 1930 left too much unattended or unaccounted for in the total realm of human phenomena. Man was lost among his works. New light was needed. In the detailed study of individuals, psychiatry, and more specifically psychoanalysis, had developed a number of working ideas, and had organized data concerning individual adaptive mechanisms, which quite suddenly shed needed light on numerous loose-lying facts that had had no place in previous anthropological systems.

In the paper that Professor Hsu sent us before the opening of this conference—the recording of his Viking Fund address on "Anthropology or Psychiatry"[2]—we have the declaration that psychiatric assumptions and findings have exerted greater influence on anthropology than has been the reverse. This has been reiterated several times during this conference without, I noted, any serious objection being raised. This is a point which I find myself accepting.

Anthropologists would do wrong to infer that this means they are more alert than psychiatrists, or more open-minded, and I have seen no evidence of smugness on the part of anthropologists that would indicate they have made this interpretation. I would say it merely reflects the fact that anthropology had greater need of psychological concepts than vice-versa. Psychiatric theory added to culture theory opens the way to new understandings of man in all his aspects, and has given to anthropology a new impetus.

I think we are seeing at work in our own field one of the most important principles of the history of science as recently stated by President Conant in his lectures "On Understanding Science." In Conant's words: "A theory is only overthrown by a better theory, never by merely contradictory facts. Attempts are first made to reconcile the contradictory facts to the existing conceptual scheme by some modification of the concept. Only the combination of a new concept with facts contradictory to the old ideas finally brings about a scientific revolution. And when once

[2] *Op. cit.*

this has taken place, then in a few short years discovery follows upon discovery and the branch of science in question progresses by leaps and bounds."

This is what is happening in anthropology today. As of this moment, however, we are apparently only in the middle phases of the second step of the process outlined by Conant. That is, diverse attempts at the formulation of adequate new concepts are in the making. Anthropology has already taken a spurt, as a result, in a few short years. It remains to be seen whether it is about to progress by leaps and bounds.

That, I think, will depend on two conditions: First, and obviously, whether our personality and culture specialists succeed in finally shaping adequate new concepts; and, second, whether they corrupt concept-making into speculative absorption of their mental energies, or follow up with adequate empirical testing and observations. I don't worry about the second threat too much, because the tradition of empiricism in anthropology is deep-rooted and strong. But I am more concerned about the realization of the first. The reason is as follows.

The accomplishments of the productive thinkers in this field to date do appear to bear the quality of highly suggestive insights and leads that open the door to fuller understanding of the human animal in relation to culture, rather than as conclusive and scientifically verified results on an extensive scale. The illumination that these insights yield is that of the spotlight, perhaps even the photoflash, rather than what we might call the "field light," which brings all aspects of the complex field into view.

The difficulty is that, although the field has been fertilized by the adoption of many new concepts, no adequate new master concept has as yet been enunciated.

This would seem to result from the fact that the flow of concepts has been largely from psychiatry to anthropology. Except for recognition of our master concept of culture—and the subsidiary concept of patterning—psychiatrists have absorbed but little from anthropology in terms of our more specific working ideas.

As I have reflected on Professor Hsu's paper, I have become more and more impressed with the importance of the distinction between the essential aims of psychiatry and anthropology: the one, the pathology of the mentally deviant; the other, the physiology of whole societies.

The concepts which come to anthropology from psychiatry are, it seems, inadequate to the anthropologist's tasks on two counts: (1) again, as has been stated several times, they are in too large a degree derived from the study of the socially inadequate and too little from the socially normal individual; and (2) they rest too much on clinical rule-of-thumb assumptions and too little on objectively verified, point-by-point substantiated data. I think this was beautifully pointed up by Dr. Saslow's enumeration of the extant experimentally determined data that needed to be fitted into assumption-based psychiatric theory, and which apparently have not been.

Now, psychiatric concepts, by virtue of their newness to anthropology when used in anthropology, of course, proved tremendously stimulating. But again we ask: Can they permanently serve as key concepts for a full science of anthropology?

For example, the importance of infancy experience in the shaping of the personality is not to be denied, and no one has here denied it, although Dr. Hsu in his paper came close to denying it. But the importance of the infancy period has surely been inflated in the work of anthropologists in the last decade and a half. In pioneering of any sort, new discoveries always loom larger and more exciting than they really may be or will seem to be when they come to be taken more for granted.

In the primitive area, almost anything observed by an anthropologist between 1935 and 1950 with respect to early child training was a new discovery. But now that we have had our measure of fun, it is time to put infancy experience into its more proper perspective, and this means more sociological and psychological emphasis and less psychiatric. And that, Dr. Winch, is why I think you and others of the related social science fields who don't bear the labels "anthropologist" or "psychiatrist" are here.

It means a revival of the importance in our thinking of the basic tenet that the nervous systems of men at large are highly plastic, and that they remain plastic and adaptable through and beyond adolescence, even though the general direction may be set in childhood. The average person in any society spends more years as an adult than as a child—that is, assuming he doesn't die in infancy. In another aspect, the adult is more socially significant than the child: It is only adults who can biologically perpetuate the group and sustain the society. And societies have to work constantly upon adults to hold them to limited lines of behavior. The needs of society are surely as important as those of the individual. In a sense they are more so. Although societies are made up of individuals, they can always get along without any individual individual. No individual can do without society.

All this adds up to an agreement with the position that the time is now at hand for a shift in the emphasis of personality and culture studies. Anthropologists can well continue to learn from psychiatrists, and they should not fail to do so. But the main—and by main I do not mean exclusive—but the main problem of human behavior will always remain, I think: How does the individual conform to culture?—not, How does culture adjust to the individual?

While the physiological and psychic needs of the individual organism impose imperative demands on every culture and limit the ultimate bounds of culture, the demands are for the most part highly generalized and could be met in a large variety of specific ways. But the integrative needs of society require that for the members of each particular society the variety of ways expressed in the behavior of its individuals must be limited and, in a relative sense, specialized.

What we have been saying thus far must not, and I am sure it will not, be taken as a disparagement of the role that has been played and will continue to be played by psychiatry in the development of the interrelations of personality and culture. The revelation of the building of adjustive mechanisms by individuals in reaction to social experience can hardly be overvalued, or overvaluated, in its contribution to the study of individual idiosyncrasy, and, indeed, to the reciprocal shaping of culture itself.

This has been well indicated, if we take as an example Kardiner's work on material that was made available to him primarily through the yeoman work of Ralph Linton. But if we look at Kardiner's contributions as representing the most fully developed conceptual scheme yet formulated in the field we are here considering, and keeping in mind it works primarily from psychiatric concepts—that is, works on anthropological data, with ideas and principles evolved from psychiatric experience—we see that it is self-avowedly a limited conceptual system. I think it attempts only two things: first, the identification of the basic personality structure and the process of its formation as a reaction to child-care customs; and second, the carry-over effect of the basic personality patterns into certain of the larger institutional structures of the society.

Kardiner has candidly acknowledged that no attempt is made to determine how the primary institutions, the child-care complexes, came into being. He says: "The primary institution is treated as the taking-off point for the individual, not for the culture." Furthermore, it assumes that certain aspects of the culture, for the purposes of his analysis, have no direct bearing on the basic personality structure and hence can be ignored. And yet further, it acknowledges that in many cultures there are institutions that lie outside of and independent of the projective system.

My own impression is that a good deal more lies outside the projective system than falls within it. And a greater proportion of culture *in toto* falls in the category of activities that have no direct bearing on the basic personality structure. But they do have direct bearing on adult personalities, and, indeed, in certain phases, on child personalities.

Thus, while genuinely enthusiastic in my response to the analytical usefulness of the Kardinerian system within the limited area to which it applies, I as one anthropologist am left restless when contemplating the vast areas of the whole, which it leaves untouched. It is not the embracing conceptual and methodological approach that must ultimately be achieved in the maturity of personality and cultural studies. And this again, we say, is well recognized by Kardiner, who treats it, I think, as an experimental effort in a limited field.

Thus, although a continuing teamwork between anthropologists and psychiatrists will and must continue on a basis of mutual stimulation, and each must continue to learn from the other and both continue to co-ordinate their efforts, it does seem clear, as has already been noted by others, that the great revolution in this phase of science is not likely to occur until anthropologists working in the personality and culture field shift from the psychiatrists' view of society as a series of factors which frustrate and limit the individual's impulses and desires, back to an emphasis on culture as set solutions to problems, both individual and societal—as a means through which personality develops and the individual is enabled to engage in modes of activities and goal achievement that without society and culture would be quite impossible.

Audrey Richards, in commenting on the collection of papers in Kluckhohn and Murray's *Personality in Nature, Society, and Culture,* in the January 1951 issue of *Man,* concludes in these words: "This book confirms my view [i.e., Richards' view] that the next contribution to this important type of study is to be made by the anthropologist, and that it consists in the systematic classification of schemes of values in different cultures and the use of such classification as a scheme for the collection of data in the field with the anthropologist's own methods and own tools."

The focal point of attention in the application of such a scheme would be the uniformities which govern the formation and maintenance of values and their expression of the particularistic details of culture—and, through culture, of normal social behavior and the concomitant "common expression of emotional attitudes by peoples of different temperament and situational determinants on the conscious level." I am of the impression that in this area will be found the key concept that may reduce the present kaleidoscopic array of disparate facts of personality and cultural interrelationships to a reasonable order.

It strikes me as highly significant that two of the papers we heard yesterday were working attempts oriented in this direction, although not explicity expressed in these terms. Dr. Mowrer suggested in a generalized way an inversion of the Freudian concept in the hope that this may more comfortably fit the cultural facts. Dr. Henry sketched a concept of dialectic opposites which he hopes will breed a series of formulations of relationships between value maintenance mechanisms and individual psychological states, and conformance and nonconformance behavior.

Whatever the difficulties and insufficiencies that immediately appear in these tentatively formulated schemes, as they were so skillfully pointed out by Drs. Saslow and Masserman, they at least are indications of a felt need in the area, as has been indicated. And more of this sort of thing is assuredly in order.

In a brief recapitulative conclusion, I would say: New facts have come to us out of psychiatry. Attempts have been made, and are being made, to modify existing conceptual schemes to make place for the new facts. There is at present no scheme that enables us to handle all the facts. This has been made clearly evident in this room in the past two days. We await the development, in a repeating of Conant's words, of "the combination of a new concept with facts contradictory to the old ideas." This, by the nature of things, I think, should come from the anthropological half of the team. But if perchance it should come from the psychiatric moiety, I for one would propose for its originators honorary liaison fellowships in the American Anthropological Association, with remission of dues for life, and all the gold medals that John Gillin can wangle from the bestowers of social rewards.

Clara Thompson

PSYCHIATRY AND PSYCHOANALYSIS

I'M SUPPOSED to speak for the psychiatrists, but I also would like to say I speak as a naïve observer—because, since this is the first time I have ever attended a conference where there have been so many people of other disciplines, I really came as an observer and looked forward to finding out what was going on in other fields. I hoped I was going to get a great many things to carry back to my den and chew over for my own work. One thing I knew in advance would happen, because it always does: that hearing other people talk about their ideas was going to stimulate me to think, and this has certainly happened.

Still talking as a naïve observer, one of the first things which I learned here was that we psychiatrists speak another language, that this is something we have which seems to be all our own, and that perhaps one of our difficulties in communication is just this. This led me to stop and think about many phrases which I'd thought were a part of the common speech and clearly understandable to everyone. I began to wonder whether perhaps they were only passwords in a given guild. For instance, when I heard my colleague here talking about the child's devouring his father in order to get a superego, I started to wonder: In what way does the nonpsychoanalytical part of this conference understand this?

Also, I found myself somewhat at sea with some of the terms of the psychologists. "Learning Theory," for instance, I understand is something very important, and there is a war on about it, but I failed to find out what Learning Theory is. Finally, I found myself somewhat handicapped, in Dr. Richards' paper, by the technical terms of the Rorschach. Now this is all my fault; I am sure I should know all these technical terms, but I don't. And I think this simply shows that we ought to get together oftener and try to talk a language which we will all understand. I think that it implies that we ought to read more of one another's work. However, I think we do have to face the fact that none of us have time to become experts in the other person's field, and that, therefore, there is a minimum vocabulary which should be held in common.

In my thoughts before coming here, I wondered whether, in addition to hearing what other people were doing in their fields, we would be able to find ways in which the various disciplines could supplement one another. That is, could we really give each other insights, not only in terms of data, but could we possibly improve one another's techniques?

There is no doubt that the social sciences can give very valuable information to psychiatrists, and there's no doubt that the psychiatrists' high concentration on the individual —specifically the deviant or the borderline individual— can offer the social scientists data which they can use. In fact, I would say that the social scientists have shown evidence of appreciating this already. That is, you do already use some of our techniques and some of our approaches in getting at the roots of things. But I think that we, the psychiatrists, are the people who have not sufficiently explored the ways in which you can help *us* with *our* techniques, and here I would certainly agree with Dr. Hoebel that the psychiatrists seem to have absorbed very little of anthropology to date.

What I think we could learn from you, I would like to illustrate by what I learned at the recent meeting of the American Psychoanalytic Association in Cincinnati, at the cultural panel. Here I learned from several papers new things about my own technique. One of the papers was that of Dr. Henry, which gave me a great deal to think about. What I saw more clearly, as a result of this, was how cultural differences between the analyst and the patient can make for a real lack of communication. Since we analysts work chiefly on our own level—that is, our patients mostly come from our own social class—we are much too prone to think that if we are well analyzed and if we know our methods, that is all we need in order to understand a patient. However, what I came away from that conference with was the idea: If you do not really know the patient's frame of reference, you cannot communicate with him meaningfully. And one of the examples which Dr. Henry gave was that of the white-collar person who failed to understand two very simple little words which are used by analysts all the time.

Also, another thing which came out of that conference was pointing up the difficulty of communication with another race. I think that most of us were already somewhat aware of this as a problem.

From the point of view of a practicing psychiatrist I have found Dr. Kuhn's discussion of the Amish very revealing, and it has started me thinking about some of my own problems with isolated people. It seems to me that he has a beautiful limited and controlled experiment there with the people who are apparently so self-contained and relatively anxiety-free, and who resort to withdrawal and isolation as a means of preserving values and of producing security. This pointed out to me what has been puzzling me quite a while about understanding the isolated individual in our culture.

The Amish, in their failure to expose themselves to world problems, to any of the new gadgets, have found a kind of peace. This is the very thing which has often puzzled me about the isolated patient, when he uses such means as his individual neurotic adjustment; this is one of the reasons isolated individuals are so difficult to treat.

In passing, I just wanted to say another thing about his paper that it seems to me was not brought out in the discussion. In their failure to reach out and to grow, there must in time develop a certain lack of resilience in the personality. We have talked a great deal about the fact that too much exposure to anxiety is bad, but what we have not discussed is that people who do not expose themselves at all to anxiety tend to lack flexibility to meet it when it comes to them. This means that they have a certain inability to learn new ways rapidly. Of course, if their system is absolutely airtight—that is, quite safe—they do not need to learn new ways; but I think even the Amish are not bombproof. And it will be interesting, if we live to see World War III, to see what will happen should these people be scattered by the vicissitudes of war and have to find themselves intermingling with another culture. This, of course, is the problem of the isolated individual.

Certainly all the papers that were presented have contributed much information—and facts are very useful to psychiatrists because, compared with the anthropologist, our world of research is very limited. Freud, and analysts in general, have been trying to make a science of man on the basis of very circumscribed experiences.

Meetings such as this bring this fact home to me very much: That not only do we psychiatrists and psychoanalysts concentrate on the individual, which you all stress, but we concentrate on the individual in a special group—the upper middle class and the professionals. I even suddenly realized that my specialization is even narrower than that, since my chief business in life is training psychiatrists to be psychoanalysts. Therefore, over half the people whose life experiences I have studied and whose goals I think I understand pretty well are psychiatrists. This is really nothing but more and more about less and less. I think, therefore, the psychiatrists especially need conferences such as these, to keep us from becoming like the Amish.

I think I was really in danger of coming to view the world as it is seen through psychiatrists' eyes, as if this were really the American culture. Of course, that is a slight exaggeration. I don't think I am quite that closed-minded.

Dr. Mowrer's paper I found troublesome because, although I do not think it is the whole story, I think he has pointed up part of the truth—namely, that neurosis is essentially a sickness of the spirit and in the ego; but I think perhaps it would be a little clearer to me if I thought that he was talking chiefly about the secondary gains of illness; that is, that perhaps we could say the secondary gains of illness appear in appeasing the conscience by the neurosis.

One certainly finds at present in our society an increasing tendency to be very neurosis-conscious; that is, to forgive the criminal and what not, because he is emotionally ill.

Perhaps this is society's side of Dr. Mowrer's premise. We have already come to discover that this can be carried too far, but certainly the secondary gain, which comes from repressing the conscience, is only one aspect of the neurosis.

I have decided not to comment on all the papers; as I have said, most of the ideas presented do tend to enlarge the horizon of the psychiatrist and are, therefore, useful. But I have certain disappointments in this conference. One is that I don't think that we tried enough to find our points of agreement.

I have the impression that a great many individuals were here and that each one was very busy with his own project, without too much concern for how it fitted into the larger goal. I think that interest in one's own project is, of course, very important, but it seems to me in our next conference we could work more as a team. For instance, to take one practical idea, I wonder if it wouldn't have been helpful if the four of us reporting today could have given our preliminary ambitions for the conference on the first day and perhaps our summary on the last day, instead of keeping secret from you all these days what we were looking for. Perhaps we should have given you our preliminary ambitions even before you wrote your papers.

Secondly, I had hoped from this program to get some new slants on two things, which somehow hasn't happened. One was, can psychiatrists and anthropologists agree on the concept of "normal"? It seems to me we have quite divergent views on that at the present time, judging from Dr. Hsu's paper,[3] and if we cannot agree, it seems to me one of us ought to give up the use of the term.

I understand that one can say a thing is normal in a

[3] *Southwestern Journal of Anthropology,* 1952, *op. cit.*

given society, meaning it is a way of life that works after a fashion—that is, that one is not isolated. In this sense, I think we could say that the individuals in our homosexual subculture, which is seen especially in large cities, could be considered as normal, in that they belong to a group which accepts them. This is a group which has its own laws, it has its own loyalties, and if you have analyzed any homosexuals you will know that it has its own language, too, and its own means of communication with strangers on the street. Of course, we bring up here the favorite thing which bothers a psychiatrist: Was a Nazi in prewar Germany normal, or should we seek for another definition of normal which is really nearer to the goal of the psychiatrist, whose aim is not primarily to adjust his patient to his culture but to free him from his inhibitions and repressions, which often, at least indirectly, are imposed by the culture?

Related to this, I had hoped to learn something of the sociological angle about the goal of therapy in our society. It would seem to me, with the increasing tendency to regimentation and more rigid demands for conformity, one might well question whether one makes a patient sicker by helping him adjust or helping him become a deviant. Of course you may well say my question is academic, because there are not many people who are economically free to become deviants. Also, I would say that my questions can't be answered because of the difficulty of devising a scientific method about such vague or abstract things.

And this, by the way, brings me to a point which has been discussed here. I would like to go on the record as feeling that we still are in the hunch-intuition-sensitivity, unproven-hypothesis stage of our sciences; that attempts to organize are good, but that they can cramp us if they are accepted prematurely as the truth.

It seems to me something like this has become the problem of psychoanalysts: We are suffering from an extensive body of theory. Our tendency is to defend this theory against all odds, certainly many times to the detriment of research. In fact, in a recent review of my book I noted that one psychoanalyst criticized Sullivan's work because it did not present a complete theory. This, I felt, was a compliment rather than a criticism. Since we are all working in young sciences, it would be very good if we didn't make our generalizations too far ahead of our findings, and that when we do make them we should make them more tentative.

William A. Hunt

CLINICAL PSYCHOLOGY

BEFORE the symposium began Dr. Hsu asked me to put down in writing what I thought would transpire. Perhaps as a psychologist I should have differentiated carefully between hope and expectation, but for once I was in the happy position of not finding it necessary, since in my case the two were blended in a composite prediction. Since we are a small working group, all interested in an interdisciplinary approach and all having made previous contributions along that line, it seemed to me that some variant of the following course would be inevitable (I quote from my prediction):

"At first glance we shall seem to be devoting ourselves to a series of learned papers contributing basic data to many of our mutual problems, and this actually will be our main activity at the beginning of the symposium. The result will be both agreement and disagreement, but in any case there will be mutual stimulation, and, above all, mutual understanding. Out of this will gradually emerge some common agreement on the meaning of our terms—some common definition of the problems and of the techniques, observational or experimental, with which they are to be approached. While we will continue to listen to "factual" and "systematic" papers, their material per se will have less and less primacy for us, and we shall be more and more interested in fitting it into a broad conceptual and methodological framework. As such a framework develops, we shall occasionally drop back and reassess and reintegrate previous contributions. We shall also begin to look to the future as we highlight areas of present difficulty and see possible ways for their clarification.

"What the specific nature of our conceptual framework will be cannot be predicted. Since we all represent sciences, it will be objective rather than subjective, based on the observable datum rather than the rational principle; and since we all represent *young* sciences, there will be a heavy stress on definition of the phenomena to be studied, with observational techniques more prominent than experimental ones. The experimental designs that may emerge will be relatively simple and uncomplicated, and predominantly directed toward the testing of broad, general hypotheses. If the symposium is very fortunate it may even result in the development of a unified co-operative research program, but there hardly seems time enough for this. Semantic agreement, mutual pooling of data, and systematic integration, with some resulting guidance for the future—this is a very respectable goal. I predict we arrive at it."

That was at the beginning of the symposium. Now at its close I am tempted to say, "Gentlemen, I was robbed!" Such a statement, however, would not be quite true. I have not been robbed, but rather repaid in a coin that I had not anticipated. The symposium has been a valuable and thoroughly enjoyable one, but we have not achieved the semantic agreement, the systematic integration, and the unification of approach that I had hoped for and expected.

Dr. Gillin set the stage for such an integration in his opening paper. He laid down a broad general foundation on which we could hope to build a unified social science of man. Some details of the building I did not like, a rococo committee tacked on here, a prefabricated fellowship tacked on there; but the general plan was one I could accept. It was a plea for a scientific approach to the problems of man, and as such I welcomed it.

Apparently many of you differed with me in your response to Dr. Gillin's paper. Some of you tended to reject his experimentalism and even his fundamental empiricism. Some objected to specific aspects of his program. Some of you sensed an autocratic authoritarian element in his suggestions, and some of you even reacted to things that I didn't think were in the paper. In fact, I was amazed to see how many different things different people got out of Dr. Gillin's remarks. It even occurred to me that for a scientific population Gillin possibly had developed in this paper a much better projective device than the Rorschach Inkblots or the Thematic Apperception cards.

This "projective" quality of our response (we might liken it to the psychoanalytic phenomenon of countertransference or even use Harry Stack Sullivan's term paratactic distortion) should remind us that even when we perform as scientists in the austere atmosphere of a symposium, we are still basically all human beings, subject to all the dynamisms and defensive mechanisms that plague our favorite object of study—the man in the street. As Gillin pointed out in his paper, as psychiatrist, anthropologist, sociologist, or psychologist we are forever stressing the way the other fellow's point of view is influenced by his personality, his problems, his social milieu, his culture; and yet we forget that our own thinking is also influenced by these things. It was unfortunate that we could not have had more time to discuss this aspect of Dr. Gillin's paper. Perhaps every symposium should begin by agreeing to use psychology, sociology, anthropology, and psychiatry in understanding the conferees, and to apply these sciences in interpreting and facilitating the actual work of the symposium itself.

This led me to realize that before any attempt can be made at the integration of our various disciplines, certain fundamental requirements must be met. Integration must be preceded by an agreement on its demands: mutual understanding, personal tolerance, systematic permissiveness, agreement to abide by the rules of logic, and the acceptance of certain basic ground rules of science. It is rather like the diplomatic situation in which many long and arduous preliminary sessions are necessary before an agenda can be worked out for the final task of attempting to reach diplomatic agreement.

In Dr. French's discussion of Dr. Gillin's paper, many of these points became clear. I sensed in French's remarks (and there might have been some paratactic distortion on my part) a reluctance to accept Dr. Gillin's complete experimentalism, at times almost an abandonment of empiricism itself. There were echoes of many of the old controversies that always have plagued science when it approaches the study of man himself—empiricism versus pure rationalism, experimentation versus intuition, relativism versus absolutism, intellectual curiosity versus faith; with a continually lurking fear in the background that somehow science is not equal to the task of understanding man, and that its application to man's problems may somehow pull the entire structure of civilization down about our ears. It is a common attitude in the clinical psychology and psychiatry of today, and it represents a defeatism that the clinical disciplines must overcome if they are to assume their rightful place among the medical sciences. It is as though psychiatry feared that science would somehow deprive it of something valuable, that something would be lost, as though there existed in the attitude of psychiatry toward science some terrifying fear of libidinal restriction, some reawakening of an early castration complex. In a discussion of this problem, Dr. Boyer suggested to me that psychiatry may be trying to intellectualize its problems, to subjugate the devils of insecurity by verbal exorcism, and that the reality principle inherent in the scientific approach threatens this mechanism of defense.

Certainly as social scientists we should all agree that our most pressing problems today seem difficult to transpose to the controlled conditions of the psychological laboratory. Valuable as the study of the white rat has been to psychology, it still offers us relatively little of immediate value in solving the problems of human adjustment at either the individual or the social level. Science as a whole, however, is much broader than any of its parts, and its methodology is not limited to a brass-instrument approach.

There are any number of simple, relatively obvious but still serviceable, nonlaboratory experimental designs which can be applied to the problems of psychiatry if the psychiatrist wishes and has the courage to use them. It is possible to make explicit diagnostic or therapeutic predictions and then to check on their accuracy. It is possible to make an explicit statement of the symptomatic behaviors subsumed under any diagnostic category, and then through descriptive psychiatry to check the validity and consistency of such symptomatic groupings. These are simple procedures, but they are basic, and a discipline as youthful as psychiatry still has need of them.

That the resistance of the psychiatrist to the experimental method is a defensive one, based on some latent insecurity, is shown by his enthusiastic acceptance of the method when it "turns out right" and reaffirms rather than challenges his clinical preconceptions.

The need for further objective scientific evidence in the field of psychiatry is evidenced by Dr. French's attempt to justify the "clinical" approach by pointing to the growth of therapy. It is only fair to ask him, "Where is the objective evidence of this growth? Is it genuine biological growth or merely chaotic cell-proliferation?" Therapy is certainly increasing its tenets and its methods, its practitioners and its patients. In this sense it is growing, but whether it is growing like a weed or like a flower is not yet established, and too little critical energy is going into its scientific appraisal.

This fear of science comes out again in Dr. French's remarks about propaganda. He is afraid that a science of man will mean the perfection of propaganda methods which may be used to lead man astray. This seems logical, for certainly a perfect science of man would include the development of perfect tools of propaganda; but Dr. French, if he would espouse science, must take the bitter with the sweet. Nor need we despair, for a perfect science of man might also demonstrate the evils of propaganda and evolve methods for its control or elimination. Science *can* be misused, but that is little reason for abandoning the scientific approach itself and falling back on methods that offer even greater opportunity for deliberate misuse and the promulgation of error. Again one senses the lurking fear, the desire to avoid the personally unpleasant, and the preference for a harmless science that reaffirms our beliefs but does not challenge them.

The opening session was followed by many excellent papers designed to be informative and to acquaint the members of the conference with many and various specific approaches to our problems. The result was interesting but somewhat overwhelming, and I felt rushed along many times when I should have liked to pause for further discussion. Personally I should have liked to discuss with Dr. Henry some further applications of his formulae, and I should have liked more discussion of Dr. Masserman's reactions to Dr. Henry's paper, for Masserman led us back to the basic semantic and methodological problems upon which we must find agreement if we are to integrate.

At first my reaction at the close of the symposium was that there had been too many factual, informative papers, and insufficient consideration of basic methodological problems, but then I realized that if we are to achieve any unity in the science of man, the disciplines concerned must first understand one another. This, I think, the symposium achieved. We became acquainted with one another's techniques and methods, and with one another's prejudices and biases. This is a necessary preliminary if we are to achieve any genuine integration. I only wish we could have adjourned over the week end and met again on Monday. Then we could have set to work on the unified approach to our problems that I hoped for in my original predictions. As it was, our sessions were profitable—so profitable that I hope we can all meet again to go on from here.

Dr. Mowrer said have bearing on this, and I wish we might pursue this point further.

There is also a matter of assumptions about the therapy itself which I would like to mention. I am still not convinced that the process of analysis which is supposed to straighten the patient out necessarily prepares the individual to meet his social world afterward. Will the reorganizations of one's drives, values and attitudes—brought about by a successful analysis—really leave sufficient inner resources that the individual, when he returns to "normal" life again, will be able to live satisfactorily—I do not say happily—with his wife and children, or with other relatives, or other people with whom he has repeated contacts? The doubts I am raising are implicit in my own social psychological standpoint, namely, that of social interaction. From this standpoint the individual's behavior is determined not only by his inner and often unconscious motivations and adjustive mechanisms but by the external situation as well. If there is, then, a dual basis of any successful reaction, the individual in question must be prepared to meet further difficulties which may arise in the environment rather than from his internal elements. Just how the psychoanalysts meet this issue is still not clear to me.

Another of my concerns has to do with the whole topic of the possible experimental testing of various assumptions, hypotheses, and findings of psychoanalysis—and I am following Dr. Hunt here in his meaning of experiment. Of course, we all know people, certainly some psychologists included, who contend that these matters are not worth testing. I should like to suggest, if another such conference is held, that it would be enlightening for someone to survey the efforts to check the reliability and validity of psychoanalytic work along the lines which R. R. Sears did in his critique for the Social Science Research Council in 1943. (See their Bulletin No. 51.) While thoroughly critical, Sears did show that some, at least, of the Freudian hypotheses had been demonstrated in the laboratory and in various controlled observational studies. Since the publication of his work, a great deal of further testing has been carried on.[4] All such effort may be regarded as valuable in bringing about a more satisfactory rapprochement between psychology and psychoanalysis.

R. LINTON: There are two points I would like to take up, one of them in connection with this matter Dr. Young has just been talking about. Your successful culture, after all, is the one which manages to condition the individual successfully and provide him with enough rewards so that he will be satisfied in being a good, functioning member of society. That is the way all societies keep their members in line—not by the use of continuous police forces, et cetera, but by the development of a socially desirable type of superego, something that will represent a compromise between what would be the complete satisfaction for the individual, and what is necessary for the survival of society.

I do think, like you, with all respect to the psychoanalysts, that they are frequently highly unrealistic . . . as, for instance, when you get a case of a male homosexual in our society and the analyst tells him that, after all, he is a homosexual, and therefore he should express these tendencies instead of repressing them, and so on.

B. BOYER: Who says that?

R. LINTON: I could cite you three or four—I won't do it here—by name. But I know definite cases where this sort of thing, it seems to me, has been completely unrealistic as far as the external or situational accompaniments of the case go.

---

[4] For example, Winch, R. F., "Some data bearing on the Oedipus hypothesis." *Journal of Abnormal and Social Psychology,* 45, 1950, pp. 481-489; and "Further data and observations on the Oedipus hypothesis: the consequence of an inadequate hypothesis." *American Sociological Review,* 16, 1951, pp. 784-795.

The other point I would like to make: I have sat in on a great many of these conferences and attempts to get a meeting of minds, and particularly to understand one another's language and technical terms, and I would have one suggestion to make here—that is, if one employs plain English in a great many situations, it will be generally understood.

You know, there is the story of one of the newspaper editors in New York in the early days who was asked by a reporter how he should write up the news. His answer was: "Tell it so Sweeney Vanderbilt will understand it." Well, in the same way, I think that most ideas which have really been worked through, and which the individual himself understands, and in which he does not have to retreat behind a smoke-screen of technical terms, can be expressed in plain English that anybody can understand. This doesn't mean there is not any amount of use for technical terms; but where you are dealing with people of other disciplines it is not the place to trot them out. (By the way, anthropologists are just as guilty of this as anyone else.)

The third point I would like to make is that, after seeing a number of attempts of the different disciplines to get together in various ways, symposia and otherwise, I am convinced that the one way they really get together is when three or four representatives of different disciplines are put together on a problem. Here, as various things come up, they are going to find: "Well, this man has got the answer on that one; So-and-So has got the answer on something else."

For instance, in this past year at Yale I have been working with a psychiatrist, a man who has been psychoanalyzed, but who is also an M.D. of the practicing variety, with strong, shall we say, physiological leanings. I think this has contributed very much to the education of both of us, and in fact to the clarification of several points. It's very interesting as to what constitutes a psychosis when the symptoms are so obviously culturally shaped. The most vital question in this connection is: Is this individual completely out of touch with reality—in the ordinary definition—or not? You can show that from our work at Yale. I might say that apparently we get all the basic types of psychosis in any of the societies on which there have been adequate reports, societies other than European, but the symptoms do differ tremendously one from another.

B. BOYER: Well, I am the youngest of the psychoanalytic group represented here, and I think possibly it would be of value to have each of us express certain orientations in regard to these things. As the youngest, perhaps I should state what I understand to be the presently dominant aims of therapy by psychoanalysis. It has been stated that the aim of psychoanalysis is to free people of inhibitions and repressions. While this is to some extent true, it is a misrepresentation of facts. To say that a homosexual . . . (*Here Dr. Boyer was interrupted.*)

R. LINTON: I said three or four, but I can specifically say two cases.

B. BOYER: It doesn't matter. I have heard this sort of thing before.

R. LINTON: Where this is done?

B. BOYER: According to my orientation in psychoanalysis, such things are just not done except in the most isolated of circumstances—and psychoanalysis is not being employed, but the analyst, for specific reasons, is using some other sort of therapy. My therapeutic aims with my patients are precisely what Dr. Linton would desire—to help condition the individuals successfully to become useful, functioning members of society, with socially desirable types of superego and without the need of external conscience. Within this framework, the object is to have them do whatever they wish, and without the need of employing deviant patterns of action, harmful to themselves or others. To my thinking, this goal is the therapeutic aim of psychoanalysis. In the earlier days of psychoanalysis extensive personal analyses were not part of the learning curriculum. Dr. Siegfried Bernfeld once told me that he was a training analyst before he had his own psychoanalysis. However, since then ego-psychology has flourished, and the earlier goals of psychoanalysis, which were primarily to free inhibitions, have long since been superseded.

Another point: Dr. Mowrer raised the question, which I think is really germane to this whole discussion—and I think it brings together the diverse opinions of the psychiatrist or psychologist and anthropologist—of what is normal and what is abnormal. I hear all the time, "Well, you psychiatrists deal with deviates and the information you are giving us isn't really applicable to our work, because we deal with normals." Dr. Hunt asked me the question: Do we, each of us, in a symposium like this, have a fear that science will in some way take something away from us as individuals? This is something which I find every day in my clinical practice—that intellectualism is used as an ego defense, and that we do make our own patterns of thinking into neurotic symptoms frequently; and I think this is a very real problem among all of us . . . that we are afraid to give up these intellectual patterns which we have established as some of our defenses and are symptoms of our own little private neuroses. I don't think this is an unusual thing at all. I think this is widespread.

Certainly the anxieties aroused among us during this conference have illustrated this point. A couple of times I have become angry. Others have gone to sleep while points contradictory to their theses have been presented. Some have presented papers and then left the room while their discussants spoke.

The last question which Dr. Linton raised was that of the number of satisfactions, the rewards, in the society which make it into a successful society. I want to ask a question in return. I don't know the answer to his question. I was just thinking of the Alorese, who are presumably an old society. It would appear that they are, and yet there seem to be very few satisfactions and rewards in the Alorese society.

R. LINTON: That is quite true; but it is interesting to note—and this, by the way, has a general reference to anthropological work—that Dr. Dubois never succeeded in establishing contact with any of the successful men in the Alorese society. They were much too busy going around dunning people for loans and trying to extract loans. It would be interesting to ask how many members of boards of directors of the larger corporations among ourselves have been contacted by either socio-psychiatrists, psychoanalysts—or shall I say psychologists. They are likely to wind up in their hands. But there must be certain satisfactions in this society, and here again you have to take into account the particular slant of the observer. For instance, those of you who have read *The Patterns of Culture* may remember tho horrific picture of the Dobuan society. If you read the Dobuan material, you will find, however, that the man and wife alternately spent six months with first the husband's people and then the wife's people. Either party was safe for half year. What is played up is the stress period here. Now, someone else, who believed that the world was bright and beautiful, would probably have played up how happy the partner in residence was during this period. There are many kinds of satisfactions, but there are certainly degrees also. There are many cultures which—I think you can say definitely—provide more satisfactions for the individual and impose fewer stresses on him, culturally, than others.

R. P. WANG: I want to say, from my own experiences as a psychiatrist, the only way we can interest a psychiatrist in the substance of this symposium is to engage him in a definite, concrete problem. If it were not for the fact that I participated in a research project and did some field work in New York's Chinatown two years ago, I would never quite appreciate the kind of things we discussed at this conference, and no amount of reading is going to help the situation much. If you have not done any practical work in cross-cultural studies, you will not care to read about anthropology, and what you do read you do not understand.

I am in full agreement with those who said we should be problem-minded. Only by working together on a definite problem can we persons from different disciplines learn from one another and achieve better understanding. Just this morning, an anthropologist and I were talking about the excessive interest the Chinese immigrants in Chinatown showed toward the news stories on rape in the Chinese-language newspaper. After I heard the story, I asked the anthropologist: "What is your interpretation?" He said it showed the pattern of social behavior among the immigrant group toward the old culture, etc. I said that I saw that too, but as a psychiatrist I felt more keenly in seeing through this incident an indication of the mechanism of releasing anxiety and tension among the first-generation Chinese-Americans by reading about the forbidden, or something like that.

My point in bringing up this conversation is that this is a good example of how the same event is seen differently by people of different disciplines. The anthropologist also saw what I had seen, but, to borrow a Gestalt terminology, to him the cultural and social features are "the figure," and the personality feature is "the ground." To me, as a psychiatrist, the personality feature is "the figure," and the social and cultural features are "the ground." This is precisely the value of teamwork in having people of different disciplines work together. We all look at the same thing, but we have a different degree of sensitivity toward certain aspects of the same thing.

Therefore we can further enrich one another's experiences, broaden our perspective, and deepen our understanding.

Another comment I would like to make concerns the entire relationship between anthropology and psychiatry. We all know Freud was the first person who tried to cross the border of psychiatry into anthropology, although by this time his early work, *Totem and Taboo,* is, I understand, already a taboo among the anthropologists.

In recent decades Kardiner, Linton, and others were the first to bridge the work of anthropology and psychiatry by a systematic application of psychoanalytic principles to the study of the entire culture. In the original concept of the basic personality, Kardiner called the childhood disciplines and other matters the primary institutions, and the folklore and religion the secondary institutions or projective systems; therefore, the basic personality structure, or cultural pattern, was seen as a product of child-rearing. Nowadays we are more inclined to think that the personality structure and cultural pattern are undoubtedly greatly influenced by childhood experiences, but many other factors also come into play, and these further influence the method of child-rearing. We also think that religion, art, and philosophy are not necessarily the result of childhood experiences or projections of personality conflicts, but they may have values by themselves, ideologically or otherwise. In other words, we do not regard these as only compensatory mechanisms for personality conflicts, but believe they may have positive values of their own.

Linton has later gone beyond that and seen that the basic personality concept may be all right for a simple uniform society like that of the primitive culture of a village group on a South Sea island. Linton has conceived the idea of the status personality, as he so well stated in *The Cultural Background of Personality.* In that concept of status personality, he sees that people in different statuses in the society may have different personality configurations; that of men differs from that of women, that of the employers differs from that of the employees, et cetera. Therefore, he conceives of the status-linked response configuration or status personality as a further differentiation from the basic personality concept.

Now, I understand that Linton and Erich Fromm are working together on the application of the concept of social character in the seminars at Yale. As I see it, the social-character concept is in some way similar to that of status personality in that it is "that part of the character structure that is common to most members of a group." Therefore, it can be any group; the upper class or the lower class, the employers or the employees, and so on. However, it further differs from basic personality in that Fromm believes the social character is not only influenced by the method of child-rearing or childhood experiences, but is also the result of interaction of various other forces, such as the social, economic, and ideological forces. This, certainly, is a much broader concept than that basing upon purely individual or strictly psychoanalytic orientation.

These may sound very elementary, but I thought it might be helpful to review some of these basic concepts.

R. LINTON: Might I say just a word to this. When I had barely begun an interest in the field of personality and culture (when I came to Columbia), what I knew about before I had contact with Kardiner is pretty well summed up in one chapter of my *Study of Man.*

Then I worked with Kardiner, and I learned a great deal in the process. However, I never agreed with him on this matter of primary and secondary institutions, which Kardiner himself had never figured out. Essentially the idea was, you see, the particular cultural patterns of child-rearing would normally produce such-and-such a personality configuration: but as an anthropologist I necessarily, naturally, was quite unwilling to accept that this then in turn would make the rest of the culture. One of the things I find in psychoanalysts who attempt to work with anthropological material is always their assumption of a sort of a primo-Garden of Eden, in which a set emerges, made up of individuals who are *tabula rosa,* who are newly born and who are going to be shaped. As a matter of fact, all societies have a very long history. Most of their content comes by borrowing from the outside. The one way in which the personality, the basic personality, does come into play here is that an institution which is fundamentally at variance with the attitudes, and so forth, which are common to the group and which are basic to the rest of their culture, isn't going to be received. For example, you would not be able to introduce prize fighting as a form of amusement into the Amish community. You have the particular predisposition, shapings, which the child has experienced, influencing the way he will react to the adult culture.

Well, now, this is completely different from the idea that the basic personality is really the common denominator, which would include a number of attitudes and values and certain concrete understandings as to what is proper behavior, not only for the individual himself, but for other individuals. Now, I think you can show there *is* such a thing as basic personality for small, culturally homogeneous groups. As I tried to say the other night over here, we tried out a three-directional approach on it, and the results of a study of the culture itself, of what we assumed from clinical experience in our own society to be the probable results of certain patterns of child-training, and the results of projective tests obviously do not check 100 per cent. If they did we would know somebody was lying; but they do check fairly well, enough to show there is something definite here.

When it comes to national character, you are dealing with a different situation. A modern nation, in the first place, is usually a more or less accidental political aggregate. Within this you have different local groups; you also have class distinctions; you have age and sex differences, and so on. Now, each of these groups or categories that society sets up is expected not only to behave in certain ways but also to have certain emotional reactions and certain values, and these are expected to differ from one group to another within the society. The basic personality under these circumstances, or the national character, would seem to be the common denominator of the status personalities, as I have called them, for all these various groups, and it wouldn't amount to very much, I think, in the average modern nation.

C. BABCOCK: Are you using those two terms, basic personality and national character, synonymously?

R. LINTON: Decidedly not. The basic personality has been used for small homogeneous groups. National character is a term that involves the interactions of large heterogeneous units. And I might say you can do this for a national group. You can say, in general, they share certain ideas and values; but these are much less than that sort of thing that is involved in the basic personality.

C. BABCOCK: Would you then say that, since you say one might be heterogeneous and the other homogeneous, they share things in common?

R. LINTON: Only in the case where certain values are recognized by everybody in the group. But the point is that in your national group the number of elements that are shared, that are held in common, relative to the local culture, are certainly much less than in a small homogeneous group like an American Indian tribe.

M. KUHN: It seems to me we are still in danger of not meeting the very first requirement that Robert Winch put forth—that we come to grips with the range of issues that need to be clarified. We will not even become aware of this range of issues as long as we deal with one after another of the prevalent theories of personality—Freudian, Hullian, Lewinian, and the like.

One way to go about the identification of the issues is to set forth *the criteria for a personality theory which our present social science findings impose.* The first criterion is that the personality theory structure *the nexus between the individual and society* in such a way as to square with the universals of original nature on the one hand and with the differentials of contrasting cultures on the other. Freudian theory is deficient in both respects: Lewinian theory affords a structuring only for the second; Hullian theory is moot in respect to the assumptions it makes about the first. The second criterion is that the personality theory must structure the locus of culture.

R. LINTON: Is there a locus of a generalization?

M. KUHN: Of course not. I will revise this second criterion to make it clear what I have in mind. The second criterion is that *personality students and social scientists must agree on what they want the term culture to mean.* And following this, there must be, in an adequate personality theory, an adequate structuring of the *acquisition of culture by the individual.* This latter requirement would constitute a third criterion.

A third criterion for personality theory is that it must afford a structuring of *the personality concomitants of cultural homeostasis and cultural change.* Cultural rigidity and cultural change must have some kind of reference in the individual members of a society. Culture doesn't just change in a free-floating way, or stand still in a free-floating way.

A fourth criterion which social science places on personality theory is that it structure adequately *the process of social interaction*—that is, of mutual modification and mutual support in this realm that has come to be called, in some ways unfortunately, "interpersonal relations." One of the special problems in this realm for the social scientist is that of the leader-follower process. I believe it would be fair to say that most social scientists find the contemporary theories of personality deficient in structuring this process, or, more precisely, in structuring the personality components relevant to it.

A fifth criterion for an adequate personality theory is that it afford a structuring of *both directed and undirected behavior.* The Freudian theory and most of its variants are preoccupied with undirected or indirect behavior. Other theories are, for the most part, concerned only with directed behavior.

A sixth criterion requires that personality theory specify *the function of language* in overt behavior, thought, and fantasy.

A final criterion is that an adequate personality theory must structure *the process of internalization*—the whole realm of phenomena variously referred to as "identification," "introjection," "role-taking," "having a model or hero," "acquiring an imago," etc.

It seems to me that the issues to which Robert Winch referred fall in these categories, and a further conference ought to address itself to them.

DR. HENRY: I would like to address myself for a few minutes to two problems: How shall psychiatrists, psychologists, sociologists, and anthropologists come to understand one another? And, secondly, what do we mean when we say they should work together? I speak on the basis of two and a half years' participation in a faculty seminar at Washington University in which were included psychiatrists, psychiatric social workers, anthropologists, psychologists, and experimental psychologists; and two other seminars, in which participated zoologists, anthropologists, and psychologists. The latter were devoted to the general problem of basic psycho-biological concepts.

One of the things that struck me was the fact that individuals participating in the seminars frequently showed an unwillingness to read in the other person's field. Now, this became a terrific obstacle. The anthropologist in presenting his position had to start from very simple basic notions, and he might be given an hour or an hour and a half to present his point of view. I found that in the seminar with the zoologists I was the only one who knew anything about primate behavior, not to mention anthropology. Of course, zoologists, as you must know, are very often concerned with the performance of cells and the performance of very low forms, and deal relatively little with primate behavior. So, it seems to me absolutely essential that people take time off and learn the field of the other fellow. This is a basic problem in arriving at mutual understanding. Then the matter of working together on a problem: What problems are the representatives of anthropology and psychiatry to work on? How is this working together to come about? How shall anthropologists and psychiatrists come to know one another? Shall the anthropologist present a program to the psychiatrist and say, "Look how I can enlighten you," or are the psychiatrists going to come to the anthropologists with the exceedingly difficult problem, the solution of the problem of an individual's behavior disorder, and say to them, "We need light on this; we want you to help us"? So it seems to me the problem of what one is to work on, and how this collaboration is to come about, must be solved.

Personally, my work with the clinicians has come in an entirely informal way on the basis of friendship, general discussions and, finally, by taking some of the psychiatrist's material and working over it and saying, "This is what I have come out with." This sometimes seemed of interest to the psychiatrists and sometimes not.

Then, if the psychiatrist feels that these things are interesting, we pick a common problem and work on it together. This has been my experience. That is to say, I have come to collaborate with psychiatrists largely on the basis of informal contacts, and I wonder whether other pathways are open.

The problem of projection was raised by Bill Hunt with respect to John Gillin's paper. This seems to me to be an ever-present danger. I remember presenting an analysis of a family case record from the child guidance clinic at one of the seminar meetings of the psychiatrists, anthropologists, and psychologists. One psychiatrist shook his finger at me and said, "You are maligning good psychiatry." This came as a blow to me. I still don't know exactly what I was doing that made him feel I was maligning good psychiatry. But what I feel was present in this group was the *anticipation* of maligning, and I think we must constantly guard against the danger of projection. There is involved in this something that Dr. Thompson said: Our weakness is in not extracting from what others have said at this conference the positive aspects. This is because we sometimes tend to project into what the other person says what we fear he is liable to mean.

O. KLINEBERG: I have just two points I should like to make. One is related to the discussion of the whole morning. I wonder whether we can speak of the collaboration or co-operation of anthropology and psychiatry in general, or whether we have to ask *which* psychiatrists can work with *which* anthropologists. It seems to me that there is such a tremendous range of points of view in anthropology and such a tremendous range of points of view in psychiatry—and, of course, that applies to sociology and psychology as well—that to put it in these general terms, as if it were possible for the *two sciences* to come together, is misleading. We should rather think in terms of what *individuals* are doing in these various fields, places where they can get together on a problem, of those anthropologists and psychiatrists who can talk one anothers' language sufficiently to be mutually comprehensible. That is perhaps a more fruitful way of looking at the problem of co-operation.

If I may be personal for a minute—there are a number of anthropologists with whom I can communicate, and there are a number of anthropologists with whom I simply cannot communicate. They say things which I misinterpret, or they say things which I can't understand, unfortunately. There are some whose language I can speak and some whose language I cannot speak; in this latter case, mutual communication becomes quite impossible.

The second point I want to make refers to the exchange between Miss Babcock and Ralph Linton about the concept of national character. I would like to suggest to both of them—and I would like to hear Ralph's comments in particular—that it is an extreme restriction of the concept of national character to think of it as applying only to those things that are held in common by all the people in a particular nation... and again I am afraid I am repeating myself. Let me take a specific example. I was looking over the material on suicide a while ago. Suicide, of course, is never something which is held in common by all members of a national group; but it turns out that regularly, year after year, over a long period of time, there are just about ten times as many suicides in Austria as in Ireland—just ten times as many—and that ten times as many stays pretty constant. In the periods of years over which I looked at the data, the variation is between three and four suicides per hundred thousand in Ireland and between thirty and forty per hundred thousand in Austria. Well, that may give us a lead to some interesting differences between the frequency of certain types of problems in the two groups. This example clearly does not refer to something common to all the members of two groups, but it still has a bearing on the question of national character.

Now the point I made yesterday about homogeneity and heterogeneity, which is similar to something you had in mind,

Miss Babcock, is also, I think, pertinent. When we speak of particular characteristics of groups I believe we ought to consider the whole range of behavior and not just the common denominator. I think we would restrict our area of activity, and also restrict unduly the knowledge that might be important, if we thought only of those characteristics which were held in common by all the members of a national community.

R. LINTON: May I speak to that? What bothers me is why you should regard the suicide rate of a group as necessarily indicative of the personality, of a personality norm for the society. Why not regard it rather as a culture pattern? As a Japanese friend of mine, who certainly I would say had a personality of a type that I could easily match among Europeans, once remarked, "Suicide frequently avoids embarrassment."

K. YOUNG: But that in itself is personality.

R. LINTON: But is that personality or is that culture pattern?

O. KLINEBERG: Why must we make that distinction?

R. LINTON: Is there no distinction between personality and impact of culture pattern?

F. HSU: I have just one brief thing to say about suicide. No one denies that there is a Japanese culturally patterned usage of hara-kiri. But, on the other hand, I do think there is a very intimate connection between the rate of suicide and personality orientation.

This is especially clear among the Japanese of Hawaii; away from any connection with the emperor cult, but next door to Caucasian-Americans. These Japanese are first-, second-, third-, and fourth-generation Americans just as the Chinese of Hawaii are. I have compared the suicide and attempted suicide rates of the three racial groups. The remarkable thing is that the suicide and attempted suicide rates of the Japanese and the Chinese have been, for a fifteen-year period, half of that of the Caucasians. This ratio is the same when we compare only incidence of attempted suicides. That is to say, Caucasians attempt twice as many times as Japanese and Chinese. A further point of difference is found between the two sexes. Females in all societies probably attempt more suicides than they actually succeed . . . but among the Japanese and Chinese females the ratio is four unsuccessful ones to one successful one; while among the Caucasian females the ratio is over eleven unsuccessful ones to one successful one.

R. LINTON: How much of this is post-barbiturate, do you know? What I mean is the exceedingly popular American habit, especially on the West Coast, by which ladies who have had a tiff take an overdose of sleeping pills carefully calculated not to be fatal, but at the same time to punish the gentleman concerned by a bad scare and a trip to the hospital. It strikes me that this is an emergent culture pattern which may perhaps replace the "delicate health" by which Victorian ladies kept their husbands under control.

F. HSU: The fact that the attempted suicide rate for Caucasian males is twice as high as those of Japanese or Chinese would seem to rule out the post-barbiturate factor.

M. HERSKOVITS: The problem of the normal versus the abnormal seems to have been moving in and out of everything we have had to say during our sessions.

In all our discussions of this question a hidden hedonistic premise invades much of our thought, almost a utopian premise that basically must be studied so that we can avoid maladjustment of any kind. That is, we hold the adjusted, the happy, individual as the desideratum. We strive to develop the efficiently functioning individual as the ideal.

Yet a study made on the Micronesian island of Ifaluk by Spiro, where what would seem to be a utopian setting prevails as far as all outer indications of the life of the people are concerned, is enlightening. He found that on this island there were no aggressions, no competition, that no one ever raised his voice to anyone. But he also found there was a culture where there is no graphic or plastic art, where the music is extremely rudimentary, where story-telling is almost absent, and where a terrific fear of the very dangerous ghosts of evil people—there being no evil people actually in life—bedevil the inhabitants. One cannot but ask, then, is utopian behavior the thing we should strive for? Oughtn't we to look at the hidden premise in our assumption? Should we not ask ourselves what sort of human being we feel desirable? Should we not ask the individual to attain enough adjustment to get along in his culture, but not expect him to solve all his problems and perhaps thus lose much of the source of stimulation that eventuates in socially desirable behavior?

When we try to solve this problem in a cross-disciplinary way, we go to the literature . . . and there we meet with serious difficulties. Whenever the subject of adjustment or maladjustment comes up in education, in psychiatric theory, in psychology, in sociology, some reference to such people as the Zuni, the Alorese, the Manus, crop up. Now, the accounts of the psychology of these peoples is very interesting, but how is the person who is not conversant with the total range of the literature on the subject to evaluate just these presentations? How is he to guess that in none of these cultures, except one, have studies been made testing current hypotheses, and that the hypotheses tested have not always held up under reanalysis?

Even the value of factual cross-cultural material is not easy to know. Take one point that Dr. Boyer made in his attempt to go to cross-cultural materials, where he stated that among the Dahomeans a serpent-deity exists which is supposed to impregnate women and is therefore an important symbol in the conventional psychoanalytic scene. The serpent does enter very subtly in the Dahomean world view, but in no way that I was ever able to establish, in field research, does it have anything to do with conception and, by extension, with sex. Yet when I asked Dr. Boyer later his source, he cited a perfectly respectable, if somewhat outdated, monograph by Spieth on Ewe, a related people. Now how could Dr. Boyer be expected to know that Spieth was a missionary who was greatly influenced by the misconceptions of Dahomean religion set down by early travelers, wherein the serpent had been elevated to a position that it does not have in the actual cosmogony of the culture?

What the answer to that problem may be I do not know. Perhaps the only answer, as has been stated, is to develop good personal relations between these people in different fields who are interested in similar problems, and that if we center our discussions around problems, rather than around disciplines, we will then have something on which really to get together. One of our problems is a human problem. Someone who had attended many interdisciplinary seminars once said that it takes a whole year of discussion to get members of different disciplines to talk *to* each other rather than *at* each other.

If that is the case, we have not done so badly in these three days of talking *at* each other. Perhaps we have made a beginning in the difficult task of talking *to* each other.

J. GILLIN: I guess what I have to say follows right in with Dr. Herskovits. Seemingly, we all want to get together on a working basis. I would like to say that in my opening remarks to the conference, the objective was to accentuate the positive and, in order to be consistent with my own preaching, I did try to lay out certain suggestions; but I would not hold, for example, that a logico-deductive-empirical arrangement of our theoretical propositions is the only possible one, by any means. I did, however, try to offer some positive suggestions for your consideration in logico-deductive-empirical form.

Now, there has been a good deal of talk about problems, and I would like to suggest, in line with what Dr. Herskovits was perhaps moving toward, that we have a problem right here: namely, how can psychologists, psychoanalysts, sociologists, and anthropologists better understand one another? When we talk about organizing our knowledge so that we can work together, in effect, what we are actually talking about is the formation of a new, small cultural system, if you will permit that word. That is, we are trying to work out new patterns of collaboration, intercommunication, and interaction; and, of course, this is done through a group. Now, we have a group here, and this happens to be a group which was, to begin with, somewhat heterogeneous in the sense that it wasn't selected on the basis of personality qualifications or congeniality. In fact, many of the members did not know one another. We have experts in culture; we have experts in groups, sociologists; we have experts in personality. Perhaps one of our problems would be simply to concentrate on how we might organize groups of this sort, how we might develop culture patterns of collaboration, and how we possibly might select personalities who would be congenial to this sort of effort.

Now, if we know anything about these things, we know a project like this can't be accomplished in two days and a half. I ask myself, therefore, if one of the things we have learned out of this may not be that, in planning the pathways for reaching the goals that we all seem to agree upon, we shouldn't make this a major project. It may require something like a three-month co-operation, and this means more than sitting on our hard chairs here seven or eight hours a day. I would like to leave the suggestion that perhaps a summer conference might be appropriate, a summer seminar, or something of that sort. We have rubbed the rough edges off; we have worked out our own narcissism; we have gone through the sounding-board function, and so on. With a longer period together we could really get down to cases and end up with something worth while.

Now, I have attended, like a good many other people other conferences somewhat like this. By the end of three days, we usually turn out to be quite congenial; but I don't see any noticeable progress toward the integration of the human sciences, that is, noticeable in the sense we are able to handle practical problems any better on the basis of our deliberations than before. Each one of us knows more about the fields involved, to be sure, and such a conference is very valuable in that sense. But I would like to point out these get-togethers are not a matter of merely knowing something in general. For my part, I want to know something that can be put into practice, and I have to know it from other fields as well as my own.

Forgive me for bringing up things that I am concerned in ... but may I mention three research projects that I am directing now. One is the study of a culture of the inside of a veterans' psychiatric hospital—the idea is to examine the culture with the possibility of seeing whether or not it provides problem-solving experience for the patients. The big question is how to cut down the number of returnees who are sent out to their communities but get into trouble because they are not able to solve their problems on the outside of the hospital. Perhaps there is something wrong with the culture of the hospital. But we anthropologists can't answer that completely. As Dr. Lebar and the other people who are working with me know, we as anthropologists don't have all the answers. We have to talk to sociologists, psychologists, and psychiatrists, and we are glad to use them on a team of problem-solvers.

Another project in which I am involved concerns the cultural organization of Air Force bases. Ridiculous? Maybe it isn't anthropology, but at any rate the Air Force comes to us and says, "We have got a problem here we want solved. Why is it GI and officer personnel don't get along as well together sometimes as they might? . . . Why is there a certain lack of morale at certain bases?"—and so on. Well, I am perhaps foolish to get involved in such things, but I do need a concentrated human science to apply to such problems, and I think other people do, too.

A study of the political aspects of Latin-American culture which I am directing brings in political science. Anthropology is involved in it. As somebody has pointed out, we anthropologists used to go out to relatively small societies, where we played the role of economists, political scientists, theologians, and everything else to try to provide a configurated picture of the culture as a whole. When we are dealing with these problems in more complex situations, we would be silly not to make use of the skills, the points of view, and the premises that you other people have developed.

My point is this: It is hard to do unified, configurated interdisciplinary studies at this time, simply because the material is in such a disorganized, scattered form; and I think that it would be useful not only to ourselves but to the world at large in these perilous times to reach a working—not merely an ideological—agreement among the so-called disciplines concerned with human behavior.

C. BABCOCK: When I came to the conference room on Thursday, someone I had not yet met talked with me a few minutes and then said to me, "Do you speak to Dr. Thompson?" I had not yet met her, and, having looked forward to meeting her with great pleasure, said, "No, not yet." And the person said to me, "Oh, you are of another school." So, I should like to report to you that Dr. Thompson and I both know each other and speak to each other.

DR. YACORZYNSKI: I believe that this story of Dr. Babcock's illustrates some of the things that I want to say and some of the things that Dr. Klineberg has pointed out. It is probably true that all the members of this symposium have at one time or another dealt with various disciplines. I myself have had the opportunity of working with a number of psychiatrists, neurologists, neurosurgeons, endocrinologists, and so on, for the last thirteen years. And I am impressed by the fact that if we have the opinion of six different psychiatrists we usually have six different viewpoints expressed. As a consequence of these factors, I am not so much impressed by the common grounds that we are attempting to attain, because we are all agreed that our common meeting-ground is an effort to understand man. I have been impressed rather, not by the similarity of our general effort, but the differences which exist between us. Dr. Klineberg has also expressed the idea that in cultures we should study not only the similarities of the personality within the group but the differences which exist between individuals in the group. In my opinion we should do the same thing here. That is, rather than asking ourselves the question, "What common grounds do we have?" we should ask ourselves the question, "What makes the differences between us?" When we approach the problem in this manner, then we can further ask ourselves the question whether these differences are due to training or the personality of the individual. I believe that both training and the predilections of the individual involved determine to a great extent what his general orientation will be. The differences between us may exist also on the basis of the material which we handle, the subject matter, methods, and theories. I believe that we should get a clear statement of these differences, much the same as one attempts to get a clear idea of a patient and how this patient differs from other individuals. When we understand these differences between us, then, rather than orienting our effort toward finding common grounds of endeavor, we can actually determine why we differ and how these differences can be resolved.

I have found this morning's discussion extremely interesting and illuminating because it took into consideration the broader aspects of the general field. It seems to me that when we state our own problems, our own ideas, we are bound by the time and space in which we find ourselves. I mean by this the theories, tools, and methods which we propound are determined within the culture with which we deal as well as with the particular era in which we live. Suppose we had held our discussion in India rather than here, and suppose that we had under consideration the philosophies of that country rather than our own. If that were true, then our orientation would have been entirely different. I believe that sometimes we become too much enamoured with our field, so that we do not realize that we are working within the historical present. I know, for example, in my own case when I lecture to psychiatry students, I frequently ask myself the question, "What would have happened if I had been delivering these lectures thirty years ago? What would I be saying at that time?" If I oriented my lectures toward the well-accepted discipline of that era which had most of the scientific facts, I would be teaching them Titchner's existentionalism. Unfortunately, as we view these facts in our present day we find them to be useless as far as understanding the individual is concerned. Therefore, if I wanted to be scientifically rigid at that time I would be lecturing on the results of well-controlled experiments and facts that could not be controverted. I would, however, be giving them material that in time would lose all its usefulness. If at that time I happened to be a Freudian, and accepted the ideas which we expound, teach, and hold at the present time in this field, I am sure that I would have been discharged from my university position. I might have been able, if I had been bold enough, to propound the Gestalt viewpoint. Also, if I had been daring enough I might have lectured on Watson's behaviorism. Putting our present discussion into an historical perspective of that nature, we can see that in the last few years tremendous changes have taken place. If we project our thinking into the future, we can realize that what we hold dear now as to techniques and theories may be entirely different in the next few short years. In my opinion, this is one of the questions which we have overlooked, and I would have been much happier if our orientation had been toward the possibilities of what may happen in the future.

This is not to say that these possibilities were not mentioned throughout the discussion, but I think the discussants this morning pointed up that argument very well. It seems to me that the less bounded we are by our present, by time and space, the more likely are we to work out eventually in the long run, in the years to come, common ground on which most of us may work.

O. MOWRER: In connection with the issue that Dr. Young was raising, it seems to me that it is this—and I would like to state this just as sharply and unequivocally as I can: The problem that we face in the field of psychotherapy today in connection with personality as it relates to psychotherapy, and the problem that we face in part with respect to what is normal and what is abnormal, is the question as to whether we are dealing, in the psychoneurotic individual, with a case of cultural inadequacies.

I put this a little differently yesterday by suggesting that it is a question of whether we are dealing with real personal immaturity. As far as I am concerned, personally, I have taken an explicit position on this. I think psychotherapy is a cultural task and not a medical task. I take this position after previously having held the opposite one—essentially the Freudian view—but I found it untenable. I think many of the confusions and the difficulties we have encountered in this conference are the same ones that eventually drove me out of that position into a different one.

Now, parenthetically, I would like to say that as far as our purposes here are concerned, it seems to me it is not at all a question of who is going to do therapy, but it is a question of what *is* therapy. And when we get that issue settled, I think we will be in a lot better position to raise the question of professional prerogatives in this field.

So what I have to say, what I have already said and have to say now is on the question: What is psychotherapy? And for the moment I don't care who does it, except I would hope that the people who do therapy would know what it is.

Now let me pick up at a point where I more or less stopped yesterday. I spoke of dissociation as being the essence of neurosis. The essence of therapy consists in interpretation or the attempts on the part of the therapist to resist and oppose the dissociative trends in the neurotic patient. The therapist is constantly pushing back together in the patient things that belong together, which the patient, in order to resolve conflicts in a shortsighted pathological, pathogenic fashion, has pushed apart. As Freud well saw many years ago, this inevitably reactivates resistance, or transference. On the part of the patient, what does this mean more specifically? It means that in the psychotherapeutic situation there is something I like to call a therapeutic regression. It means that you, as therapist, create a situation in which an immature individual—a physically mature but emotionally and morally immature individual—can go back to that period of childhood, if you will, and pick up unresolved struggles with authority figures, parent figures, with surrogates of the culture.

Now there are two things that can happen; there are two points of view one can take here, depending on what one's theory is: If one assumes that the difficulty with this individual is that he is oversocialized, that his previous socializers have been too strict, irrational, severe, and so on, that the biological impulses have been blocked that need to be expressed, then the therapist, within the Freudian framework, needs to say, "But, oh, I don't believe these things—these things are really bogeymen out of the past. Your parents were unrealistic about this," and so on. The therapist thus tries to reduce the severity of the superego by showing that he is not this kind of a parent, that he is "accepting," he is lenient, he is indulgent, "anything goes." But when you try to do this, you run squarely into difficulties that Dr. Young mentioned. You try in effect to get the individual to go out and deal with the real world in an utterly unrealistic fashion. The alternative view, which seems to me to be much more justifiable, both pragmatically and theoretically, is this: The reason the person, this physical adult but emotional child, comes to you is that the experiences he, as a real child, had were with inadequate parents; and he comes to you and says, "Will you be my parent again and give me a second chance at becoming a better human being, a second chance at growing up, a second chance of learning about the ordered, integrated, culturally prescribed adult way of life?" What the therapist has to do, therefore, is not to renounce the culture or the ordered way of life, but to be able to give the patient a new experience with this, to present it in such a way that it will now become more acceptable for the patient; and in order to do this he has to avoid, in Freudian terms, countertransference: to avoid repeating with this person the mistakes that the original, real parents made.

Now a couple of brief points—the first one bearing on or perhaps being a continuation of Dr. Herskovits' remarks and a point that we touched upon repeatedly: the question of relativity or nonrelativity of normality and abnormality. In Dr. Hsu's paper,[5] I think he is entirely correct in saying that we cannot settle the issue of normality in the psychiatric

[5] Anthropology or Psychiatry, *op. cit.*

sense by pointing to specific behaviors in the same culture or in different cultures. This is not the level at which this issue is to be settled. He did deal with it too cavalierly in the first version of his paper by saying, "We can decide this by just simply pragmatically asking: Who is in the hands of a psychiatrist? Who is institutionalized? Who is called crazy?" and so forth. But in the second version of his paper Dr. Hsu has quite independently seen that the problem here is essentially a psychological problem, a subjective one. In the new version of the paper he has defined this issue as a question of how an individual resolves a conflict; and I think we can all agree perhaps that if a person, no matter when or where, resolves a conflict dissociatedly, that for all practical purposes is psychopathology. If, on the other hand, a person turns and faces the issue, as Dr. Hsu expresses it, then that does not lead to psychopathology; that points back to integration, normality.

Another point that follows from that is this: It is not the purpose of anthropologists or psychiatrists, or anyone else, I think, to try to create a world in which there is no conflict, in which there is no unhappiness, in which there is no suffering, no misery. This is unavoidable, and it is a part of the process of living to meet these implying threats to us as persons, and as societies, and to surmount them. But here we are not in the realm of psychopathology. We are in the realm of psychopathology only when there is an abandonment of the integrative task and the person turns back to partial self-destruction, repression, dissociation, as a means of dealing with his conflicts.

I would like to touch upon something again that Dr. Hsu discusses in his paper and which Dr. Winch referred to this morning. I really think there has been much unnecessary controversy in recent years about this question of the influence of childhood events. Are we going to have a nipple-diaper kind of anthropology?, we are asked. I think this is a perfectly simple way of cutting through this problem, which again emerges from clinical material. Let me put the dilemma this way: I have in therapy at the present time a patient who engaged in sex play with another boy when he was nine years old. Was that normal? Was that abnormal? Statistically, no, as Kinsey has shown; but psychogenetically it was, because this experience meant for this particular boy that he was thrown into conflict about going to confession. He was Catholic. He began to lie to his parents about going to church. He made them think he was a good Catholic when, in fact, he stopped going to confession at the age of nine. At twenty-one he married a Protestant girl. His parents up to this point thought all the time he was a good Catholic and that this Protestant hussy had come along and lured him away from the faith of his fathers. Eventually this young man took his wife to see his family, and you can't imagine how they went to work on her. As far as they were concerned, this was not a marriage. The man's family was therefore intent upon driving this woman away from their son, and as a result of what his deception and duplicity had thus done to his wife, this man's conscience finally began to bother him enough that he had to come into therapy.

Now these specific events in childhood which I described were not in and of themselves fateful. A person can have almost any kind of experience, including this kind of homosexual one, with or without its being pathogenic. The question is whether or not the experience drives a wedge between the individual and the significant person in his life. Or let me put it this way: It is a question of how the individual attempts to cope with this experience. There have been many boys, as Dr. Thompson indicated by her nod a moment ago, who have had these experiences, but they may have had the immediate "misfortune" of having been caught, or somebody told about it; so their guilt became ventilated and they took the consequences of their actions and then, in later years, sort of blush or laugh a little bit about it, and that is all there is to it. But the past becomes psychiatrically important only when it continues to be *a part of the present.* And the thing that was still with this man was not the fact that he had engaged in sex play with another boy for three months when he was nine years old, but that he was *still* essentially a liar and an evader and a misrepresenter and a person who got other people into trouble that they didn't deserve to be in. Along these lines somewhere lies a way of thinking that will, I believe, do much to clarify the question of the past versus the present in the genesis of neurosis.

DR. HENRY: I just want to talk a little bit to this point of the nipple-diaper anthropology. The expression, I am afraid, sounds just a little bit like an epithet. When I study the interaction of mother and child in a primitive society, day after day, when one of my students studies mother-child interaction in the immediate postnatal period—it seems to me these data are so momentous that they cannot be tossed out the window. The issue is, as I see it: What use are we going to make of these data in the development of a theory of culture?

DR. STEIN: I would like to make a few comments that are extensions of Dr. Gillin's remarks this morning. Like him, I have been concerned with the possible lack of growth or lack of integration that exists in this group at the end of the conference. To put the question differently, how much will each of us change as a result of this contact?

In fact, I believe that the lack of integration may be traced to the poor communication in the group. Several persons have suggested that we have been talking *at* each other. During the course of discussions that followed the papers, I have found that A will use a specific term, B's comments on A's remark stem largely from the significance that that term has for him, a discussion follows, and no integration is attained, primarily because the two men have been talking about very different things. There was no common frame of reference.

Might it not be of value in future conferences of this sort to adopt a procedure in which each discussant has to present *his* interpretation of the remarks he will discuss, and obtain the agreement of the preceding speaker that he has been interpreted correctly before he, the discussant, presents his own point of view? To be sure, this is an artificial technique and one which might slow up the proceedings. But such sacrifices may be necessary only at the beginning of the conference. As the group forms its own culture, it should not be as prevalent.

Another suggestion that I would like to make is that conferences of this sort might well start with a statement of the "rules of the game" or methodologies that each of us utilizes in his own discipline. Then, with the aid of one concerned with methodology, like those involved in the philosophy of science, we could abstract those factors which are common to each of our disciplines. This could be set up as a base on which we could build in the future. In following such a procedure, we might find that some of the interdisciplinary difficulties may be traced to the fact that at times we tend to look down at each other because we do not each utilize the same so-called "scientific methods." But we might also realize that there is a critical interaction between the methodology and the status of the science. Such knowledge might clear the atmosphere and encourage progress. However, if we permit our methodologies to stand in the way of our thinking and the development of new insights, or if we continue to be defensive in standing by the façades we have built up, then there is little hope of progress.

R. LINTON: My only suggestion would be that perhaps (having had quite a bit of experience with the Socratic method, on both the giving and receiving end myself), instead of having the gentleman summarize the remarks and the opinion of his victim, and then go on from there, it would be better to call on the man to really restate what his points were before these were subjected to criticism. We all know that in the restatement of another person's point of view an exceedingly deadly job can be done.

F. HSU: Let me take the last few minutes of this symposium to thank you all for coming, for making this symposium a successful one, and for teaching me, personally, a great deal. I think that, even though we have not found solutions for all the problems we have touched upon, we can all probably agree on two things. First, the experiences of the symposium have given us some intellectual stimulation. Second, now that we have had more than a passing acquaintance with each other, we ought to look for another symposium, less ambitious than this one in scope, but longer in duration, in the not too distant future.

O. KLINEBERG: Francis, before we adjourn, I think all those of us invited here would like to express our appreciation to you and the committee, but particularly to you, for the invitation, and for the very pleasant arrangements you made to bring us all together.

CONTRIBUTORS*

In Alphabetical Order

Alexander, Franz, M.D.
Director, Institute of Psychoanalysis, Chicago, Illinois

Babcock, Charlotte G., M.D.
Psychiatrist and Psychoanalyst, Institute of Psychoanalysis, Chicago, Illinois

Boshes, Benjamin, M.D.
Associate Professor of Psychiatry and Chairman of the Department of Nervous and Mental Diseases, Northwestern University Medical School

Boyer, Bryce, M.D.
Practicing Psychoanalyst, Berkeley, California

French, Thomas, M.D.
Associate Director, Institute of Psychoanalysis, Chicago, Ill.

Gillin, John, PH.D.
Professor of Anthropology, University of North Carolina

Henry, Jules, PH.D.
Associate Professor of Anthropology, Washington University

* The editor regrets that the contributions of Drs. Bryce Boyer, Charles Hyneman, R. S. Lyman, J. S. Slotkin, and Morris Stein are not available for publication.

Herskovits, M. J., PH.D.
Professor of Anthropology and Chairman of Department, Northwestern University

Hoebel, Adamson, PH.D.
Professor of Anthropology and Chairman of Department, University of Utah

Hsu, Francis L. K., PH.D.
Associate Professor of Anthropology, Northwestern University

Hunt, William A., PH.D.
Professor of Psychology and Chairman of Department, Northwestern University

Klineberg, Otto, PH.D.
Professor of Psychology, Columbia University

Kuhn, Manford, PH.D.
Associate Professor of Sociology, State University of Iowa

Lewis, Oscar, PH.D.
Associate Professor of Anthropology, University of Illinois

Linton, Ralph, PH.D.
Sterling Professor of Anthropology, Yale University

Masserman, Jules H., M.D.
Associate Professor of Psychiatry, Northwestern University Medical School

Mowrer, O. H., PH.D.
Research Professor of Psychology, University of Illinois

Richards, T. W., PH.D.
Professor of Psychology, Northwestern University

Saslow, George, M.D.
Professor of Psychiatry, Washington University

Schneider, Louis, PH.D.
Associate Professor of Sociology, Purdue University

Slotkin, James S., PH.D.
Associate Professor of Anthropology, University of Chicago

Thompson, Clara, M.D.
Director, William Alanson White Institute of Psychiatry, New York, N. Y.

Wang, Richard P., M.D.
Practicing Psychoanalyst, Princeton, New Jersey

Young, Kimball, PH.D.
Professor of Sociology and Chairman of Department, Northwestern University

INDEX

INDEX

INDEX